A CENTURY OF SCIENCE PUBLISHING

A Century of Science Publishing

A Collection of Essays

Edited by

Einar H. Fredriksson
IOS Press, Amsterdam, The Netherlands

IOS
Press

Ohmsha

AKA

Amsterdam • Berlin • Oxford • Tokyo • Washington DC

ISBN 1 58603 148 1 (IOS Press)
ISBN 4 274 90424 5 C3040 (Ohmsha)
Library of Congress Catalog Card Number: 00-112330

Publisher
IOS Press
Nieuwe Hemweg 6B
1013 BG Amsterdam
The Netherlands
fax: +31 20 620 3419
e-mail: order@iospress.nl

Distributor in the UK and Ireland
IOS Press/Lavis Marketing
73 Lime Walk
Headington
Oxford OX3 7AD
England
fax: +44 1865 75 0079

Distributor in the USA and Canada
IOS Press, Inc.
5795-G Burke Centre Parkway
Burke, VA 22015
USA
fax: +1 703 323 3668
e-mail: iosbooks@iospress.com

Distributor in Germany, Austria and Switzerland
IOS Press/LSL.de
Gerichtsweg 28
D-04103 Leipzig
Germany
fax: +49 341 995 4255

Distributor in Japan
Ohmsha, Ltd.
3-1 Kanda Nishiki-cho
Chiyoda-ku, Tokyo 101
Japan
fax: +81 3 3233 2426

LEGAL NOTICE
The publisher is not responsible for the use which might be made of the following information.

PRINTED IN THE NETHERLANDS

Contents

Foreword

In recent years interest in science publishing has broadened and now extends well beyond the narrow confines of publishing professionals. Publishers, librarians and distribution agents all have their own forums for discussion. This collection of essays is an attempt to bring professional publishers a bit closer to the large community they serve: authors, editors scientists/readers, as well as other partners and colleagues in the collection and distribution of information. Science publishing has grown as a result of the extension of services provided by publishers to scientists and experts from the outset of formation of (new) disciplines.

The time frame has been set to cover actors and developments in the 20th century, noting that major innovations like the Internet have only made an impact since 1990 and the World Wide Web since 1995. Also, science publishing has a history stretching back for many centuries. While concentrating on some of the leading actors of the past century, some characteristic features introduced before 1900 are commented upon. In the second half of the book we attempt to cover key trends and innovations which have had an impact on our industry — notably since World War II. Transition in the language(s) of science has also meant transition in the locations where management of communications takes place.

At the start of the past century there were comparatively few scientists, and that holds true (to a lesser degree) for the period around 1950 as well. Their mode of communication with colleagues, be it through correspondence by letter, visits to key colleagues and institutions, membership of societies, and attendance at conferences, is considered as background to several of the contributions. Formal publications were through books and journals and this system has been preserved throughout the 20th century. No-one denies the massive changes which have taken place over this period, the increase in the number of scientists and the large measure of internationalization. The evolution of the Internet and the Web has resulted in a large information garbage belt in which many valuable pieces can be found — sometimes only after great effort.

All participants in the science publishing chain (or circle as some observers prefer, from the scientist/author to the scientist/reader) have been affected by innovations ranging from the mechanical typewriter, photocopying, telecommunications, computers, all the way to database and search technologies. Today the Internet involves millions of servers and billions of homepages. Communication between scientists and the role of publishers and other actors are no doubt subject to change. On the other hand, last month a journalist commenting on the year 2000 performance of market leader Reed-Elsevier used the headline "a second life for the dinosaurs". Is the old saying "plus ça change, c'est plus la même chose" still applicable?

An additional reason to put together this collection has been to celebrate two of my colleagues who at this time have served 50 years in the publishing profession: Seiji Sato in 1999 and Hans Kruschwitz this year. I take this occasion also to express sincere thanks to my family and colleagues, too many to thank individually, for having made this publication possible.

E.H. Fredriksson, Amsterdam, April 2001

Publishers and Publishing

A Century of Science Publishing
E.H. Fredriksson (Ed.)
IOS Press, 2001

Chapter 1

The Birth of Scientific Publishing — Descartes in the Netherlands

Jean Galard
Cultural Department, Musée du Louvre, Paris, France

René Descartes (1596–1650) occupies an eminent place at a crucial moment in the history of thought. He played a decisive role when the medieval scholastic tradition was supplanted by the modern scientific mind. His personal contribution to the attainments of science was perhaps modest (most of his theories were soon outdated). But he incarnated a new attitude of the mind towards the world; he formulated a new method; he furnished the essential bases for the future development of knowledge.

His books, which were all written in the Netherlands, are examples of the spectacular birth of scientific publications. However, by a noteworthy paradox, they were directed against the cult of the Book. Descartes, like Galileo, relied on observation, on direct experience, aided by reasoning, at a time when intellectual authority was incarnated by the canonical books, those of Aristotle. The Cartesian moment in the history of thought is marked by a refusal of opinions conveyed by ancient books. It was the moment of the true re-foundation of thought, independent of bookish culture. An anecdote illustrates it well. A gentleman went to visit Descartes at Egmond, in Holland, where the philosopher resided from 1644, and asked him for the books of physics that he used. Descartes declared that he would willingly show them to him: he took his visitor in a courtyard, behind his dwelling, and showed the body of a calf that he was about to dissect.

Official intellectual authority, in the 17th century, continued to belong to the university. But new intellectual centres were formed outside the universities. The latter had played a brilliant role in different cities of Europe from the 13th century onwards. They were international foyers from which ideas were exported. In the 16th century, these universities started to decline. In the 17th century, dynamic thought began to blossom in private circles. During the second half of the century, scientific research flourished both in the Academies (L'Académie des sciences, in France, dates from 1658) and in the periodical press (for example the *Journal des*

Sciences, in 1664, in Paris, and the *Acta eruditorum*, founded by Leibnitz, in 1682, in Leipzig). During Descartes' lifetime, in the first half of the 17th century, new ideas were searching for a means of expression. The years 1620-1650 were of an extraordinary effervescence. They witnessed the appearance of the great works of Bacon, of Galileo and of Descartes, but also, in the philosophy of law and political philosophy, those of Grotius and of Hobbes...

Contemporary with the birth of the publication of scientific books, in which the Netherlands played a major role, there was an intense circulation of ideas by letters that the scientists exchanged among themselves. It is known that Descartes devoted several hours a day and an entire day each week to his correspondence. Those letters that have been kept and handed down to us represent about half his writings. If he spent so much time and lavished so much care on them, it proves that he knew well that they would be shown, transmitted and commented. Father Mersenne (1588-1648), who resided in the Convent of the Annonciade in Paris from 1619 onwards, occupied a central position in this epistolary circulation. Himself author of several large works against atheism and scepticism (in 1623, 1624 and 1625), author of works on music and on acoustics (in 1636 and 1637), translator of Galileo (*the Mechanics* in 1644), he was also a very active correspondent with Constantin Huyghens, Isaak Beeckman, Gassendi, Fermat, Roberval, Pascal, and many others. Questions and replies from different scientists transited through him. He was a sort of catalyst of the intellectual life in Europe of his time. His role could be compared to the present role of the Chief Editor of a scientific journal, extraordinarily active and read by the best minds of the moment. Descartes, who voluntarily lived far from Paris, kept up a considerable correspondence with Mersenne and was thus in indirect communication with the readers, admirers and adversaries of his works.

* * *

Descartes spent more than half of his adult life in the Netherlands. His first visit was during his youth when he spent fifteen months there. When he went back, during his adulthood, he had not as yet published anything and had not even started his researches, as he himself explained, on the foundation of any philosophy more certain than what was taught currently at that time. During the twenty years that he was to spend in this country he was to construct all his work. Why did he chose to live there? Chance and accident cannot explain such a long stay, especially for a man who was so keen to lead a life governed by the precepts of reason. Why were the Netherlands so convenient for him? Apart from the motives that he mentioned himself, one wonders if there was not some secret affinity that linked Cartesian thought and the Netherlands in the first half of the seventeenth century.

Descartes went there for the first time in 1618. He was twenty-two years old. He had studied at the Jesuit College of la Flèche, an experience summed up in the *Discours de la Méthode*, followed by a year of Law in Poitiers. In that year 1618, his father bought an office of Counsellor to the Parliament of Rennes for Pierre Descartes, René's elder brother. He doubtless intended his second son to follow a career in the legal profession. But Descartes felt the urge to travel. What better means to escape from the sedentary life than to choose a career in the army. The Netherlands offered, at that time, the best training in the military profession. They were not, however, at war, the Twelve Years' Truce having been signed with Spain in 1609. But the prestige of Maurits of Nassau continued to exercise its attraction and two French regiments remained in the service of the States. It is thus plausible that Descartes, joining the troops of Maurits of Nassau, followed the normal destiny of a younger son of a good family in becoming a soldier in an army already legendary. One cannot, however, say that he precipitated himself towards an opportunity of military glory. He could not ignore that the Truce had been signed nine years earlier. It was thus a garrison life that awaited Descartes.

Mere volunteer in a reserve army, Descartes received no pay. He was free to leave when he wanted. No obligation was imposed on him. He was idle. The key event of this stay at Breda was his meeting with Isaac Beeckman. The latter was thirty at that time. Not only was he a physician but he was also curious about mathematics, and physics. He had been to France on September 6, 1618, to be awarded his degree of Doctor of Medicine at the University of Caen. It is from his diary that we know that his first meeting with Descartes took place on November 10, 1618. He became, for Descartes, like an elder brother, a study companion for the young Frenchman isolated among military men. A common cast of mind incited them to study mathematics in view of their application to physics. Beeckman's diary includes the account of their discussions on falling bodies, on hydrostatics, on algebra. Descartes said that he was indebted to his friend for having escaped from the torpor that threatened him. On December 31, 1618, he gave Beeckman, as a New Year's gift, his first text, the *Compendium musicae* (Summary of Music), a mathematical theory of consonances. He gave it to him as a souvenir of their friendship, asking him never to show it to anybody, refusing that the world at large should judge a work "composed rapidly, only for you, amidst the ignorance of soldiers, by an idle man, submitted to a type of life completely different from his thoughts". From January 2, 1619, Beeckman was no longer at Breda — he was more often resident at Middelburg. Descartes wrote letters to his friend, letters that the latter duly transcribed into his diary: we thus learn that Descartes spent his time studying painting, military architecture and, above all, Dutch. "You will soon see that I have made progress in your language, for I plan to be in Middelburg, God willing, for the coming Spring".

The letters to Beeckman should also give us some idea as to why Descartes decided to leave the Netherlands so soon. On April 29, 1619, in fact, fifteen months after his arrival at Breda, he left Amsterdam for Denmark, by ship, whence he intended to go to Germany. But his intentions remain obscure. He said that he wanted to take part in the war that was being prepared in Germany, while organising a long detour and not giving up his scientific work. He seemed impatient to intervene in the battles of which he had been deprived by the Truce of Twelve Years. He was tired of the inactivity of Breda. At the same time he showed himself by no means in a hurry: "If I stop anywhere, which I hope, I promise you to undertake immediately the writing of my Mechanics and of my Geometry and to extol you as the inspirer and the spiritual father of my studies". His reason for leaving the Netherlands was perhaps simply that which had brought him there: the desire to travel, or the intention to study in the 'great book of the world', as he was to state later in the *Discours de la méthode*: "in deciding to search for no other science than that which could be found within myself, or rather in the great book of the world, I spent the rest of my youth in travelling, in seeing courts and armies, associating with people of diverse humours and conditions, collecting different experiences, proving myself in the encounters that fortune proposed me, and everywhere reflecting upon the things that presented themselves, so that I could benefit somewhat from them".

Descartes thus went to Germany. We know that he was in Frankfurt on September 9, 1619, for the coronation of Ferdinand II as Holy Roman Emperor, that he then spent the winter in solitary meditation, closed up in a room, probably in the region of Ulm. It was there that he said he discovered "the bases of an admirable science". He noted the date of this revelation: November 10, 1619. It is very likely that the admirable discovery, mentioned in his notes as a miraculous illumination, was that of the possible unity of sciences following a general mathematical method. It was the flowering of ideas that had ripened on contact with Beeckman.

The following years, Descartes continued his travels wandering "here and there in the world, trying to be a spectator rather than an actor". He went to Italy and found the heat in Rome unbearable. Then he stayed in Poitou, in Brittany and, for a longer period of time, in Paris. He associated himself with a group of scholars who were gathered round Father Mersenne. He worked on his research on optics. His reputation as a mathematician grew. He was famous for his method and for the perspectives that it opened in favour of a study of Physics renewed by

Mathematics. His conceptions intrigued. One could guess their importance, from the assurance with which he refuted the ancient ideas and the pseudo-innovators. But he still had not published anything. His friends urged him to do so. They considered him as the champion of a new philosophy, capable of combining Christian truth and scientific discoveries. The old scholasticism, in fact, was incompatible with the science that was being developed. This new science was thus considered as a possible encouragement of atheism. The time had come for Descartes to establish his system clearly and to articulate together his metaphysics and his physics. In 1628, he had his back to the wall. He had to put his ideas into form so as to present them to the public. He looked for the most convenient place to work in peace. With full knowledge of the facts, because he had already stayed there, he chose the Netherlands. He was to stay there twenty years.

The first person that he wanted to see when he landed in Holland, arriving probably from Calais, was Beeckman. They met at Dordrecht on October 8, 1628. Beeckman's journal recounts their conversation, during which Descartes related his progress: he had already elaborated an algebra applied to geometry, and this analytical geometry was in the process of constituting the instrument of all human knowledge. The esteem between the two men seemed mutual.

Descartes certainly had other conversations with Beeckman in the following weeks. We know, however, that in April 1629 he enrolled as a student at the University of Franeker. The region of Friesland offered him the retreat that he was looking for, for a peaceful and studious life, as well as the advantages of an intellectual centre. A high school, "Hoogeschool", had been founded in Franeker in 1585. Descartes was able to attend the courses of Adrian Metius, who was the author of an *Arithmeticae et Geometricae Pratica*. He lodged opposite the University, in the Castle of the Sjaerdema, a great catholic Friesian family.

But, as from October, 1629, Descartes installed himself in Amsterdam. At the request of doctor Wassenaer and of Henricus Renerius, with whom he had been in contact, he examined the phenomenon of parhelions (mock suns, comparable to haloes); he interested himself in the rainbow, then in all the phenomena which he was to describe in his work on Meteors. His correspondence with Mersenne shows that he unceasingly widened the field of his investigations. From Optics he passed on to Acoustics, Ballistics, Anatomy. The title of the work that he then was preparing bears witness to his scientific ambition: it was to be *Le Monde* (The World), no less.

From 1629 to 1635 Descartes lived in Amsterdam. His stay was nonetheless interrupted several times. On June 27, 1630, he enrolled at the University of Leiden and the *Album studiosorum* mentioned his residence in that town. He wanted to follow the courses of the mathematician Jacob Golius, in company with the astronomer Martin Hortensius and of Renerius. He also lived in Deventer, in 1632 and 1633. His friend Renerius was professor of philosophy there, at the "Illustere School"; and it was there that Descartes, far from the outside world, hoped to finish his treatise *Le Monde*. But he always came back to Amsterdam.

It was during his stay at Leiden that the unpleasant episode of his quarrel with Beeckman took place. Father Mersenne came to visit Descartes. He was already in correspondence with Beeckman, who asserted that he had been the early master of Descartes. When they met, Beeckman showed Mersenne his Journal and claimed the merit of the discoveries that Descartes considered as his own. Descartes, informed of this by Mersenne, gave vent to his anger in imprecations against his former friend and wrote him wounding letters. The violence of the rupture was in proportion to the intimacy that they had known.

At Deventer, while he completed the writing of the Physics (the treatise of *Le Monde*), Descartes learned that the Inquisitor in Florence had just seized the recent work by Galileo, *Dialogues on the Two Principal Systems of the world, that of Ptolemy and that of Copernicus.* (Dialogo intorno le due massimi sistemi del Mondo, Tolemaico e Copernicano). The thesis that had been condemned, that of the movement of earth round the sun, occupied an essential place in Descartes' own system; it could not be omitted. However, Descartes refused to publish a work "where there would be the least word that might be disapproved of by the Church". He therefore shelved his manuscript. Was it a gesture of prudence? He was however in no danger of being troubled. He was living in a protestant country, and the Dutch were then considering offering a refuge to Galileo, whose *Dialogo* was to be published, in latin, by the Elzevier brothers in 1635.

In April 1635, Descartes was in Utrecht, close to Renerius, who was there as professor at the "Illustere School" where he taught the Cartesian theses. The philosopher lived in a pavilion that opened on to the Maliebaan, outside the fortified walls. It was there that he wrote the Dioptrics, one of the three essays (with the Meteors and the Geometry), which were intended to follow the *Discours de la Méthode*, as applications of his method. It was probably there that he wrote the *Discours de la Méthode* itself. In the Spring of 1636, he went to Leiden where he was to stay for a year to oversee the printing of his book. This printing, in fact, necessitated particular care because of the woodcuts (by Frans Schooten the Younger) illustrating the three essays. The work was to be published by the Elzevier brothers. But Descartes doubtless judged the financial conditions unacceptable and he looked for another publisher. He thought of having his book published in France. But what kept him back was the fact that the preparation of the wood blocks had to be effectuated in his presence; it was thus more convenient to call upon a publisher established in Holland. We know that he wanted "the whole text to be printed with very fine characters and on very fine paper" and that at least two hundred copies should be kept for his personal use for he "desired to distibute some of them to a quantity of people". In 1637 the *Discours de la méthode* was published by Jean Maire at Leiden, without mentioning the name of the author.

Descartes took advantage of his stay in Leiden to attend the anatomy courses of Professor Van Valckenburg. He did not live in isolation. He frequented Constantin Huygens, Counsellor of the Stathouder, who had been his friend for several years and with whom he kept up assiduous conversations and correspondence. He knew and respected Pieter Corneliszoon Hooft. However, tranquillity remained his main concern. As soon as his presence at Leiden was no longer necessary, he retired to Egmond-Binnen, in the region of Alkmaar, then to Santpoort, near Haarlem.

This period was, at first happy. He had his daughter Fransintge brought to him as well as the discreet Helena Jans, mother of the child. His letters are imbued with serenity and are often cheerful. He reckoned on developing his medical research: the lengthening of human life seemed to be the goal of all science. He only received the visits that he desired: for example those of two catholic priests of Haarlem, Bannius and Blomaert, or those of his disciples, Renerius and Regius. Renerius died in 1639. He had practised the method of Descartes without, for all that, adopting the metaphysics. On the contrary, Regius, also a professor at the "Illustere School" of Utrecht, declared himself more completely faithful to Cartesian philosophy. Descartes certainly expected the University of Utrecht (the "Illustere School" had become University in 1636) to be a favourable ground for the propagation of his doctrine, thinking that it would come up against less resistance there than at the old Sorbonne. Nonetheless, it was there that the most violent hostility was expressed: that of Gisbert Voet (Voetius), a Calvinist minister and professor of theology. Voetius undertook to bar the route for the new doctrine which was threatening to invade the University. This violent conflict affected Descartes profoundly. He considered himself slandered, unjustly accused of atheism. He witnessed the disappearance of the possibility of a diffusion of his ideas in a milieu that he had thought, for a moment, to be the most receptive. He had written the *Discours de la méthode* in French, because he hoped to reach a wider public than that which could read in Latin. In 1640, on the contrary, he wrote his *Metaphysical Meditations* (Meditationes de prima philosophia...) in Latin: it was a question, this time, of convincing the world of scientists. He was to prepare, shortly afterwards, the *Principles of Philosophy* (Principia philosophiae) by dividing his treatise into articles to make it easier to use in teaching. But the learned theologians of whom he was mainly thinking did not appear in the least disposed to listen to him.

The *Metaphysical Meditations*, followed by objections collected by Mersenne from different theologians and philosophers to whom he had shown the manuscript, followed also by the replies from the author, were published in August, 1641, in Paris, by Michel Soly. A second edition was published, in May 1642, by Louis Elzevier, in Amsterdam, "more correct than that of Paris" according to Descartes, who had supervised the printing himself. As for the *Principles of Philosophy* (Principia philosophae), they appeared in 1644, as a first edition, printed by Louis Elzevier, in Amsterdam. While he was working on these two major works, Descartes lived in Leiden, then nearby at Oegstgeest, from March 1641 to April 1643, in the little castle of Endegeest which he had rented thanks to an inheritance from his father. The proximity to Leiden allowed Descartes to keep up frequent relations with the university professors. His philosophy found defenders there: Heydanus and Bannius. But there, as well as in Utrecht, he was also to meet determined opposition.

In 1643, Descartes left this ideal residence of Endegeest for a short stay at Egmond-op-den-Hoef. Then he travelled in France for four months in 1644, his first visit after fifteen years in the Netherlands. On his return, he settled in a country house at Egmond-Binnen, where he lived until his final departure from the Netherlands in September 1649.

He enjoyed talking to the peasants. He used his influence with Constantin Huyghens in favour of one of them who had been dragged into committing a murder. It seems that he chose his friends without considering their social rank, as one can see in his relationship with Dirk Rembrandtz, a boatman or a cobbler of the neighbourhood, and who became, with his help, a notable astronomer. If he kept up an important correspondence with Princess Elizabeth (daughter of the Elector of the Palatinate Frederick, ephemeral King of Bohemia, who had taken refuge, with his family, in the Netherlands), it was not that he was particularly fascinated by her rank of princess, but rather because of the intellectual vigour of the young lady and the acuteness of her questions. Also, doubtless because she was young and showed interest in his research, representing a generation on which he founded his hopes. She was thus an ideal disciple. This hope of exercising a durable influence was precious at a time when his differences with the theologians barred his way in the universities.

Descartes made a second trip to France in June 1647. When he arrived in Paris, the great question debated in scientific circles was that of the Vacuum in nature. The position of Descartes, set forth in his *Principles of Philosophy*, was that a vacuum cannot exist. His thesis seemed to be contradicted by the experiments that Pascal had just carried out; but he did not seem to be shaken in his opinion. In Torricelli's tube, according to him, a "subtle matter" passing through the pores of the glass, replaced the air. One should not consider that Descartes felt, in Paris, in the painful situation of an ageing physicist who sees his theories surpassed. He met Pascal and planned new experiments with him. He probably also met Hobbes, and renewed his acquaintance with Gassendi. His glory was evident to all. It was moreover towards the end of his stay that he received from "the King by the inter-mediary of Cardinal Mazarin, without any solicitation other than that of his friends, and by letters patent of September 6, 1647, a pension of three thousand livres, in consideration of his great merits and the utility of his philosophy and of his research based on long study brought to the human race" (Adrien Baillet, his first biographer, 1691). All, in consequence, should have kept him in France. However, he was to return to Holland. The enigma of his attachment to the Netherlands is here posed in a striking way. He was honoured in Paris while in Holland he experienced, above all troubles. Why did he go back?

On his return to Egmond, Descartes spent his time studying astronomy with the help of a telescope that he had, and above all his work of dissection, for the fifth and sixth parts of his *Principles*. He replied scrupulously, as he had always done, to the written objections that he received. He allowed himself to be questioned viva voce by a young man of twenty, Frans Burman, who came to visit him on April 16, 1648, and whom he invited for dinner. Their long conversation, which lasted several hours, transcribed by the young man, bore on the main philosophical works and corresponded to what we would today call an "interview". This was not the only example of the attention given to the improvement of young people, he also followed the progress of the sons of his friend Huygens, closely enough to foresee that Christian would become an exceptional scholar.

However, the pension announced had not yet been paid and Descartes found himself requested, on behalf of the king, to travel once more to France to receive it. This third trip took place from early May to September, 1648. A badly chosen period. It was the beginning of the Fronde uprising. On August 26, 1648, barricades were built in Paris. The day after, with all possible speed, Descartes left for Holland. He was never to come back to France.

During his last year in Holland Descartes worked on the third part of his *Passions of the Soul* (Passiones Animae), the treatise on psychology undertaken in parallel with the moral reflection that occupied an essential part of his correspondence with Princess Elizabeth. It was at that moment that a fine opportunity to favour the propagation of his doctrine arose. France was busy with political troubles, the Netherlands in the throes of theological disputes, whilst the Court of Sweden was perhaps in a position to welcome his ideas in all their developments. Queen Christina was trying, at that time, to attract to Stockholm scholars and artists of all nationalities. She was particularly interested in the Netherlands. Many Dutch engineers and architects were already in Sweden and numerous Swedish students attended courses in Dutch universities. One of Descartes' friends, Pierre Chanut, had been appointed chargé d'affaires of the French government to the Queen of Sweden. He understandably mentioned the philospher. Descartes was flattered by these testimonies of interest in his work, but when, in February 1649, he received an invitation to go to Sweden, he was embarrassed rather than pleased. The idea of such a long voyage worried him. The Queen wanted to have him near her so that she might familiarise herself with his philosophy. Could she not read his books, followed, if necessary by a long correspondence that he was ready to carry out? He put off action deliberately, but finally decided to go to Stockholm for a stay that he thought would last no longer than a few months. He left Egmond on September the first, 1649. In Amsterdam, having left the manuscript of the *Passiones Animae* with Louis Elzevier, he embarked for Stockholm. He was never to come back. He immediately missed the solitude of Egmond. He hated life at court and felt that he was wasting his time. The Queen was often absent from Stockholm for long periods and when she decided to converse with him about his doctrine, she asked him to come to the palace at five o'clock in the morning, three times a week, in the heart of the Scandinavian winter. Stricken with pneumonia, he died on February 11, 1650, at the age of fifty-three.

* * *

Descartes always felt profoundly attached to the Netherlands, among other reasons, because this country always remained for him the place where he experienced, during his youth, the first true intellectual stimulation. It was Isaak Beeckman who was the inspirer of the studies which were to occupy him for a long time: "You alone, in truth, awoke me from my idleness". The souvenir that Descartes was to keep of their meeting can certainly explain, for a large part, the choice that he was to make in 1628 to settle in the Netherlands — the place where he was to orchestrate his work. The country where he had known friendship, the enthusiasm of his first discoveries, and the revelation of his vocation.

When Descartes, later, convinced himself that he had discovered the principles that were to make possible an extraordinary development of science, he saw in the Netherlands the most propitious place to continue his studies and to publish them. Firstly because it was there that he found liberty and security: the maintenance of public order guaranteed his daily tranquillity. At the same time this country was rich with personalities open to the new scientific spirit, to whom Descartes was able to put his ideas to the test.

The Netherlands, on the other hand, offered precious possibilities of publication. One should not go so far as to state that it was the only country where he could have his works printed. These were also publishable — and indeed were published — in Paris. The publication in the Netherlands of French works was only to become important after 1680, with the growth of anticalvinism in France and the increase in non-conformist writings. Only then were French works printed in Holland that could not be printed in France. Let us say rather that during the time of Descartes, Leiden and Amsterdam were towns where it was possible to find publishers capable of meeting the requirements of the most exacting authors (and we have seen how demanding Descartes was, concerning the quality of the paper, of the typography, of the illustrations). It was only necessary that the authors should be able to negotiate and be ready to assume the financial investment.

As for the question of the diffusion of the new ideas, the biography of Descartes carries several pieces of information. Firstly, let us repeat, the circulation of letters was, at the time, an essential means for the communication of knowledge (letters formed about half of the writings of our author). Publication in book form, however, was a moment of paramount importance in the expression of a thought, a moment on which it was important to lavish all possible care. Secondly, this transition to the printed word was not without danger, even in the Netherlands. Descartes renounced the publication of his treatise *Le Monde* after the condemnation in Florence of the *Dialogo* of Galileo, and the works that he had published brought about long discussions and troubles with the theologians of Utrecht and Leiden. Thirdly, the appearance of a book, even if it escaped controversy, was not conceived as an end in itself. Furthermore, it was necessary for the ideas it contained to reach the greatest possible number of different minds. Hence the hope that Descartes placed in possible "relays": the universities (this hope was soon disappointed), or certain young people (Princess Elizabeth, Frans Burman...), or finally, Queen Christina of Sweden. Fourthly, a clear contradiction appears, with Descartes, between the desire to see his ideas widely diffused and the desire to keep them as his property. The painful rupture with Beeckman shows clearly that Descartes was torn between the sincere desire to serve truth and a susceptibility of an author who wanted his name to remain associated with his discoveries.

Descartes, incontestably, has left his name to posterity (he has even left an adjective: "Cartesian"). However, even though he was singular, this thinker was highly representative of a whole world: that of the years 1620–1650 in Europe. This was the period when the continent was bathed in blood by the Thirty Years' War.

Paradoxically, the date of 1648, with the signature of the Treaty of Munster, is perhaps the time when Europe became conscious of herself. At the same time, in an apparently independent way, another Europe existed: that of the philosophers and scientists, who remained in close contact with each other regardless of frontiers. Mersenne, Huyghens, Torricelli, Pascal, Hobbes, Gassendi, Fermat... were all intellectually cosmopolitan, like Descartes. This Europe was in the process of conceiving a world based on the principle of causality, and no longer on the finalism of Aristotle. Nature in its immensity was not animated by secret correspondences and symbols: it was a great machinery, delivered to man, who, from then on has power over her. The world ceased to be an ensemble of signs to be deciphered according to the teaching in The Book; it became an ensemble of objects, analysable experimentally, in view of transmissible knowledge by books. The modern era was born.

A Century of Science Publishing
E.H. Fredriksson (Ed.)
IOS Press, 2001

Chapter 2

Academic Publications before 1940

Alan Cook
Selwyn College, Cambridge, UK

Summary

The overall scope of this book is scientific publishing from 1900, but 1900 is a somewhat arbitrary date in the history of academic publishing which, for the most part from 1900 to 1940 was a continuation of that in earlier times. There were substantial changes from about 1850 and then after 1950, so that it is natural to consider the hundred years between those dates as a whole. There were considerable advances in physics in 1900, which also influenced chemistry, and they had consequences in publishing, but the journals founded before 1900 continued into the new century and relatively few new ones appeared after 1900. The procedures and economics of academic publishing up to 1950 also remained much as they had been for almost two centuries. Thus something must be said about the development of academic publishing in science from the end of the seventeenth century onwards in order to understand its nature in the first half of the twentieth. That is the plan of this chapter.

The physical sciences underwent greater developments and were generally more advanced by 1900 than were the biological sciences, and that is reflected in the greater prominence given to the physical journals in this essay. Most attention is also given to publishing in English, not because that in other languages was negligble but because it was on the whole parallel, and the account of English language publishing covers most of the issues that arose in other languages.

Early academic publishing in natural philosophy

The natural philosophers who started the so-called scientific revolution about the middle of the seventeenth century differed from the hermetic scholars of the Renaissance who preceeded them by making their thoughts and discoveries public and by open correspondence with others at home and abroad. In so doing they not only disseminated natural knowledge, but by developing peer review they authenticated it, and so steadily augmented the stock of confirmed understanding of the natural world. Thus in the first half of the seventeenth century students of magnetism published some notable books. In 1581 Robert Norman described in the *The Newe Attractive* the dip needle that he had just constructed. William Gilbert in his *De Magnete* of 1600 studied the Earth as a great magnet, and Guillaume de Nautonier in the *Mecometrie de Leymand* of 1602–1604 put forward somewhat similar ideas. Athanasius Kircher, the Jesuit polymath of Rome, wrote a small book, *Ars Magnesia* in 1631, with a substantial list of magnetic observations at ports and other places round the world, and a suggestion of how a balance might be used to measure forces between magnets. He followed it in 1641 with the far longer *Magnes*, in which he again had a list of observations, and also described the idea of a chart showing lines of equal magnetic declination. Lastly in 1644 René Descartes gave an extensive account of his ideas about magnetism as part of his comprehensive *Principia Philosophiae*. All those books were written before there were any serial journal publications, and before there were permanent academies in England or France. They were however contemporaneous with the Accademia dei Lincei, founded in Rome by Prince Federico Cesi, Duke of Aquasparta, of which Galileo was a fellow. Fellows of the Lincei certainly published privately, but the Lincei itself brought out two works of Galileo, the *Letter on Sunspots* of 1613 and *Il Saggiatore* of 1623. They were the first works published by an academy, although not as journals. Slightly later the Accademia del Cimento, founded and actively supported by the Medici princes, Ferdinando II and Leopoldo (later cardinal), enjoyed a brief life in Florence during which it published the *Saggi di naturali esperienze* of 1667, a cooperative account of the researches conducted by its fellows as part of its corporate life.

At the same time a few individuals maintained a lively correspondence in which they gave news of what their colleagues were doing and sought similar information from their correspondents. Henri Justell in France, Henry Oldenburg in England, and P. Eschinardi in Rome were three such letter writers. Justell was associated with Montmort's informal academy in Paris, Oldenburg became secretary of the new-born Royal Society in London, and Eschinardi was a member of the Roman Accademia Fisica-Mathematica in which Queen Christina of Sweden, then living in Rome, was interested. People who had no official connection with an academy might also maintain a substantial correspondence, as did, for example, the astronomer Johann Hevelius of Danzig. Scientific journals seem to have arisen from that extensive letter writing. Henry Oldenburg began the first with the *Philosophical Transactions* of the Royal Society of London in 1665. Others soon appeared, notably the *Journal des Sçavans* in Paris (1665) and the *Acta Eruditorium*, but they were private not corporate endeavours. The Académie Royale, founded in Paris shortly after the Royal Society, began to publish its *Histoire* (later *Memoires*) *de l'Académie royale des Sciences* in 1699, more than thirty years after those of

Inscriptions and Belles Lettres. At first the Royal Society also published books by fellows, no doubt because by its charter it had licence to do so independently of the powerful Stationers' Company of London. Its experiences were not happy. The *Historia Piscium* (1686) by Francis Willughby, completed after his death by John Ray, was a financial disaster for the Society, and on that account, and because many of the most active fellows were engaged in helping to bring it out, the Society could not itself undertake Newton's *Philosophiae naturalis principia mathematica* (1687), but had to rely on Edmond Halley to finance it and see it through the press. From then onwards, the Society left book publishing alone and concentrated on the regular publication of Philosophical Transactions that effectively set the pattern for scientific publishing in Europe for the next century.

There had been natural philosophers in the English colonies in North America from at least the time of the foundation of the Royal Society, which included among its early fellows a Mather and a Winthrop. There was much interest in natural history and astronomy in Jamaica as well as the northern colonies, and that is reflected in contributions to *Philosophical Transactions*. Then in the middle of the eighteenth century publishing by academies extended to North American when the American Philosophical Society was founded in Philadelphia in 1769; it also had members from Jamaica.

In the first academic journals like *Philosophical Transactions*, all life was there, from mathematics to mycology, and much else besides that we would not now count as natural knowledge. The *Histoire de l'Académie royale des Sciences* in Paris, the journal of the American Philosophical Society, and the *Transactions* (1832) of the Royal Society of Edinburgh, were all devoted to natural knowledge of the most comprehensive sort.

The second half of the nineteenth century

Towards the end of the eighteenth century so many people were engaged in certain fields of science that they needed more and more specialised journals than those of the older comprehensive academies. Thus in Britain the Astronomical Society was founded in 1820 (the Royal Astronomical Society from 1850). It and the Geological Society of London (1826) both published learned journals, the *Memoirs* and the *Monthly Notices of the Royal Astronomical Society* from 1827, and the *Quarterly Journal* and *Memoirs of the Geological Society* in the previous year. The Linnaen Society (1874) and the London Mathematical Society (1865) similarly served biologists and mathematicians. Those societies were primarily devoted to original science, although that does not mean that all their fellows were professionals who earned their living by doing science. Far from it: the Royal

Astronomical Society always had many amateur astronomers among its fellows, and there were many amateurs in the Geological Society and in the Linnaen Society. That is not surprising, for those subjects depended strongly on observation in their early days, and amateurs, especially country clergymen, could make valuable contributions. There was, and to some extent still is, great scope for the amateur observer in ecology.

The year 1850 seems to mark the beginning of a considerable increase in professional science throughout Europe. In that year the British Government first made a grant to the Royal Society for the support of work by scientific men, and it seems very likely, if not certain, that the ideas associated with the Great Exhibition of the following year led the government to agree to do so. The foundation of the Kensington colleges of science and engineering was the most important outcome of the Exhibition. The government grant supported significant investigations in the physical sciences in the late nineteenth century, as well as geological and biological expeditions, while the Kensington colleges were new centres of research in universities. Scientific work increased greatly in Britain, and became more specialised and professional as the numbers of university staff and the resources available to them increased.

In consequence of those developments, the volume of papers in *Philosophical Transactions* increased considerably, and in 1867 the Royal Society divided it into two series, A and B, physical and biological. In the early years of scientific academies, many fellows could attend meetings in person and did not need to be told what had gone on at them, but later people wanted to have published reports of meetings as distinct from the papers presented to them. Already in 1800 the Royal Society started its *Proceedings*. At first it contained reports of meetings and brief summaries of papers that would be published in full in *Philosophical Transactions*. In the same way the Académie des Sciences had its *Comptes Rendus* (1835) and other academies likewise had such subordinate journals. They themselves came in time to take shorter original papers while the older journals took longer ones. In 1905 *Proceedings* also was divided into two series, A and B. A similar pattern was followed by the *Accademia dei Lincei* which was refounded in Rome in 1870 after the reunification of Italy and began to publish its Atti in 1873. It subsequently published Rendiconti with short papers and Memorie and other occasional publications with more substantial contributions. Each of the early issues of the *Proceedings* of the Royal Society contained lists of presents among which were copies of journals received from other academies: those lists show how numerous academic publications were around 1870.

There were three major developments in academic publishing in the nineteenth century that to a large extent set the pattern for the early twentieth century. Regional comprehensive academies were formed in Europe, especially in those lands, particularly Germany and Italy, that had no central government. There were academies all publishing journals in Turin, Milan, Venice, Bologna, Naples and Palermo, and in Göttingen, Hamburg, Berlin, Munich and Vienna. Britain had the Royal Society of Edinburgh (1832) and the Royal Irish Academy.

In the second development new specialist societies were founded. They included in Britain the Physical Society, the Chemical Society, the Linnean Society, the Royal Meteorological Society, the Royal Microscopical Society, and the Zoological Society, all with one or more serial publications.

The third development was the appearance of comprehensive academies outside Europe. Scientific research was developing in the British dominions, and Royal Societies were formed in Canada, Australia and New Zealand, and published their own journals. However, many scientists from those countries, and even more from India, continued to send their important papers to the Royal Society in London.

Comprehensive academies such as the American Philosophical Society were relatively less important in the United States where academic publishing became dominated by the major societies, among them the American Physical Society, the American Geophysical Union and the American Astronomical Society, all three of which and others published the most important work in their fields, whereas in Europe, and especially Britain, the work published by the established national academies continued to include important investigations in most fields.

The first scientific institutions supported by public funds were a few physic gardens and the royal observatories in Greenwich and Paris. In the course of the nineteenth century other public institutions came into being, the geological surveys of Britain and the USA, for example, and meteorological and magnetic observatories. They were institutions with responsibilities to the public generally, and they saw it as their duty to publish their work in their own journals in a quasi academic manner, for the dissemination of knowledge and not for commercial profit. Their publications complemented those of academies and other societies. They were for the most part the means of preserving and putting on record the work of institutions that were supported by public money. Although like the publications of academies they did not in general depend on outside sales, some publications were sold widely to the public, in particular The *Nautical Almanac* from the Royal Observatory in England and the *Connaissance des Temps* from the Bureau de Longitude in Paris, two annual publications essential for seamen.

In the nineteenth century, medical men in hospitals did more research in the life sciences related to medicine. Early maps of the brain, for instance, were made in mental hospitals. A few hospitals, including mental asylums, were under the control of local or central government, but most were institutions of charitable foundations, and some were associated with universities. Journals such as *Philosophical Transactions* published work done in them, but scientific medicine, like other burgeoning fields, produced its own journals, in particular the *London Journal of Medicine* which became the *British Medical Journal.*

Engineering Institutions are not considered here, for they have functions that include representing the professional interests of their members and certifying that they are qualified to practise as engineers. They do however also publish academic journals, and like the purely scientific societies they grew in numbers and functions throughout the latter part of the nineteenth century

The amateur composition of many scientific societies in the late eighteenth and early nineteenth centuries had a considerable influence on the economics of their publications. For the most part a member of a society received its publications free in return for his subscription. Additional sales were few. Many copies were given free to individuals or institutions that in return presented the academy with copies of their own works. Societies and institutions such as observatories, commonly developed their library collections of learned journals in that way. When members, especially amateurs, were reasonably well to do, when the cost of the manual labour of printing was by comparison low, when the sizes and volumes of journals were small, and editorial work was done voluntarily by a few members, the subscriptions of the members could cover the costs of production. Academic publishing was not a commercial business, it was undertaken to promote and disseminate knowledge, and in the circumstances of the times it did not have to be run on commercial lines.

At the same time as the specialist societies were coming into being, other societies were formed to develop an interest in science and the understanding of it, but not to pursue it as such. The British Association for the Advancement of Science was formed in 1835, and in addition to its annual metings, published a journal to promote wider support for science. The Royal Society of Arts had somewhat similar aims, though more technological, while the Royal Institution, although not an academy, also published a similar general journal. The American Association for the Advancement of Science was likewise founded in the USA.

The first half of the twentieth century
The patterns that had been set in the latter part of the nineteenth century continued in the first half of the twentieth. The established general journals continued, with some modifications, as did the publications of the more specialist societies that had been formed in the nineteenth century, as well as the obligatory pub-

lications of public scientific and technical institutions. At the same time changes were taking place foreshadowing the major rearrangements of scientific publishing that occurred after 1950. Most may be traced to the great increase of scientific activity and to the change from a partly amateur to a more wholly professional pursuit. Active scholars and teachers found it increasingly difficult to read for themselves all the relevant papers in their field, and so journals came into being that published reviews for whole topics. Two early ones were *Reviews of Modern Physics* (1929) from the American Physical Society and *Reports on Progress in Physics* (1934) from the Physical Society in Britain.

While it is true that calendar dates are in general arbitrary milestones in human history, it so happens that two developments around 1900 had a significant influence on academic publishing. National laboratories for standards and other physical research were founded in Germany (the Physikalische-Technische Reichsanstalt in Berlin), in the United States (the National Bureau of Standards in Washington DC) and in Britain (the National Physical Laboratory in Teddington, 1900); they had been preceded by the Bureau international des Poids et Mesures at Sèvres. All had a responsibility for making their work publicly known, and like the Bureau international the German and American laboratories published their own series of reports, the National Bureau of Standards through the US Government Printing Office. The National Physical Laboratory, however, was initially guided by a committee under the Royal Society and so published important work in the journals of the Society, although it also issued annual reports. In addition, it collaborated with the Institute of Physics to publish the *Journal of Scientific Instruments* (1923) which, in responding to the growing importance of instrumentation in science, was like the *Review of Scientific Instruments* of the American Physical Society.

The turn of the century was notable for the evolution of quantum mechanics and relativity, both of which led to a great increase in experimental as well as theoretical investigations in the new subjects and consequently to larger and more numerous journals of physics and chemistry.

New sciences emerged early in the twentieth century. Geomagnetism had been studied on traditional lines since the work of Edmond Halley in 1700, but when the Smithsonian Institute in Washington began to publish its studies in geomagnetism it did so in its own *Journal of Terrestrial Magnetism and Electricity*. Papers on geophysical topics, mostly theoretical, had been published in the journals of the Royal Society and of the Royal Astronomical Society, and then in 1922, the Royal Astronomical Society began a small journal, the *Geophysical Supplement to the Monthly Notices of the Royal Astronomical Society*, in which at first most papers were on seismology, then just developing as a major observational study. Similarly the American Geophysical Union published its *Transactions* (1920) that became the *Journal of Geophysical Research*.

In summary, the important developments that occurred in the early years of the twentieth century were the foundation of journals for new subjects such as geophysics, for scientific instruments, and for reviews as distinct from original contributions.

The economics and methods of academic publishing differed little after 1900 from those before. An honorary officer of a society would decide on the publication of a paper after receiving one or more reports from referees, and would probably assemble the articles to make up an issue. He (almost never she) would be assisted by a small paid staff in the office of the society where a few members, perhaps no more than one, would deal with the correspondence (receiving papers, sending them to referees), undertake the copy editing, send copy to the printers, check and distribute proofs, and maintain a mailing list.

Many journals were produced by small printing firms among whom Taylor and Francis in London were prominent. Type was still set by hand until early in the century the larger printers adopted the monotype machine in which individual characters were cast at the touch of a key. Small mechanical presses would print small numbers of journals. Journal printing for many smaller societies was still a sort of cottage industry.

As in the late nineteenth century, so at first in the early twentieth century, a large proportion of the print run of many academic journals would be distributed free, either to members of the society in part return for their subscriptions, or by exchange with other societies. Sales for profit were few.

So long as journals could be produced in that way without a net loss to a society, there was no need to market the journal agressively to libraries and individuals, nor to give the journal a superficially attractive format. Societies did find in these years that their journals were increasingly sought by university libraries. In 1850 there were few universities with scientific laboratories and libraries, by 1950 there were very many, especially in the English-speaking countries. That was the time in which great universities in London and the English industrial cities grew up, in Bristol and Birmingham and Manchester and Newcastle and elsewhere. Even more, in North America the original universities of the East coast were supplemented by state universities — every state of the Union wanted its own college. Many were like the University of Colorado, founded with the state in the Centennial year of the Union. It was at first a very small college, but it gradually accumulated a substantial library and supported research. The University of California at Berkeley, founded in the nineteenth century, acquired a substantial library and active research departments; in the 1930's an additional campus was started in Los Angeles. Those two parts of the University of California, together with the California Institute of Technology in Pasadena, supported important early work in astronomy and in geophysics, especially seismology. All those developments generated demands for the existing academic publications, especially in English, and also led to the establishment of newer academies, such as the Astronomical Society of the Pacific, and associated journals. In the first half of the twentieth century American science came to exceed European science, especially in physics, chemistry and the earth sciences, and journal publishing and sales followed suit. The expansion of science was however, not confined to Europe and America, and the early twentieth century saw the foundation of academies elsewhere, for instance, the Imperial Academy of Tokyo in 1912.

Aftermath

The second world war brought about very great changes in academic publishing. Developments already seen before the war speeded up, but in addition, new subjects came to the fore, in the physical sciences, for example, microwave radio engineering, nuclear physics, geophysics and space research, and in biology, molecular biology. At the same time the cost of producing journals increased drastically, so that academies have had to behave more as commercial publishers, and seek to obtain a profit from their publications, but now in severe competition with the real commercial publishers. Another development, again begun in the previous years, has been a great increase in the number of univerities and industrial and public research institutions, all wanting to acquire runs of journals, not only in the USA and Europe, but even more outside, in India, Russia, China, South America and the older British dominions. At first most of those institutions had ample funds to buy journals for libraries, but not now, so that commercial pressures on academies have increased as sales have fallen. The costs of printing were reduced by replacing traditional means of composing and printing by electronic systems, but they have not entiely solved the problems, and now academies face the need to introduce electronic publication. How, in these circumstances to maintain a public duty to publish and authenticate reliable natural knowledge, as they have done for three hundred and fifty years, is a serious issue for academies.

Academic publishing before 1940
List of Journals

This list is far from complete, and does not adequately represent academic publishing in Europe, but does give an idea of how academic publishing expanded up to 1940. The greatest number of new journals appeared in the nineteenth century.

1665	Philosophical Transactions (A/B, 1887)	1874	Proc. Linnaen Soc.
	Journal des Sçavans	1880	Astrophys. J.
1699	Histoire de l'Académie royale des Sciences	1883	R. Soc. Canada
			Edinburgh Math. Soc.
1769	American Philosophical Soc.	1889	J. Inst Elec. Eng.
1780	Mem. Acad. Roy. de Belge	1893	Physical Rev.
	Naples, Acad. royale	1896	Aeronautical J.
1783	American Academy of Arts and Sciences		Geol. Soc. France
1786	Acad. roy. de Turin	1897	Proc. Inst. Chem. G.B. & Ireland
1799	Annalen der Physik	1898	R. Acad. Sci., Amsterdam
			Physics Abstracts
1800	Proceedings, Royal Society (A/B, 1905)	1899	Proc. Washington. Acad. Sci.
1826	Proc. Geol. Soc. London		
1827	Mon. Notices, R Astronom. Soc.	1900	American. Math. Soc.
1830	Proc. Zool. Soc. London	1904	Proc. Amer. Chem. Soc.
1832	Proc. Roy. Soc. Edinburgh	1905	Faraday Soc.
1835	Inst. de France, Comptes Rendus	1912	Imperial Academy of Tokyo
	Mem. Ist. Nat. Genève	1915	Proc. Nat. Acad. Sci., Washington, DC
1841	Mem. Chem. Soc., London	1920	American Geophys. Un.
1843	Cambridge Philosophical Society		J. and Proc. Inst. of Chem.
	Istituto Veneto		Zeits. f. Physik
1849	Astronom. J.		Phys. Berichte
1861	Trans. Roy. Microscop. Soc.	1922	Geophysical Supplement
1861	Proc. Roy. Met. Soc.	1923	J. Sci. Instrum.
1865	London Math Soc.	1929	Rev. Modern Physics
1873	Atti. Acad. naz. Lincei	1934	Rep. Progress Phys.

A Century of Science Publishing
E.H. Fredriksson (Ed.)
IOS Press, 2001

Chapter 3
The Growth and Decline of German Scientific Publishing 1850–1945

Heinz Sarkowski
Historian of German Publishing, Germany

Summary

The development of commercial scientific publishing companies in Germany commenced in the middle of the 19th century. University and Academy publishers never had a chance. Scientific society publishers emerged only in 1921/1923 during inflation, but had little impact. German publishers dominated in particular in Mathematics, Physics and Chemistry. In 1909, 45% of the articles covered by the *Chemical Abstracts* were from German publications. Until 1933 the German language was the "lingua franca" of Europe's scientific community. The export of German science publishers was significant, and in 1930 around 60% of Springer Verlag's turnover came from export. The international significance of German science can be seen from the large number of Nobel Prizes bestowed on it: 15 German scientists were recipients from 1901 to 1915, 16 from 1918 to 1932. After 1933 many highly qualified scientists fled the Nazis and found refuge in the Western world, constituting the start of the decline of German science. During World War II German science literature was reprinted on a large scale and sold worldwide. After the War the German language had definitively lost its world significance and German companies concentrated thereafter on production of textbooks and journals for the home market. In the sixties they also commenced publication of research literature in English.

From 1901 until the First World War one third of all Nobel Prizes in the fields of physics, chemistry and medicine were awarded to German scientists. This documents the immense significance of German science before the First World War. The names make this clear:

1901: Wilhelm Conrad Röntgen (Ph)	1909: Ferdinand Braun (Ph)
1901: Emil von Behring (Med)	1909: Wilhelm Ostwald (Ch)
1902: Emil Fischer (Ch)	1910: Otto Wallach (Ch)
1905: Philip Lenard (Ph)	1910: Albrecht Kossel (Med)
1905: Adolf von Baeyer (Ch)	1911: Wilhelm Wien (Ph)
1905: Robert Koch (Med)	1914: Max von Laue (Ph)
1907: Eduard Buchner (Ch)	1915: Richard Willstätter (Ch)
1908: Paul Ehrlich (Med)	

The German language had become the "lingua franca" of the science community. "Physicists and chemists in Britain and the USA could not do without reading German if they wanted to keep abreast of the developments in their own fields" [1]. In 1909, for instance, 45% of all (literature) citations referred to in *Chemical Abstracts* came from German journals [2].

German universities and science libraries provided a model for American and also for Japanese science. The German book trade, its organization and central services in Leipzig, were internationally the most exemplary. The British publisher Sir Stanley Unwin, who spent some time in the Leipzig book trade as a trainee, wrote in his memoirs in 1960: "The German book trade organization was in those days, and up to 1914, the finest and most complete that the world has ever known… The destruction of Leipzig in the Second World War, and its subsequent occupation by the Russians, almost entirely disrupted it" [3]. This complex and well organized book trade in Leipzig — where most of the science publishers were also located — together with the highly developed graphics industry, as well as local book-exporting science antiquarians like Gustav Fock, Otto Harrassowitz and Anton Hiersemann, were the reason for the export success of German science publishers.

In the predominantly regionalised German publishing industry a clear specialization in natural science and technical books became evident around 1850. Before that the mixed-list publisher, with output in literary work alongside theology, law and history, also randomly published work in science and technology. To illustrate the latter for the year 1850 I found a total of 34 titles, which had appeared from 24 different publishing houses. Friedrich Vieweg was represented with four titles, the classics publisher J.G. Cotta with three. The remaining 27 were divided among 22 further publishers.

Vieweg in Braunschweig was the first German publishing house to dedicate itself to the natural sciences (chemistry, mathematics, physics and technology). Liebig, Poggendorff and Wöhler were among their first authors. As early as 1826 in Berlin, August Hirschwald was the first who specialised in medicine.

Julius Springer, who had founded his publishing house in 1842 alongside a bookstore, turned in 1859 towards natural sciences, publishing a pharmaceutical journal and later a handbook of pharmacology [5]. After the founding of the German Empire in 1871, business, technology and science witnessed an unprecedented development. The sons and grandsons of Julius Springer expanded into technology, mathematics and medicine. The starting point of their activities was usually a journal: in 1889 Springer already published 20 science journals. In 1911 it was 41, in 1928 — when biology, physics and chemistry were added — 106 and in 1933 128 titles, among which were several abstracting journals. Springer also improved its market position by purchasing publishing houses with similar orientation — J.F. Bergmann in 1917, August Hirschwald in 1921, F.C.W. Vogel in 1931 — as well as by the acquisition of single items like *Beilsteins Handbook of Organic Chemistry* in 1916 and individual journals. Through Springer's determined effort after the First World War to establish its Mathematics Press, the respected publisher B.G. Teubner lost its leading position in this field. When inflation had abated in 1924, Springer enjoyed a dominant position not only on the German market. This is illustrated by the fact that in 1931, when their production reached 381 books and 125 journals, almost 60% of its turnover came from abroad.

In the second half of the 19th century a substantial number of other publishing houses were founded, which covered areas in natural sciences or began to specialize, often in medicine: Ferdinand Enke, founded in 1837, already produced more than half of his publications in medicine by 1874. F.C.W. Vogel, a company founded in 1730, also specialized in medicine from 1862. Newly founded were Urban & Schwarzenberg (1866), J.F. Bergmann (1878) and Gustav Fischer (natural science and medicine). An older company, Veit & Comp. strengthened its activities in natural science and medicine in 1876 and Georg Thieme became active in 1886. Johann Ambrosius Barth, after a change in ownership, specialized in natural sciences (*Annalen der Physik*) and expanded its program into medicine in 1894. S. Hirzel, a much older company, also covered medicine alongside humanities, after 1894. S. Karger (1890) was a newly founded medical publisher, as was Theodor Steinkopff (1898). The Akademische Verlagsgesellschaft, founded in 1906 by the antiquarian Leo Jolowicz, was a publisher active in all areas of natural sciences and in a relatively short time became the most important science publisher in Germany after Springer.

As well as journals, multi-volume handbooks, in which the current knowledge in a discipline was assembled, usually by a number of specialists, belonged to the program of these companies. From 1924 to 1933 Springer published 319 volumes of 19 handbook titles [6]. These handbooks included not only "established" knowledge but also new research results, illustrated by the fact that, in their bibliography of the "most important contributions to the literature of medicine", Garrison/ Morton included 8 Springer handbooks. There was fierce competition in this field: from 1924 until 1929 Springer published its 24-volume *Handbuch der Physik* while at the same time Akademische Verlagsgesellschaft started publishing a *Handbuch der Experimentalphysik* which was completed in 1937, and in 1925 Friedrich Vieweg reintroduced his *Lehrbuch der Physik* after Müller-Pouillet in 14 volumes, published since 1842.

For German science publishers the combination with a house-owned printer was rather the exception. Vieweg in Braunschweig, Rudolf Oldenbourg in Munich (Engineering, Technology) or B.G. Teubner in Leipzig (Engineering, Mathematics), for example, possessed their own technical companies. From 1911 Springer participated increasingly with the Würzburg printer H. Stürtz to have its strongly growing production less dependent on the market power of the Leipzig companies.

Some of the provisions of the Versailles Treaty were to prevent German science from regaining its pre-War status. German scientists were not admitted to a number of international congresses. The use of the German language was also forbidden, which was still the dominant scientific language for Dutch and Scandinavian scientists. Also these restrictions (lifted under the Locarno Pact of 1926) clearly hindered to a large degree the export of German science literature. Germany was essentially excluded from scientific communication for 12 years. Therefore, it is a sign of the world standard of German science that from 1918 to 1933 again one third of all Nobel prizes for physics, chemistry and medicine were awarded to German scientists:

1918: Max Planck (Ph)	1925: Richard Zsigmondi (Ch)
1918: Fritz Haber (Ch)	1927: Heinrich Wieland (Ch)
1919: Johannes Starck (Ph)	1928: Adolf Windaus (Ch)
1920: Walter Nernst (Ch)	1930: Hans Fischer (Ch)
1921: Albert Einstein (Ph)	1931: Robert Bosch (Ch)
1922: Otto Meyerhof (Med)	1931: Friedrich Bergius (Ch)
1925: James Franck (Ph)	1931: Otto Warburg (Med)
1925: Gustav Hertz (Ph)	1932: Werner Heisenberg (Ph)

After the end of WWI there was a significant gain in prestige for German exporters in that orders from enemy states' libraries had not been cancelled but stored up. To their surprise the libraries could close the gaps created through the War after a short time. The income in hard currency earnings was very welcome during this period of German inflation.

During inflation the founding of university and society publishing houses was actively discussed, but with the strong position of the German science publishers, their chances were small. There were also legal obstacles for the founding of university presses. However, during these years scientific societies founded their own companies — for instance the Association of German Engineers (VDI) started the VDI-Verlag, the Association of German Chemists the Verlag Chemie and the Association of German Electrotechnical Engineers the VDE-Verlag, to mention but a few — but as of today only a few of them have survived. On the other hand, science associations started their own journals, but usually had these taken care of by commercial publishers.

Also in these times Springer succeeded not only in maintaining its international position, but also in expanding it. In this the scientific journals played a significant role. Especially the *Zentralblätter* (abstracting journals), of which 38 were founded by the company or taken over from other publishers, found a world-wide market. Medicine was central in Springer's aspirations to build a comprehensive information system on natural science publications. The first abstracting service was the *Zentralblatt für die gesamte innere Medizin* started in 1912. The *Zentralblatt für die gesamte Chirurgie und ihre Grenzgebiete* followed in 1913. (Both publications had the support of the corresponding societies.) In the mid-20's Springer annually published about 175,000 abstracts in their *Zentralblättern*, for which 3300 domestic and foreign journals were reviewed.

In particular Springer's relations with the Soviet Union intensified. In 1932 18.8% of all exports by Springer-Verlag went there, totaling 4,637,000 mark. In second place followed Japan with 16.3% and in third place the USA with 11.9% [7]. Russian mathematicians often visited Göttingen and its Mathematical Institute, among them Paul Alexandroff, Andrej Kolmogoroff and Alexander Khintchine, and they also published their works with Springer in order to secure the copyright.

In 1931 exports suffered much from the devaluation of the English pound, and all currencies depending on it, from 20.43 to 12.43 mark. German book exports to Japan were halved in the period up to 1935. The US dollar was also devalued by 40%, in April 1933.

After the National Socialists came to power, Jewish and Marxist scientists were expelled from universities and institutes. An exodus on an unprecedented scale ensued. Among the emigrants were: Hans von Baeyer, Max Born, Richard Courant, Albert Einstein, James Franck, Fritz Haber, Rudolf Höber, Rudolf Ladenburg, Lise Meitner, Richard von Mises, Otto Meyerhof, Carl Neuberg, Rudolf Nissen, Wolfgang Pauli, Peter Pringsheim, Georg Schlesinger, Erwin

Schrödinger, Eduard Teller, Hermann Weyl and Richard Willstätter, to mention only a few. A List of Displaced German Scholars, which was published in London in 1936, included 1652 names of scientists who had been forced to leave Germany, most of whom had not been able to find appropriate positions. Some science publishers also emigrated to the USA. For instance Walter Jolowicz (later Walter J. Johnson) from the Akademische Verlagsgesellschaft, who in 1941 founded Academic Press together with his brother-in-law Kurt Jacoby (and in 1945 also the Johnson Reprint Corp.); or Erik Proskauer, who became involved with the founding of Interscience Press (later part of John Wiley). S. Karger, who had founded his medical publishing house in Berlin in 1890, emigrated with his company to Basel (Switzerland).

From now on German scientists of Jewish origin published almost exclusively in the for them unfamiliar English language. In the Netherlands Martinus Nijhoff founded the journal *Physica* — which was open to scientists who until then had published in Springer's *Zeitschrift für Physik*. In the first issue, published in November 1933, of the eight contributions by Dutch physicists four were still published in German, and the others in English. In the mid-30's M.D. Frank and J.P. Klautz visisted German publishers to establish contacts with, for instance, the medical publisher Georg Thieme and the Akademischen Verlagsgesellschaft whose Jewish owner family Jolowicz, was under increasing pressure. The publishing houses Elsevier and North-Holland were interested in translation and co-productions, but before these efforts could have any great success the War started.

The race laws were also an immediate threat for the Springer publishing house. Both grandsons of the founders, Ferdinand (II) and Julius (II), were considered through the marriages of their fathers to be either fully Jewish, or less compromisingly, as mixed-race of second grade. In this context Julius (II) Springer had to leave the company in 1935. His stock was taken over by the trusted director Tönjes Lange. After a further sharpening of regulations, in 1942 Ferdinand (II) Springer also sold his shares to Lange. In the eyes of the National Socialists the company was now theoretically "judenfrei". In the circumstances the company name, which until then was "Verlag von Julius Springer", was also changed, into "Springer-Verlag". Both Springer cousins regained their rights after 1945, but they had not been able to prevent the father of Julius (II) Springer and two of their uncles becoming victims of the Holocaust.

The devaluation of the most important western currencies had a negative effect on the export of German books. German science publishers were naturally particularly hard hit. Therefore, on 9 September 1935, a general price cut of 25% for all exported books was introduced, the costs of which were essentially covered by the state. Companies like Springer, which had had a comparatively high contribution from Jewish authors and editors, suffered even more damage. It was now also noticeable that foreign publishers began establishing journals, which started to compete with German journals. Because of this, Springer's export went down from 44.3% of turnover in the year 1931 [9] to 19% in 1941 and 12% in 1942. In this context it should be noted that exports — be it in strongly reduced quantities — to countries with which Germany was now at war were conducted through book traders in neutral foreign countries, for instance Switzerland or Sweden. The shortsightedness of the German authorities can be illustrated by the fact that in November 1939 they pointed to the importance of exports of science literature to neutral states which continued to be subsidized.

Instructed by the American "Alien Property Custodian" (APC) and on the basis of the "Trading with the Enemy Act", renewed on 21st April 1942, the Ann Arbor firm of J.W. Edwards in 1943 and 1944 alone reprinted 874 volumes from German science publishers, 390 of which were from Springer-Verlag and 89 from Akademische Verlagsgesellschaft.

Publisher	Titles	Volumes	Total list prices	%
Julius Springer	238	390	4357.35	48.6
Akademische Verlagsgesellschaft	48	89	949.85	10.6
Verlag Chemie	10	45	482.95	5.4
Walter de Gruyter	12	36	421.95	4.7
Georg Thieme	9	18	316.05	3.5
Dr. Theodor Steinkopff	48	47	287.75	3.2
Urban & Schwarzenberg	2	13	249.00	2.8
Ferdinand Enke	32	33	240.70	2.7
Johann Ambrosius Barth	29	31	204.90	2.3
Gebr. Borntraeger	14	15	198.85	2.2
S. Hirzel	23	25	180.05	2.0
Friedr. Vieweg & Sohn	10	10	108.35	1.2
44 others	114	122	968.90	10.8
Total	589	874	$8966.65	100.0

Publications in the field of chemistry figure most prominently. In addition there were countless reprints from journal volumes, as well as microfilms from individual publications for research projects. (One can assume on the basis of this that most American scientists were still able to read German.) The importance of this reprinting program for American war research [10] can be seen from a letter of the then publisher of *Chemical Abstracts* to the Alien Property Custodian: "There is not the least doubt in my mind, that your republication program was one of the factors which made the atomic bomb possible" [11]. The gaps in German research literature in American libraries were clearly not only caused by the dollar devaluation of 1933. In the twenties, American libraries were already conducting a restrictive purchasing policy with respect to German primary journals because of their high prices. (The reasons for these were that the German journals were financed by private companies and not by societies, and there were no page charges required from authors.)

After the German surrender on 8 May 1945, and the division of the country into four occupation zones, book production was at first impossible and functioned later only in a very limited fashion. The acute lack of paper and the destruction of many production companies, especially in Leipzig, contributed to this. Export of stock which had survived the war was almost impossible at first, and later possible only under allied control. Universities and institutes were not yet fully operational, their libraries had suffered substantial war losses and their holdings were mostly stored elsewhere. And, on the other hand, German scientists had run up an information gap of at least a decade through the lack of foreign primary information. It was also a handicap that numerous important books continued to be reprinted in the USA and came on the world market at very low prices [12]. In this situation it is not surprising that German scientists were prepared to accept foreign job proposals. Numerous ambitious students soon followed them.

On the other hand, reprints of the journal volumes often had the advantage that American libraries in particular became interested in taking up subscriptions with the publishers or with their importers (journal agents). This, of course, in cases where the journals were of active interest to their users.

Only in 1949, after the foundation of the Bundesrepublik Deutschland and the Deutsche Demokratische Republik, could production be resumed in any significant way. In Leipzig, however, which had previously been the site of preference for science publishers, most companies became state enterprises and their owners had to re-establish themselves in the West. In both German states, moreover, priority was given to the re-publication of textbooks for students as well as practice books in, for instance, technology. Export of German science literature was also limited by the fact that the German language had largely lost its worldwide significance. Not only had English definitively become the "lingua franca" for scientists, but American, English and Dutch companies had taken the lead. Only since the sixties, when German publishers hesitantly commenced the publication of research literature in the English language, has the situation slowly improved.

German publishers were forbidden to have direct contacts with foreign clients; thereby making export of books and journals impossible. However, in the Summer of 1947 Springer succeeded via the JEIA (Joint Export and Import Agency) by an indirect route in exporting stocks of books and journals which had survived the War. In this context Robert Maxwell was of help, at the time working as British press officer in Berlin. He founded the European Publicity and Advertising Company (EPAC) in London, and on 1 September, 1947, also in London, the firm Lange Maxwell & Springer was founded. Using these firms Springer realised exports to the value of 20.5 M DM between 1 February 1948 and 31 December 1958. Other German science publishers could also export along these routes.

Through a contact with Paul Rosbaud, who until the end of the War was a leading employee of Springer's, a joint venture company with the British publisher Butterworth was established, whereby Springer contributed publishing rights and Butterworth the venture capital. After two years however the collaboration was dissolved. The publication rights were acquired by Robert Maxwell for his own Pergamon Press [13].

From the 1950's German publishers could again export directly. They also started to publish books and journals in the English language, initially with some hesitation. When Springer opened its New York office in 1964 the company also gained direct access to American authors. Later offices in London, Tokyo and Paris followed, but these developments would require a separate treatment.

References

[1]   van Leeuwen, J.K.W. (1980) The Decisive Years of International Science Publishing in the Netherlands after the Second World War. In: *Development of Science Publishing in Europe.* A.J. Meadows (Ed.) Elsevier, Amsterdam, New York, Oxford, p. 251.

[2]   Spence Richards, Pamela (1990) Der Einfluss des Nationalsozialismus auf Deutschlands wissenschaftliche Beziehungen zum Ausland. In: *Von Göschen bis Rowohlt. Beiträge zur Geschichte der deutschen Verlagswesens.* Monika Estermann und Michael Knoche (Hrsg.) Harrassowitz, Wiesbaden, p. 234.

[3]   Sir Stanley Unwin (1960) *The Truth about a Publisher.* George Allen & Unwin, London, p. 70.

[4]   Sarkowski, Heinz (1) (1988) Die Entwicklung ingenieurwissenschaftlicher Verlagsprogramme im 19. Jahrhundert. In: *Buchhandelsgeschichte*, p. 3.

[5]   Details on the Springer-Verlag from Heinz Sarkowski (2) (1996) *Springer-Verlag. History of a Scientific Publishing House. Part 1: 1842–1945.* Springer-Verlag, Berlin, Heidelberg, New York.

[6]   Sarkowski (2), l.c. p. 258.

[7]   Sarkowski (2), l.c. p. 324.

[8]   Sarkowski (2), l.c. p. 345 and p. 372 f.

[9]   In addition, deliveries of German exporters amounted to an estimated 20% of turnover.

[10]   Nemeyer, Carol A. (1974) *Scholarly Reprint Publishing in the USA*. Bowker, New York, p. 34–51. — Spence Richards, Pamela (1981) Gathering Enemy Scientific Information in Wartime, *Journal of Library History*, **16**(2), pp. 253–264. — Sarkowski, Heinz (3) (1987) Amerikanische Nachdrucke deutscher Wissenschaftsliteratur während des Zweiten Weltkriegs. In: *Buchhandelsgeschichte*, pp. 97–103.

[11]   Richards, Scientific Information, p. 254.

[12]   Sarkowski, Amerikanische Nachdrucke, p. 102. — Tabel: from Sarkowski, Springer-Verlag. p. 381. — "List prices" refers to Edwards' prices, which were usually only half of the German selling prices. *Belsteins Handbuch der Organische Chemie* in a complete reprint sold at 20% of the Springer price (Sarkowski, Springer-Verlag, p. 397, note 46).

[13]   Götze, Heinz (1996) *Springer-Verlag. History of a Scientific Publishing House. Part 2: 1945–1992.* Springer-Verlag, Berlin, Heidelberg, New York, pp. 14–17 and pp. 78 ff.

A Century of Science Publishing
E.H. Fredriksson (Ed.)
IOS Press, 2001

Chapter 4

Ohmsha, its Birth and History

Seiji Sato
Ohmsha, Ltd., Tokyo, Japan

The Age of Beginning 1914–1929 (World War I and Birth of Ohmsha)

Half the Life of Seiichi Hirota, the founder of Tokyo University of Electrics and Electronics and Ohmsha, and the Influence of Europe on it

Established on November 1, 1914, Ohmsha celebrated its 86th anniversary in 2000. The company name Ohmsha comes from the title of its first magazine *Ohm*. It also coincides with the initials of the founders of Tokyo Electrical Engineering School (currently Tokyo Denki University), Shinkichi Oogimoto, Seiichi Hirota and Ryozo Maruyama.

Seiichi Hirota was born in 1871. He graduated from the Electrical Engineering Department, Engineering College of Tokyo Imperial University and joined Takada & Co., an importer of electrical equipment. He was sent to Siemens company in Germany to do research into electricity. While there and on his way back home, he visited other European countries and the United States. Many of his later activities were influenced by what he saw and learned during those days.

Steam engines were essentially the only industrial power source. Hirota and Oogimoto met around this time and formed a close friendship. They believed that "Engineers with university or college backgrounds were not sufficient to support future development of the Japanese electric industry. A great number of technicians are needed and must be trained as soon as possible". This led to the foundation of Tokyo Electrical Engineering (EE) School. It was just after the Russian-Japanese War ended and future growth of Japan's electric industry was expected. In reality, however, kerosene lamps were still used in most middle class Japanese households, and gaslights rather than electric lights.

Although they established the school, its financial base was weak because private schools received virtually no financial support from the government at that time. So they started a publishing business as a means of ensuring the school's survival. Most of the books on engineering were imported and those written in Japanese were inferior in terms of content. They felt that the publishing business would contribute much to the study of electrical engineering in Japan and, at the same time, provide much needed income.

Ohmsha was formally established in 1910 as the publishing department of the school and started publishing textbooks for correspondence courses and transcribing lectures delivered at the school. Hirota published the *Ohm* magazine on November 1, 1914, intending it to be an educational and training tool for young engineers around the country. The publishing house was named Ohmsha. He wrote in the first issue of the magazine that "The word Ohm reminds me of the many obstacles I expect to encounter in my path of duty. Nevertheless, I hate to tread on the paved path of conventional ideas. So I am determined to cultivate a new road leading to the development of sciences unique to Japan". When World War I broke out, it found Japan opposing Hirota's beloved Germany. His strong desire to see Japan's own electrical technologies develop was behind his address.

The first issue of the *Ohm* magazine ran the answers to the 1914 national qualification test for electrical engineers. This test started in 1911 and comprised Class 1 through Class 5 tests (currently Class 1 to Class 3). The *Ohm* magazine was the first to publish all the test answers.

The 1091st issue of *Ohm* magazine (fifth issue of volume 87) came out in May, 2000 without missing a single issue, even during such historical events as the Great Kanto Earthquake of 1923 and World War II.

In September 1922, Ohmsha was incorporated and made independent of the EE School with a capital of ¥ 30,000 (¥ 20 per share, 1,500 shares, all paid-up). Forty-three of the 44 shareholders were employees of the Electrical Engineering School (including seven Ohmsha employees). The remaining one was Tomoo Namioka who was invited by Hirota to be the chief editor of *Ohm*. All shares were transferred to them free of charge. A general meeting of the Ohm society was held on August 27 at the EE School. The first board of directors comprised Senior Managing Director Namioka (later to become the second representative director of the company), Directors Oogimoto and Kato, and Auditor Sakuma. The office of president was left vacant. The senior managing director served as the representative director.

When the capital was increased by ¥ 20,000 to a total of ¥ 50,000 in 1924, the management of related electrical companies and college professors as well as a certain number of *Ohm* subscribers were invited to become shareholders (a rare practice even now). The only time Ohmsha was forced to miss a dividend payment was in the aftermath of the Great Kanto Earthquake of 1923.

The Japanese electrical industry was burgeoning then. The Schottky effect was invented in Germany in 1918 and Hull fabricated the dynatron electronic tube in the USA. The age of the vacuum tube had begun.

Ohmsha published its first book, entitled *Hyaku Koshou Shissaku* (Hundred Failures and Errors), in 1918. Interestingly enough, Ohmsha at that time was engaged not only in publishing but also in retailing such products as slide rules and nichrome wires. Ohmsha installed its printing plant in the company yard the same year and started printing *Ohm* magazine from the November issue. Typefaces were gradually increased to support English words and numerical expressions. The point system was also employed for characters used in the plant. Ohmsha in this period created and published original books and magazines.

The Osaka office was opened in 1919 as the base of operations in the Kansai area.

1920: Denki Kosakubutsu Kitei (Electrical Work Procedure), still a best-seller today, was published.

1921: Denki-ka Nikki (Electrical Engineers' Diary — its revised edition is published every year to this day) was published.

1922: The publishing rights to *Denki Shinpo* (Electric News, later the *Denki Shinbun*), were transferred to Ohmsha. The *Denki Shinpo* became independent in 1926, but close relations were maintained between the two companies.

1923: Ohmsha's Tokyo office was burnt down during the Great Kanto Earthquake of 1923. So, the company was forced to publish the *Ohm* magazine from the Osaka office.

The following is a description of the day of the disaster obtained from old records. "It was 11:58 on September 1, 1923 when a strong earthquake struck Tokyo. Koji Koga, the third representative then, saw the concrete school building sway to the north and south. He prepared for the worst, as the wooden Ohmsha building would be crushed under the school building at any moment. The school building, however, withstood the earthquake as well as the fire that broke out as evening came. The wooden office was engulfed in flames and burnt down during the night. During severe quakes, an emergency stack of documents was transferred to the adjacent school building. Since flames were approaching the school building, a boy named Miyata who was staying there that night wrapped them in a piece of cloth and carried them out, thus escaping from the fire. These documents included the subscriber cards for the *Ohm* magazine and *Electrical Industry News*. This was very fortunate for future sales activities because most of *Ohm*'s readers were subscribers.

Since the Ohm printing plant was also burnt down, Namioka set about printing the magazine in Osaka where he had many friends. On September 4, he sent Horii (later to become the second president of Ohm bookstore) to Osaka giving him full powers to secure a printing firm for the *Ohm* magazine and *Electrical Industry News*. Horii, then aged 20, was a salesman.

On the following day, editors of the *Ohm* magazine went into town and found embers still smoldering on the streets, and a smell of death engulfed the town.

Since the Tokaido Line was suspended, it took 30 hours for Horii to arrive at Osaka after a long detour using the Shin-etsu, Chuo and Tokaido Lines. Through the efforts of Horii, the Chuo-Do printing house agreed to do the printing.

The October issue of the *Ohm* magazine was titled "Special Disaster Issue", and it featured articles on and pictures of seriously damaged electrical facilities, traffic facilities and electrical plants. This issue also listed the new addresses of large companies, stores and plants that were forced to relocate, along with detailed information on how they were recovering from the damage.

The *Ohm* magazine thus responded to reader needs without missing a single issue. Since the subscriber cards were safe, Ohmsha could send this issue to every subscriber without delay, thereby ensuring their confidence in the company. Horii said later that "All employees had nothing but the clothes on their backs. We experienced a kind of socialist society, with no one claiming ownership of property or money. These things were shared equally among us. Publication of the *Ohm* magazine was only possible as the result of such efforts". Since the *Electrical Industry News* was a weekly paper, its publication was interrupted but printing was restarted on October 2, only a month later, thanks to the cooperation of Osaka Kon-nichi Shinbunsha (Osaka Daily News Inc.). This first issue was unique among competitive trade papers in that it was printed on a rotary press, rather than the lithograph used by competitors.

The burnt down company office was rebuilt in 1924 along with a new printing plant. Books published there included *Denki To Sono Machigai* (Misconception on Electricity) and *Saikin No Hoso Musen Denwa* (Recent Developments in Wireless Telephones).

1926: Ohmsha erected a gravestone for Donsai Matsumoto (1763–1836) at the Nenbutsuji Temple in Osaka Tennoji. He lived in the Edo period and wrote the first Japanese book on electricity, entitled *Oranda Shisei Erekiteru Kyurigen* (Principles of Electricity Developed in Holland). In 1935, a meeting was held at the Nenbutsuji Temple to commemorate the centennial of his death, initiated by Namioka and others. Memorial publication of Donsai's writings successfully ended in 1940. When the Donsai's book was reproduced in 1983 as an appendix to *Gendai Denki Koji Taikei* (Complete Works on Contemporary Electrical Work) consisting of 46 volumes, it was highly valued as a precious historical document.

Taking the opportunity afforded by the visit of Chinese electrical engineers to Japan, the *Ohm* magazine added columns written in both the Chinese and English. The foreign languages used in the column were increased to include German,

Esperanto, French and Russian. The foreign language columns continued until 1938 when the situation leading to World War II turned critical.

1927: Commemorating Seiichi Hirota's first visit abroad, Ohmsha held its first Ohm lecture meeting at the Denki Club in Tokyo. For the benefit of the magazine readers, Ohmsha conducted a practice examination of the national qualification test for electrical engineers. It was the first of many events to be offered to readers. The *Ohm* magazine held the first ever prize contest for reader's essays on electricity. Ohmsha increased its capital to Y70,000 this year, at which time the total number of shareholders increased to 138 because the company encouraged employees to hold company stock if they wished to do so. That year, Ohmsha published *Denki No Gainen To Roden No Yobo* (Concept of Electricity and Leakage Prevention), *Hatsuden Suiryoku No Keizaiteki Riyo* (Economical Application of Water for Hydraulic Power Generation) and *Zenkoku Dai Hatsudensho Ichiran* (List of Big Power Plants in Japan).

1929: Dr. Ryoichiro Isono, Dr. Matsujiro Oyama, Dr. Sadatoshi Betsugu, Dr. Yasujiro Niwa and Shigeru Mori, who was a technical officer of the Ministry of Posts and Telecommunications, joined *Ohm* as advisors. Chief editor Koga introduced a special section in the *Ohm* magazine called Footlight and invited five young elite electrical engineers to contribute essays each month for it. The column continued for five years, running 83 essays in all, and enhanced the reputation of *Ohm* magazine in government, industry and academic circles.

1930–1950 (Trial Installation of Automatic Public Telephone in Tokyo, Osaka and Yokohama)

World War II and Restructuring of Publishing Industry (From Integration of Magazines to Integration of Publishing Firms) due to Wartime Control

Hirota was a bright, resolute and challenging person as well as being affectionate, but he was not blessed with good health. His history of striving for the company was also the history of his struggle against illness. After appointing Namioka as the second representative of the company, he offered his services to the administration of Tokyo Denki University and in the establishment of Kobe Technical College (currently Kobe University).

In 1930, he wrote *Hirota Seiichi Bunshou* (Selected Essays of Seiichi Hirota) while he was hospitalized. In November of the same year, he was bestowed with the Third Order of Merit. He died aged 61 on January 25, 1931.

Ohmsha's operations so far had mainly involved the *Ohm* magazine. In the 1930's, however, it began to publish a series of electrical-related academic books focusing on technical innovations in this field. Such publications included *Wa Ei*

Doku Denkijyutsugo Daijiten (Encyclopedia of Electrical Terms in Japanese, English and German) in 1932 and *Denkikogaku Hanron* (Introduction to Electrical Engineering), consisting of 3 volumes, in 1934.

A bestseller in 1935 was *Denki Koji Dokuhon* (in 3 volumes) (Electrical Work Reader). It was published immediately after regulations governing electrical engineers and technicians were enacted, selling tens of thousands of copies within a very short time, thanks to the publication timing. This book contributed greatly to the building of a new office in 1937.

In 1939, in celebration of its 25th anniversary, Ohmsha awarded the first Ohmsha scholarship to those who successfully passed Class 1 of the national qualification test for electrical engineers. This scholarship continues to this day. The following year, 1940 (2600 according to the Japanese calendar) was also the year of a munitions boom sprung from the Sino-Japanese War. People were seen all over the country praying for victory.

This was the year that the Metropolitan Police Headquarters introduced magazine controls and, as a result, Ohmsha and Denki No Tomosha were specified as surviving electricity-related publishing firms. There was a growing trend toward prohibiting the use of enemies' languages. The name of the magazine *Denki Zasshi Ohm* (Electrical Industry Magazine Ohm) was changed to *Denki Zasshi Omu* (the word Ohm being replaced by the Japanese equivalent), then forced to employ the name *Denki Nihon* (Electrical Science in Japan) in 1942. In 1943, the regulations governing publishing firms were enacted. Ohmsha changed its name to Denki Nihon Sha (Electrics Japan Co., Ltd.). Its articles of incorporation were modified accordingly and the company employed its first president instead of a representative director.

The first president was Koji Koga. He was born in 1888 and graduated from the Electrical Engineering Department of Tokyo Imperial University. He guided the company superbly through difficult times, during and after the war. He was gentle, sincere, punctual, and above all, patient, as well as affectionate. After retiring to take responsibility for a conflict which occurred at Daido Printing Inc., he was re-elected president without the right of representation. In 1965, Koga, who was a counselor then, was bestowed with the Fourth Order of Merit, and died at the age of 85 in 1973.

According to the second set of regulations governing publishing firms, the government drafted the facilities and materials of printing plants with 200 or less employees. Ohmsha's printing department was also merged with six other small to mid-size printing companies in the Kanda area into Daido Printing Co., Ltd. (with about 250 employees). That year Ohmsha's printing department ended its 20-odd-year history.

Daido Printing went bankrupt in 1957, but Ohmsha still maintained close relations with the six printing firms as affiliates after they became independent from Daido soon after the war.

The tide of the war was turning against Japan and Tokyo came under frequent air attacks. Kanda Nishikicho, where Ohmsha was situated, and its vicinity were almost totally destroyed but fortunately our office buildings survived, though part of the wooden building was burnt. Our paper molds, printing paper and office supplies, which had been removed to the countryside during the war, were brought back afterwards.

Although the war had ended, the country was devastated. People were forced to stand in a long line for books in front of the Kyoto sales office (later Kyoto branch office) every day. Books were sold on the spot until stocks ran out. Employees and directors worked day and night. Sales of the Kyoto office contributed to the company's financial state at a time when the headquarters were having difficulty securing materials for publishing magazines and books.

The following were some of topical events at that time.

In 1945, Ohmsha's Osaka office was burnt down during an air raid.

In 1946, Ohmsha opened its Kyoto office. New magazines *Gijutsu Shinron* (New Technological Review), *Kokumin Keizai* (National Economy) and *Onkyo* (Sound) were issued. Ohmsha joined the newly organized "Shizen Kagakusho Kyokai" (Natural Science Publishers' Association of Japan).

In 1947, the company name Ohmsha was restored. A new magazine *Shin Denki* (New Electrical Science) was issued targeted at people preparing for Class 3 of the national qualification test for electrical engineers.

In 1948, the sales department became independent as Ohm Bookstore. Ohmsha's Sunaga proposed and organized "Kogakusho Kyokai" (Technology and Engineering Publishers' Association of Japan), inviting 25 publishers of engineering-related books.

The Age of Reconstruction 1950–1970 (The Electrical Laboratory developed the ETL Mark 1 relay system computer in 1952)
Publishing activities benefit from high economic growth

In the late 1950's, the petrochemical industry began full-fledged production, the electronics industry was burgeoning and industrial machines were becoming increasingly more sophisticated accompanying Japan's economic growth. Against this background, Ohmsha and Ohm Bookstore expanded their operations rapidly. Ohmsha successively published new magazines titled *Electronics*, *Denki To Koji* (Electricity and Electrical Work), MOL and *Setsubi To Kanri* (Facilities and

Control). The first issues of some of these magazines were reprinted, thanks to positive requests from readers.

To satisfy increased public interest in nuclear energy, Ohmsha published *Genshiro Note* (Reactor Note), *Genshikaku Kogaku Sokutei Gijutu* (Measurement Technologies in Nuclear Engineering) and *Genshikaku Kogaku Nyumon* (Intro-duction to Nuclear Engineering) in 1955. This same year Gozaburo Tanaka (born in 1908) became the sixth president succeeding Koga. After graduating from a junior high school in Taiwan, Tanaka studied electrical engineering at the Electrical Engineering School attached to the current Tokyo Denki University. He passed the Class 2 test of the national qualification test for electrical engineers on his own.

The following lists major publications and topics during this period.

1950: Musen Kogaku Pocket Book (Radio Engineering Pocket Book) and *Denki Kogaku Pocket Book — Junior Edition* (Electrical Engineering Pocket Book) were issued.

1951: Sokuryo Gijutsu Koza (in 8 volumes) (Survey Engineering Course) was the first Ohmsha publication in the field of civil engineering.

1952: The Japan Publishers Confederation was formed by the nine representative publishing bodies (currently, the Japan Book Publishers' Association). Publication of Ohm paperbacks began with *Atarashii Zetsuen Zairyo* (New Insulating Material).

1953: The Publisher's Association for Asian Cultural Exchange (currently, the Publishers Association for Cultural Exchange) was founded. A ceremony was held to mark presentation of the first Ohm engineering prize. This prize was established to commemorate the signing of the San Francisco Peace Treaty.

1954: Ohmsha held the centennial of G.S. Ohm's death at the Yamaha Hall in Ginza. This year Ohmsha published *Georg Simon Ohm — Sono Shogai To Gyoseki* (Georg Simon Ohm — His Life and Achievements), *Denki Gijutsusha No Tameno Jidoseigyo* (Automatic Control Technology for Electrical Engineers), *Sokuryo Gijutsu Binran* (Surveying Techniques Handbook) and *Musen Kogaku Handbook* (Radio Engineering Handbook) as well as the bestselling Ohm paperback, *Jidoseigyo Nyumon* (Introduction to Automatic Control).

1955: The Japan Society of Electrical Engineers was established and its secretariat located in the Ohmsha office.

1956: Ohmsha published the *Electronics* magazine, a new magazine specializing in electronics.

1960: The first issue of *Denki To Koji* (Electricity and Electrical Work) was published and sold so well as to require reprinting. In the same year, the first issue of *Joho Shori* (Information Processing) edited by Information Processing Society of

Japan was published.

1961: Ohmsha started publication of *Gendai Denki Kogaku Koza* (Electrical Engineering Today), consisting of 50 volumes.

1963: The first issue of the chemical technology magazine *MOL* was published, and *Introduction to Automatic Control* was published in English by Elsevier Publishing Co. of Holland, becoming the first Ohmsha book to be published abroad.

1964: Commemorating the 50th anniversary of Ohmsha, a variety of events were held including a memorial lecture and publication of *Ten Great Handbooks.* These comprised *Shinpan Musen Kogaku Handbook* (Revised Radio Engineering Handbook), *Hakumaku Kogaku Handbook* (Thin Film Engineering Handbook), *Jikayo Denki Shunin Gijutsusha Handbook* (Handbook for Qualified Engineers at Non-Utility Facilities), *Sequence Jido Seigyo Binran* (Automatic Sequence Control Handbook), *Handy Book Denki* (Handy Book on Electricity) and *Kenchiku Study Book* (Architecture Study Book). An extra memorial dividend was paid to shareholders to reward their support.

1967: The first issue of *Setsubi To Kanri* (Facilities and Control). It was targeted at the building and plant maintenance market. This same year, the government issued the Basic Law on Environmental Pollution Control. Ohmsha's capital was increased by ¥ 14 million to ¥ 30 million.

1968: Masamitsu Mitsui (currently an Executive Advisor) was elected as the seventh president to succeed Tanaka. Tanaka became chairman after serving 12 years as president. A long-awaited warehouse was built adjacent to the headquarters building. Ohmsha achieved record high production, sales and ordinary profit, thanks to internally promoted Ohm Move, aimed at achieving Originality, Humanity and Motivation, its three main goals. The house organ was published in May as a tool for training employees as well as for establishing better communications with them. The first seminar for those taking the national qualification test for electrical engineers was held in Tokyo and Osaka. This seminar is still being held to this day.

1969: Ohmsha published 13 computer and information related books to meet reader needs in the age of computers and information. *Nyumon FORTRAN* (Introduction to FORTRAN) and *Nyumon COBOL* (Introduction to COBOL) were super bestsellers, cultivating a strong readership among businessmen.

The Age of Information Technology 1970–1990 (New Tokyo International Airport (Narita Airport) was opened)
The age of major change: oil crisis and threat from copying machines
The age of computers was here. It was also the time when government con-

trol over environmental pollution became increasingly more severe. The Osaka International Exposition was held in 1970. The size of Ohmsha's magazines was enlarged to meet the needs of the times.

Focusing on trends in factory automation, Ohmsha published the *Syoryoku To Jidouka* (Energy Saving and Automation magazine).

1971: Japan shifted from the fixed exchange rates to a floating system following the so-called "dollar shock". Measures to prevent environmental pollution were promoted more than ever through the newly established Environment Agency. Anticipating introduction of the first national qualification test for environmental pollution control engineers, Ohmsha published such bestsellers as *Kogai Gairon* (Introduction to Environmental Pollution) and *Kogai Boushi Kanrisha Mondai Kaitou 600* (600 Selected Exercises for Those Taking the Environmental Pollution Control Engineer Test).

1972: This was the year that large-scale general strikes began. Labor disputes arose all over the country. In the publishing industry, the so-called "net problem" became more serious than ever among publishers, distributors and retail stores. Publishers made big compromises in order to settle the boycott by retail stores. Ohmsha published *Audio Hyakka* (Complete Book on Audio), consisting of four volumes.

1973: The Vietnam War ended at the beginning of this year. Japan experienced the so-called "oil crisis" due to economic problems both at home and abroad. The Japanese economy, in general, suffered not only as a result of the oil crisis but also from a shortage of electric power and a scant supply of paper. The publishing industry was no exception. Economic conditions were changing rapidly as the result of four successive hikes in the official bank rate following four successive reductions the previous year. The government budget saw a 124.6% year-on-year increase. Publishers had trouble setting prices because of soaring production costs and a labor shortage.

1976: Ohmsha's *Hikari Fiber Tsushin Nyumon* (Introduction to Optical Fiber Communications) was awarded the authorship prize by the Institute of Electronics and Communication Engineers of Japan and translation rights were sold to American and French publishers. Ohmsha published *Microcomputer Nyumon* (Introduction to Microcomputers) and *Microcomputer Kokoroe Cho* (Microcomputer Guide), forerunners of the microcomputer boom in Japan. This was followed by publication of the first issue of the long-selling *Zukai Computer Series* (Illustrated Computer Series). Ohmsha's *Gendai System Kogaku* (System Engineering Today) was awarded the authorship prize by The Institute of Electrical Engineers of Japan.

1978: The current headquarters building (1 floor below ground and 8 above with a total floor space of 4,907.08 m²) was erected in Kanda Nishiki-cho. Ohmsha's *Denjiha Kairo* (Electromagnetic Wave Circuits) was awarded the authorship prize by The Institute of Television Engineers of Japan.

1979: Ohmsha opened a booth at the world's largest book fair in Frankfurt. This same year, Ohmsha published *Denshi Tsushin Handbook* (Electronic Communication Handbook) and *Sougou Energy Koza* (General Energy Course). Copyrights to *Digital Audio Nyumon* (Introduction to Digital Audio) were granted to the USA and Italy.

1980: Ohmsha published some large handbooks, including *Shinpan Johoshori Handbook* (Revised Information Processing Handbook), *Antenna Kogaku Handbook* (Antenna Engineering Handbook) and *Television Gazo Kogaku Handbook* (Television and Image Electronics Handbook).

1981: Ohmsha, jointly with Elsevier/North-Holland, started publication of the *JARECT* Series (Japan Annual Reviews on Electronics, Computers and Telecommunications), to introduce state-of-the-art Japanese technologies to foreign countries. It also published *Cho LSI Gijutsu* (Basic VLSI Technology), *Seidenki Handbook* (Electrostatics Handbook) and *Kuki Seijo Handbook* (Environmental Clean Air Technology Handbook). *Onsei Joho Shori No Kiso* (Fundamentals of Speech Signal Processing) was awarded the authorship prize by the Institute of Television Engineers of Japan.

1982: Ohmsha published *Zukai Wordprocessor Dokuhon* (Illustrated Word rocessor Reader), the first electronic publication in Japan based on FD-saved manuscripts.

1983: Ohmsha published the first issue of *Computer & Network LAN* magazine. The company also began participating in business and data shows to exhibit its publications. Ohmsha started publication of the English academic journal, *New Generation Computing*, which focused on fifth-generation computers. This journal is distributed worldwide by Springer-Verlag. Our largest project began this year: the publication of *Gendai Denki Koji Taikei* (Complete Works on Today's Electrical Engineering) consisting of 46 volumes to be marketed through door-to-door sales.

Hikari Fiber (Optical Fiber) was awarded the authorship prize by the Institute of Electronics and Communication Engineers of Japan. Publication of *Zukai Mekatoronikusu Nyumon Series* (Illustrated Introduction to Mechatronics Series) was started. Ohmsha and Elsevier/North-Holland mutually exchanged staff for training.

This year Norikazu Taneda was elected as the tenth president, succeeding Mitsui who served as president twice for a total of 12 years. Taneda was an engineer who worked with the company as chief editor of the magazines and manager of the general affairs and accounting departments.

1984: Ohmsha held the second seminar for those taking the Class 2 national qualification test for information administrators in Tokyo. It published *Data Tsushin Handbook* (Data Communication Handbook), LSI *Handbook* (LSI Handbook), *Shin Kenchikugaku Pocket Book* (New Architecture Pocket Book) and *Sougou Zairyo Kyoudogaku Kouza* (General Course on Material Strength).

This year Ohmsha celebrated its 70th anniversary. All Ohmsha magazines invited readers to enter essay contests titled *Development of Technology*, *Education* and *International Cooperation*. The number of essays contributed far exceeded expectations. In June this year, ex-president Gozaburo Tanaka died after 60 years of service at Ohmsha.

1985: Ohmsha started publication of *Shin Ohm Bunko* (New Ohm Library). Our *Chishiki Kogaku Nyumon* (Introduction to Knowledge Engineering) received the first engineering and science book prize awarded by the Nikkan Kogyo Shinbunsha (Daily Industrial News). The Tsukuba International Exhibition of Science was held in Tsukuba University Town. Ohmsha fully supported the operations and exhibitions. We participated in the Exhibition, holding a book fair for 184 days at Papyrus Plaza pavilion. Mitsui was the executive chairman of the book fair. This same year, he was bestowed with the Fourth Order of Merit. After graduating from Tokyo Denki University, he worked for some time at the Naval Technology Laboratory before joining Ohmsha. When Japan lost the war, he returned to Ohmsha after having been detained in Siberia. He played an active part both in Ohmsha and the trade. Currently, he holds the post of executive advisor of the company. He was my tutor in the management of Ohmsha.

One of our subsidiaries, NPS, was inaugurated the same year. As part of our creative team, NPS is currently playing an active part in production of Ohmsha publications.

1986: Ohmsha started publication of *New Diamond* and *Jinkouchinou Gakkaishi* (Journal of Artificial Intelligence Society) as well as *Chishiki Kogaku Koza* (Knowledge Engineering Series) consisting of 10 volumes.

1987: Ohmsha published *Denki Kogaku Pocket Book* (Electrical Engineering Pocket Book) and *Kenchiku Setsubi Shusei* (Complete Book on Architectural Facilities). *Fuzzy System Nyumon* (Introduction to Fuzzy Systems) was a bestseller.

1988: Ohmsha exhibited its electronics publications at data shows. It started trial operation of the Ohm-net, a PC communication system. *Denshi Joho Tsushin Handbook* (Handbook for Electronics, Information and Communication Engineers), *Kagaku Gijutsu Waei Daijiten* (Japanese-English Science and Engineering Dictionary), COM *Series* (COM Series) and *Keiei Johogaku Koza* (Management Information Course) were also published.

The Age of Energy and Environment 1990 — Today (Kyoto Meeting for Prevention of Global Warming was held in 1999)

User-friendly technology and knowledge: expanding the computer market

1991: Ohmsha introduced the *Super Beginner Series* targeted at beginners in personal computing. *Chikyu Kankyo Kogaku Handbook* (Earth Science & Engineering Handbook) was awarded the technology and science book culture prize.

1992: Minna No Chikyu (Green Earth, Our Planet) and *SE Crisis* were bestsellers.

1993: The total number of issues of the general electric magazine *Ohm* reached 1,000. Ohmsha published *Kagaku Gijutsu Eiwa Daijiten* (English-Japanese Science and Engineering Dictionary), *Chodenndo Teion Kogaku Handbook* (Super Conduction and Low Temperature Engineering Handbook), *Sentan Device Material Handbook* (Advanced Device Material Handbook) and *Digital Shingo Shori Handbook* (Digital Signal Processing Handbook). It also published *Chikyu Kankyo Seminar* (Global Environment Seminar) consisting of 8 volumes, and publication of *Shin Computer Koza* (New Computer Course) was also started.

1994: Ohmsha held a lecture at the Ashahi Hall in Yurakucho to commemorate its 80th anniversary. It also held a seminar for those taking the national qualification test for data processing system administrators. Publication was started of *Techno Life Sensho* (Techno-Life Series) planned to commemorate the 100th anniversary of the Japan Society of Mechanical Engineers.

Translation from the German of *Denshi Bussei No Kiso* (Basics of Physical Properties of Electronics) was awarded the 31st Japan Translation Prize.

1995: Shinpan Jouhoushori Handbook (Revised Information Processing Handbook), *Kagaku Gijutsu Eigo Hyougen Jiten* (Dictionary of English Scientific and Technological Expression), *Zukai Denki No Daihyakka* (Illustrated Encyclopedia of Electrical Technologies) and *Zukai Computer Daihyakka* (Illustrated Encyclopedia of Computers) were published.

1996: Opened Ohmsha homepage on the Internet. *Haikibutsu Handbook* (Waste Management Handbook) and *Energy Shigen Handbook* (Energy Resource Handbook) were published. Ohmsha started publication of *Denken Sanshu Kanzen Koryaku* (How to Successfully Pass the Class 3 National Qualification Test for Electrical Engineers).

1997: Ohmsha published textbooks titled *Inter-University Series* to be used with the semester system. *Zukai Kisho No Daihyakka* (Illustrated Encyclopedia of Meteorology) and *Kankyo Yogo Jiten* (Dictionary of Environmental Terminology) were also published.

1998: The first issue of the Ohm Mook *Robocon Magazine* (Robot Contest Magazine) was issued. Ohmsha also published *Encyclopedia Denshi Jouhou Tsushin*

Handbook (Handbook for Electronics, Information and Communication Engineers), *Ouyo Butsuri Yogo Daijiten* (Dictionary of Applied Physics Terminology), *Shinpan Seidenki Handbook* (Revised Handbook of Electrostatics) and the *Journal of Visualization*. Ohmsha established Beijing Oriental Kelong Computer Typesetting and Production Co., Ltd. as a joint venture with IOS Press and Science Press of the Chinese Academy of Sciences.

1999: The first volume of the information magazine *Techno-Info* was published. Commemorating its 85th anniversary, Ohmsha published *Tokusoban Techno-Life Series Gijutsuya No Fukken* (Techno-Life Series — Reinstatement of Engineers), *Tatakau Dokuso No Yu Junichi Nishizawa* (Junichi Nishizawa, The Seeds of Creative Talent) and *Robokon Hakase No Monozukuri Yuron* (Dr. Robocon's Introduction to Handcrafting Robots for Competitions). The Ohmsha anniversary book fair was held in various cities throughout Japan.

2000: Ohmsha published a translation of IEEE's *Engineering Tomorrow*.

The next century

We believe that the mission of publishers is to publish good books. A good book is one that optimally meets the needs of the readers of the age. Now in the year 2000, the net business is rapidly growing and the number of ECs is also steadily increasing despite warnings issued regarding the computer networks.

Living in such an age, I celebrated my 50th anniversary at Ohmsha in 1999. Ohmsha grew in step with the development of science and technology in support of Japanese industry. Ohmsha has been managed democratically since its foundation as a non-hereditary company, which is exceptional among Japanese publishing houses. I celebrated my 10th anniversary (from February 1990) as the 11th president, observing the ambitions of the founders despite the severe environment surrounding the publishing industry. Since joining the company, I have not confined myself to the fields of electrics and electronics, but launched into other fields, including information, communication, machines, architecture, civil engineering and environmental facilities, chemical and science in general. I believe that I was appointed president because the books I planned and marketed sold best.

Now, 55 years after the war, parts of the Japanese social system are beginning to show signs of fatigue. We must realize that we are living the age of cohabitation of man and machine. It is not technology or computers that make careless mistakes. The problem lies in the interface that connects man and machine. I believe, however, that man will be able to live peacefully with machines as typified by the robot contests frequently held these days, where mismatching of the two is eliminated in fine style.

A Century of Science Publishing
E.H. Fredriksson (Ed.)
IOS Press, 2001

Chapter 5

Science Press
(Longman's Book Co., Ltd.)

Wang Jixiang
Science Press, Beijing, China

1. Initial period (1930–1938)

Longman's Book Co., Ltd., was founded in 1930 by Yan Youzhi. As a teacher who often experienced difficulty in acquiring high-quality, competitively priced books for teaching, he realised that there was a gap in the market and established his own publishing house. Business rose sharply, with orders from major universities as well as individual subscribers, and in 1932 the company started a small printing house. In 1934, in order to introduce advanced technology from foreign countries, Yan Youzhi decided to go abroad to study. Before leaving the country, he organised it so that Longman's printing, publishing and distributing business would operate as normal. Yan Youzhi studied for more than three years in England and Germany, first studying maths, physics and metallurgy at Manchester Science and Technology College and Manchester University, and in 1936 attending Leipzig Printing College, Germany, and studying printing technology there. In the spring of 1937, he predicted that the Japanese were preparing to declare war against China. In May of that year, he returned to China. On 13 August the Japanese bombed Shanghai, destroying Longman's Printing House. When Shanghai was occupied by the Japanese, Longman's cleared up, invited the workers who had been evacuated to the countryside to come back, bought some broken printing machines and had them repaired, leased a temporary factory, and thus restored production. In its first seven years, Longman's published almost 1,000 titles for schools and universities.

2. Combined development period (1938–1945)

After 13 August 1937, the people in Shanghai were nervous; the publishing industry was moribund, competition was intense, and profits had dropped sharply. In order to regain profits, Yan Youzhi had the idea that eight publishing houses should combine their resources and operate together. Longman's issued shares, of which the original Longman's Book Co. held 32%. A board of directors was appointed, and Yan Youzhi was appointed the general manager. At first, marketing was contracted out to a Shanghai journal publisher, but in 1938 it was taken back and carried out by Longman's. Longman's also built a printing house and set up a distribution centre and bookstores; sub-branches for distribution were also established in Peking and Tianjin. From then on, Longman's integrated its publishing, printing and distributing operations. This new combined company used a simpler administration; it cut costs and increased its efficiency levels.

At that time, Longman's consisted of only about 16 people, fulfilling the roles of secretary, accountant, publishing, general affairs, stockroom and wholesale departments. Although Longman's was not big in size, it published a wide variety of books; but it suffered a permanent cash-flow problem. As time passed, money management became the most outstanding characteristic in Longman's operation and management, which set high standards for the turnover time of raw materials and the storage time of finished products and semi-finished products. Therefore, learning by their experience, Longman's published books in accordance with supply and demand, and fixed production quantities based on sales. Most of the manuscripts were provided or recommended by the universities and colleges that planned to use them. Longman's set up several warehouses for storing semi-finished best-sellers and large or thick books. This meant that Longman's did not have to pay immediately to have books bound; they could bind them when needed. The quantity of books to be bound could be changed according to selling status, so this was very flexible. Most of the board of directors of Longman's Combined Book Co. came from education. They knew that their staff were the key to success or failure of their undertaking, so they took good care of them. Many were young people; probationers accounted for one-third of the staff. In this way, the company saved money and trained new recruits from the ground up. The development of Longman's business was often restricted by a shortage of funds. In order to save money, from 1942 on, the Company cut down on its stock dividends (to 0.8%) and bonuses.

Longman's understood the importance of distribution: only when books had sold out could they make profits and reprint where necessary. The company was careful never to let best-sellers go out of print, and equally they were careful not to overstock slow-selling books. At that time, the direct cost of publishing books was about one third of the list price of the book (not including administrative expenses and taxation). Trade discount was 40%; sometimes a greater discount was given in retail sales for purchasing a large quantity of books. Longman's advertised in newspapers and journals, distributed book catalogues, etc., all of which obtained good results. The company tried its best to supply books as long as the titles of those books were listed on the catalogue. No matter whether readers came to buy books, bought books by mail or purchased books by telephone, a catalogue would be sent to them together with the books they had purchased, to encourage them to buy again from Longman's. Longman's invested heavily in distribution, and the company set up a number of distribution centres in a short time. When the Japanese invaded China, the Nationalist Party government was passive, and was defeated again and again. It moved its capital to Chongqing, Sichuan Province. Many universities followed its suit. From 1939, Longman's had to transport large numbers of books to Sichuan Province to sell them there, thus alleviating to some extent the urgent demand for science and technology books.

3. The Turning Period

In the autumn of 1945, after the war had ended, publishing became more competitive. Longman's decided to set up a scientific and technical book division with Mr. Cheng Keyou as Director, to meet China's needs. Selected topics were recommended; after preliminary approval, the commissioning editor would exchange views with professors at several universities or experts in the subject to determine potential demand and readership. Then authors (or translators) had to be selected. They would sign a contribution contract which stated the royalty rate to be paid (generally 10–12% of the list price, the royalty would be paid each season based on copies sold). Printruns and list prices were decided by General Manager Yan Youzhi and Director Cheng Keyou. Longman's employed few general editors, preferring part-time editors with specialised knowledge.

At this time, editing and proofreading were combined, so that editors and staff jointly designed and proofread a book, thus all gaining wide experience of different skills. Longman's also persuaded 23 university professors, each experts in their own field, to form an advisory committee for the publication of engineering titles. Within two years of establishing the scientific and technical books editorial division, nearly 200 titles had been published, many of which became textbooks or reference books for universities and schools, being reprinted many times and used for many years. At that time, printruns were generally about 3000 copies, with seldom more than 10,000 copies being printed. To begin with, Longman commissioned, typeset, printed and bound the books it sold, but with the increasing volume of scientific and technical books being published, it began to outsource typesetting, printing and binding. Before long, Longman's had signed long-term contracts with many other companies to have these tasks done out of house.

4. New Historical Period (1949–1954)

After Shanghai was liberated in May 1949, Longman sent employees to Shenyang Xi'an, etc., and set up bookstore branches, thus expanding its distribution service. From 1950 on, in order to increase its sales, and facilitate libraries, scientific research institutions and the general public to purchase scientific and technical books, bookstore branches in Beijing and Hankou, among others, also sold scientific books published by other publishing houses besides Longman's. This was welcomed by readers. According to statistics, in Beijing branch, the percentage of books sold in one month which had been published by other publishers was as high as 70% of the total volume of sales during that period. In 1953, Longman's strengthened its editorial and proofreading departments and improved their working environments. Before this, Longman's publications were sold basically through its own distribution network, so the publishers and the readers interacted directly with each other. After the liberation of China, Longman's publications were given to Xinhua Bookstore and China Book Distribution Corporation for sale and distribution. In order to further expand distribution, in August 1951, Longman's, together with China Scientific Books and Instruments Corporation, Lixin Accountant Books and Utilities Company and Xinya Bookstore, organised a combined distributing institution called the China Combined Scientific and Technical Books Distribution Agency (CCSTBDA). Yan Youzhi was appointed the Director of this organisation. Longman's sales outlets and those of the other members of this organisation all became CCSTBDA sales outlets, and bookshops were set up in many other cities. In the Movement Against the Five Evils (1951–1952), public opinion was against CCSTBDA; it was thought that it was in rivalry with the state-owned Xinhua Bookstore and China Book Distribution Corporation. Therefore, after this movement, CCSTBDA was disbanded and, except for the bookshops in Shanghai and Beijing, branches of Longman's in other parts of China were all closed and its distribution business was handed over to the Xinhua Bookstore for operation. Thereafter, Longman's made contact with Ministry of Higher Education, and accepted the task of compiling, translating and publishing scientific and technical textbooks from the USSR. At that time, few Longman's editors understood Russian, so they had to learn quickly. Because Longman's had previously combined editing and proofreading, this work was split between the staff, to undertake the three stages of proofreading. It was required that the proofreader check the translation manuscript carefully against the original. There were only a few members of staff, the task was a time-consuming and onerous one, and funds were low; the manuscripts of a book had to be sent for typesetting and proofreading in several batches in a streamlined process, so the work was very intense. Longman's also placed orders for processing, and at that time the production volume was increasing rapidly. Take the case of the paper used for printing books, for example: if the paper use amount in 1949 was 100, in 1950 it was 385, in 1951 it was 1073 (in 1952 it was 599, because the Movement Against the Three Evils and the Five Evils occurred during this time), and in 1953 it was 1679. In the meantime, Longman's book distribution also increased. If the distribution amount of 530,037,769 yuan (old RMB) was 100 in 1949, by 1953 it had reached 5728. As sales of books increased, expenses grew relatively smaller: in 1949 expenses accounted for 27.24% of the distribution cost, and in 1953 this had decreased to 14.23%.

5. The founding of Science Press

In view of the importance of publishing work to scientific research, on the day it was founded (November 1, 1949), the Chinese Academy of Sciences (CAS) set up the Compiling, Translating and Publishing Bureau (later changed to the Compiling and Translating Bureau) in the headquarters of the CAS, hosting publishing work. This was the first science and technology compiling, translating and publishing organisation of its kind established after the founding of New China. At that time, the Bureau's tasks were to publish the journals edited by various CAS societies, science and technology monographs by Chinese scholars, to translate and publish scientific works from foreign countries, and organise the compilation, examination and approval of natural science terms. In the meantime, it was to accept the entrustment from the State General Administration of Publication, and undertake the tasks of examining science and technology book manuscripts offered by Commercial Press and Longman's. Moreover, the Bureau collected selected topics and book manuscripts from various universities and scientific research institutions, and in turn recommended them to Commercial Press and Longman's. In February 1954 the CAS thought it necessary to enhance their publishing work, and they established the Compiling, Translating and Publishing Committee, to lead and plan the publishing work of the whole Academy, and decided that the Compiling and Translating Bureau should be the working body of this Committee. Since the Compiling and Translating Bureau was not an independent publishing unit, it was restricted in its manuscript-organising activities. The only way to solve this problem was to enhance its editing and publishing departments and establish its own publishing house, thus freeing the Compiling and Translating Bureau. At that time, the socialist reform of private industries and commerce by the state was in full swing. In accordance with this, the CAS proposed a plan of public–private joint operation with private publishing enterprises, so as to cover the manpower shortage of the CAS. In this way, under the hosting of the General Administration of Publication, talks began with Longman's on public-private joint operation. After two very successful talks, "A Transcript of Talks" was published. On 26 May 1954 the General Administration of Publication formally gave a written reply to Longman's, saying: "Your company originally has some government shares and has already undertaken the task of placing orders for processing for the state. At present, conditions are ripe for overall public-private joint operation, and our Administration agrees that your company can adopt public-private joint operation, and has decided to regroup it into Science Press". From April 1950, Longman's had submitted several applications for public-private joint operation; it was one of the first private publishing companies to adopt public-private joint operation.

In 1954, the CAS appointed Yang Zhongjian, a famous paleontologist, former Director of the Compiling and Translating Bureau, as President of Science Press, and Longman's recommended Shen Suming, the original President of Longman's, to be Vice President. On 27 July Science Press held the first meeting of its Board of Directors. Zhou Taixuan and Yan Youzhi both made reports on the process of preparatory work for the founding of Science Press. Finally, it was agreed that the formal founding date of Science Press would be 1 August, and the inaugural meeting would be held in advance on 29 July. The guiding principles and tasks of Science Press approved by the Culture and Education Committee of the Government Administration Council on 28 July, 1954 are as follows:

The guiding principles and tasks: In accordance with the general tasks of the State in the transitional period, to organise, compile and translate Chinese and foreign scientific works, to promote scientific research work, so as to serve the socialist construction of China. Its concrete tasks are:

1. Publish sorted data collected by and monographs on the investigation and research achievements obtained by researchers in the research institutes of the CAS and other research institutions;

2. Publish scientific journals and bulletins of various specialised scientific societies and research institutions;

3. Edit and publish materials and treatises of China's history of science, serial journals of scientific treatises of modern times, scientific abstracts and translation journals;

4. Compile, translate and publish world-leading scientific treatises and classical works, mainly from the USSR;

5. Compile, translate and publish theoretical natural science titles;

6. Edit and publish other related scientific books and journals within the publishing plan approved by the Compilation, Translation and Publication Committee of the CAS.

As approved by the Culture and Education Committee of the Government Administration Council, Science Press was under the governance of the CAS and the General Administration of Publication, with the CAS as the main factor. The CAS was in charge of the leading principles of editing work, work plan, vocational work and administrative management, etc., while the General Administration of Publication was in charge of publication business, enterprise management, etc. The editorial department, managerial department, and Shanghai branch were set up under the President, Editor-in-Chief and Manager, and within the departments, corresponding sections were set up to deal with day to day work. The Board of Directors of Science Press only held two meetings, the first on 27 July 1954 when Science Press was founded, and the second on 27 December 1955. In the second meeting, Zhao Zhongchi, Vice President, gave a report on "Work from August 1954 to December 1955", manager Yan Youzhi gave a report on "Financial Statement from August to December 1954", and Zhao Zhongchi also gave reports on "Draft Statutes of Science Press" and "Additional Remarks on the Draft Statutes". All these reports were passed. Finally, the meeting decided that no Council Meeting would be held in the future, unless it was necessary. By that time, the Board of Directors of Science Press had accomplished its historical mission.

6. Great development period of Science Press (1954–1966)

After its founding, under the leadership of Guo Moro, the President of the CAS and leaders at various levels of the CAS, Science Press gradually became known for three 'heights' (high grade, high level and high quality), its guiding ideology of 'quality first' and 'preciseness and accurateness', and the working styles 'solemnity, strictness and tightness', and became the largest academic publishing house in China. In accordance with the demands of the CAS, the Compilation and Translation Bureau of the CAS and Science Press proposed, in succession, the "Draft Outline of 15-Year (1953–1967) Long-term Planning", the "Draft Outline of 12-Year (1956–1967) Long-term Planning of Scientific Publication", and formulated the "Ten-year (1963–1972) Publishing Planning of Science Press" for internal circulation. The drawing up of these documents played a positive role in coordinating and reflecting China's scientific research work status and achievements, providing publications for various scientific disciplines, fostering alliances and promoting the development of science and technology. In 1958, in order to meet the needs of its broad readership, with approval from the Publication Administration of the Ministry of Culture, Science Press decided to set up bookshops in China's main cities, to assist local Xinhua bookstores and post offices to sell books and journals for Science Press across the country. Science Press thus set up 19 bookshops in cities such as Beijing, Shanghai and Nanjing. The establishment of this distribution network led to increased profits. For example, in 1963, the sales of books and journals from the various bookshops accounted for 41% of the total distribution amount in the same year. Over the three difficult years from 1960 to 1962, a total of eight bookshops stopped operation, and eleven other bookshops closed down due to the impact of the 'Cultural Revolution'. In 1961, in accordance with the provisions of Publication Hu No. 66 of the Ministry of Culture, "Notice for Transferring the Tasks of Publishing Books and Journals in Philosophy and Social Sciences Undertaken by Science Press and other Related Publishing Houses", the task of publishing books and journals in philosophy and social sciences that had originally been undertaken by Science Press was handed over to the People's Publishing House, Zhonghua Book Co. Ltd., Commercial Press and Historical Relics Publishing House. During this period, Science Press published more than 5,000 prestigious academic books and over 100 science journals. As well as this, from 1958 onwards, Science Press translated, compiled and published several monographs and proceedings concerning the new atomic and hydrogen bombs and satellite technology. In 1965, it published more than 100 titles related to atomic development and exploitation, thus retaining its original characteristics of publishing 'high grade, high level and high quality' titles. On 27 October 1959, Chairman Mao Zedong visited the Exhibition of Natural Science Leap Forward Achievements of the CAS, where books and journals published by Science Press were displayed.

7. 'Cultural Revolution' period and subsequent restoration period (1966–1978)

After the start of the 'Cultural Revolution', editing and publishing stopped at Science Press. In 1970, after the three scientific organisations (State Science and Technology Commission of China, the Chinese Academy of Sciences and the National Science and Technology Association) had been incorporated, China System (1970) No. 1 Document formally dismissed Science Press and Popular Science Press, and preparations were made to establish a new publishing house, to be called China Science Press. Its name was subsequently changed back to Science Press. During this period, publications were mainly the products underway before the Cultural Revolution and a few new books. In 1972, the Atlas of Higher Plants of China was published, and nine new journals were begun or resumed. At that time, the company reorganised itself, took on new staff, and editing and publishing work gradually developed again. Science Press was to take on the publishing of books and journals relating to basic disciplines, frontier disciplines and new technologies. In 1974, the CAS organised a working group with participants from

Science Press to implement the translation and publication of China's Science and Civilisation (by Joseph Needham). In 1975, Science Press published a large character version of the Fossils and Zoology journals to serve as a reference for Chairman Mao and other leaders of the State. In 1978, Science Press formulated the 8-Year (1978–1985) Publication Planning in order to modernise its publishing processes in line with the Party's Central Committee and the State Council decrees. Science and technology publication work was thus resumed. Publication began of the monograph series Pure Mathematics and Applied Mathematics, and the Science and Technology Encyclopedia. In order to increase staff expertise, Science Press began to hold lectures on editorial work and other relevant topics as well as foreign language training courses for personnel.

8. Practice reform and opening up to the outside world to recreate splendour (after 1979)

In order to make up the loss caused by the 'Cultural Revolution', after the Third Plenary Session of the 11th Central Committee of the Communist Party of China, in accordance with the guiding principles of publication: 'laying emphasis on basic science, laying emphasis on improvement, and concurrently giving consideration to popularisation', Science Press' staff served scientific research by publishing a huge amount of monographs, proceedings, books and journals in high and new technology (500 books and more than 140 journals annually, on average), and at the same time actively promoted the development of science and technology publishing and the cooperation with foreign publishers in co-publication and distribution.

Science Press set up cooperation relationships with Springer Verlag, Germany and forty other publishers, and co-published a large number of excellent books and journals, such as Ligand Field Theory and Method, Physical Geography of China, Engineering Controlling Theory, Value Distribution Theory and Its New Research, and Chinese Soil. Since 1982, more than 200 books published by Science Press have won prizes and critical acclaim, and it has consistently been at the forefront of publishing excellence in its chosen subjects. In 1984 and 1992, in order to develop scientific publications, the CAS and the News and Publication Administration agreed that Science Press could publish audio-visual and electronic publications. After the reopening of Shanghai Branch, Guangzhou, Changchun Shenyang and Chengdu editorial departments and Wuhan Branch were set up in turn. In 1985, National Natural Science Terms Committee was formally established under the leadership of the State Science and Technology Commission and the CAS, and its office was attached to Science Press. In accordance with Decision of

Strengthening Publication Work and the guiding principles of running the CAS, Science Press formulated its guiding principles and tasks and drew up 'Key Points of Three-year Planning of Science Press (1988–1990)' and the 'Outline of the 8th Five-year Planning for the Development of Science Press'. In 1985, Science Press was approved to become an institution (not an enterprise). In 1987, the CAS agreed to the three-year operation goal determined by Science Press. In 1990, in order to support the publication of excellent science and technology books and journals, the CAS decided to set up Science Publication Funds, for which the CAS would appropriate three million yuan (RMB) per year from science operating expenses. The office of the CAS Science Publication Funds Expert Committee was set up in Science Press. All publications receiving support from the publication funds were to be published by Science Press, and the publication of a number of excellent academic monographs resulted from this. The long-term goal was to turn Science Press from a production company to a production-operation company, from a company selling only to China to an international company. At the same time, Science Press proposed the new working strategy 'support books with books, supplement the internal with the external, and supplement the main profession with side lines', in order to enhance its strength and development ability. Science Press then set up C-EScience Press Ltd. (HK), Science Press New York, Ltd., and the Golden Lion Company (Moscow) respectively in Hong Kong, New York and Moscow in the form of joint ventures or using its own capital. Science Press also put in place a series of measures for optimising selected topics, strengthening its operation and reducing losses. In August 1993, with approval from the State News and Publication Administration, Longman's Book Co., Ltd. resumed trading, mainly publishing books in the fields of culture, education, and popular science. In October of the same year, Science Press, together with 14 other Chinese publishing houses, became the first National Excellent Books Publishing Organisation to be jointly commended by the Propaganda Department of the Central Committee of the CPC and the State News and Publication Administration. In May 1993, the joint meeting of the Party and the administrative leaders of Science Press passed the General Plan for the Reform of Science Press. On this basis, in January 1995, Implementation Opinion on Transforming the Systems of Science Press and Promoting Structural Adjustment was passed. In July 1995, the 'Science in China' Periodical Press was set up with the approval of the CAS. In 1996, Science Press underwent a review of all company costs, practices and accounts and adopted many new management practices, including target management and implementing a new and comprehensive index check-up system. After several years of trial and error, the development goals of Science Press were clear, and they were as follows: guiding

principle, one goal, two traditions, three services, four characteristics and five measures. One goal: Making Science Press into China's largest international publisher,
publishing at the highest academic level and the most comprehensive range of
books. Two traditions: 'three heights' characteristics, and 'three strictness' working
style. Three services: With the CAS as backing, these 'services' were to serve scientific research bases, serve the development of high-tech and new industry bases, and
serve the talent-fostering bases. Four characteristics were as follows: 1. Series of
monographs, basic theories and basic materials, all at an international level;
2. Series of high and new technology and applied technology; 3. Series of high-level
textbooks for teaching purposes; 4. Series of dictionaries and handbooks. The five
measures were: insisting on opening up to the outside world; continually making
structural adjustments within the company; further transferring mechanisms; fostering talents; and optimising environments.

Science Press proposed a 'three point strategy': intensifying the highest point,
developing the growth point and fostering the profit growth point. In 1996, it over-
fulfilled its annual plan, achieving a production value of 46 million yuan (RMB) and
realising a profit of 4 million yuan. In 1998, Science Press proposed the goal of
putting emphasis both on spiritual civilisation and material civilisation. It proposed
the guiding principle of development into groupment, 'getting together with those
concerned, forming an inner core, transforming mechanisms, introducing and fostering talents, expanding and fission'. In the same year, Science Press achieved a
production value of 250 million yuan, a sales income of 120 million yuan, and a
profit of 22 million yuan.

After three years' rapid development, in 1999, the management of Science
Press stated that they would set out on a journey, being based on the source of
knowledge innovation projects, to disseminate and transfer knowledge, and popu-
larise knowledge innovation achievements, thus making Science Press the largest
international publishers in China; the highest level academic publishers and the
most comprehensive and, on this basis, organising the China Science Publication
Group. In 1999, Science Press achieved a production value of 302 million yuan, a
sales income of 240 million yuan, and a profit of 25 million yuan.

Over the last 45 years, Science Press has published over 20,000 titles and 300
journals. Currently, it publishes over 2,000 titles (of which over 30 are in foreign
languages) each year, with science and technology titles accounting for 12.5% of the
total books published in this subject in the whole country. It also published over
150 journals (of which 29 titles are in foreign languages), the academic journals
published accounting for 15%of those published in China. In recent years, Science
Press has also actively developed audio-visual products and software, CD-ROMs and

other electronic publications, with science and technology as a main subject matter. Since 1982, Science Press has ranked first in seven successive sessions of National Excellent Science and Technology Book Appraisals; over 40 books published by them have won first-class awards or special-class awards, and over 200 books have won book prizes at ministerial level or above. Science Press has set up bookshops or distribution centres in large cities such as Shanghai, Wuhan, Shenyang, Changchun, Chengdu and Shenzhen. In order to open up to the outside world, and strengthen contact with foreign countries, Science Press has set up Science Press New York, Ltd. and C-E Science Press Ltd. (HK) in New York City and Hong Kong respectively, and has also forged cooperation relationships with over 80 publishers from 10 countries.

From the above, it can be seen that Science Press is marching forward in its reform and opening up to the outside world! Earnestly hoping that science and technology experts and colleagues in publishing and marketing circles in China and overseas will cooperate with Science Press, to go forward hand by hand, in order to make a greater contribution to the dissemination of science, the popularisation of science, the promotion of civilisation and the progress of mankind.

A Century of Science Publishing
E.H. Fredriksson (Ed.)
IOS Press, 2001

Chapter 6

The Dutch Publishing Scene:
Elsevier and North-Holland

Einar H. Fredriksson
IOS Press, Amsterdam, The Netherlands

International science publishing activities in the Netherlands in the first half of the twentieth century came about through contacts with German publishers, many from Leipzig, Germany's publishing centre, which contained important companies such as Akademische Verlagsgesellschaft (Aka), where young, aspiring Dutch publishers received their training. When the Nazis came to power, many German scientists, especially those of Jewish origin but also others, began to face difficulties in publishing their scientific work.

The first Dutch publisher to recognise this situation and its implications was J.P. Klautz, managing director of Elsevier Publishing Company in Amsterdam, who offered Jewish German scientists the chance to publish their work via his company, thereby becoming the major player in foreign language scientific publishing in Holland in the years before the Second World War broke out.

Elsevier was founded in 1881 in Rotterdam at the initiative of a local bookseller — using the name of the famous Elzevier dynasty of the seventeenth and eighteenth centuries. Before the Second World War Elsevier published general titles in Dutch, encyclopaedias and so on. In 1887 Elsevier moved to Amsterdam, the cultural and publishing centre of the Netherlands. One of its central works was the Winkler Prins encyclopaedia, and in 1883 Elsevier obtained the rights to illustrations from Brockhaus' famous series of encyclopaedias. (Ferdinand Arnold Brockhaus founded his company in 1805 in Amsterdam, but moved to Leipzig in 1817.)

J.P. Klautz (1904–1990) visited Brockhaus in 1929 for the preparation of the fifth edition of Winkler Prins. While he was there he saw on the office wall of the director, Hans Brockhaus, two photographs, one of a middle-aged woman and one of a rather unattractive man. Brockhaus explained that he kept these photographs on the wall for the benefit of young editors on his staff and added: "the lady is Mrs Johanna Schopenhauer, a novelist of moderate ability but whose books were bestsellers. She was therefore held in high esteem by us. One day she showed us a short manuscript on philosophy by her somewhat eccentric son. We saw nothing in this manuscript, but wanted to please one of our best-selling authors by publishing her son's work. We published more and more of her son Arthur's work and today nobody remembers Johanna, but her son's works are in steady demand and contribute to Brockhaus' reputation" [3].

During the early 1930's, Elsevier had to cope with serious financial problems, which had arisen even before Klautz had been appointed director of the company in 1930. The Winkler Prins encyclopaedia was to carry the company financially, and it remained the policy of the owners that the non-fiction works should subsidise fiction publishing, but there were to be years, especially during the Second World War, when best-selling fiction titles would contribute significantly to the survival of the company. In 1936 Klautz wrote a memo for the Elsevier board on the opportunity of publishing scientific books in German by Jewish scientists facing difficulties in Germany. In 1937 he went to Germany, Austria and Switzerland to further investigate the market for scientific books in German. In Leipzig he visited Aka and G. Thieme, learning that over 50% of their science books (in German) were sold abroad. Dutch booksellers confirmed this estimate.

As to the situation in Germany, Klautz also learned that works by Jewish authors were allowed to be bought and that such titles could be imported into Germany, but it was uncertain whether Germans would be allowed to use foreign currency to pay for them. When Klautz reported his findings to the board, he was met with scepticism: Elsevier's main activity was in Dutch language books, including translations from foreign languages, and to start to publish works in German, primarily for export markets, might only yield results in the long term.

Klautz realised, however, that not only the right to publish works in German, but also the right to publish scientific works in English by German authors might be of interest. In Leipzig he also discussed, therefore, English language rights for some important titles. Elsevier therefore ventured into publishing a mix of German and English language book titles before the war. It should be borne in mind that Elsevier had no more than 10 employees when the war broke out, and that the total number of foreign language titles it published remained low up to 1940. Klautz also had a good relationship with the Rubber Foundation in Delft and his discussions there encouraged him in his determination to move into scientific publishing, especially in the field of chemistry, and started the preparation of two major works in English: Karrer's Handbook of Organic Chemistry and Richter's Organic Chemistry.

At the same time, Klautz took the daring initiative in 1939 to set up a US branch of Elsevier. Since the mid-1920's an Amsterdam bookseller, Dekker & Nordemann, which specialised in the mail order selling of German science books and journals, had played an important role in facilitating his contacts with German publishers. In the late 1930's these contacts would prove to be important to Klautz. The first attempt by a Dutch company to establish a science publishing foothold in the United States was by the Nordemann Publishing Company, which was established in 1937. It anticipated collaboration with the German company Aka. When this failed, Klautz was contacted, and plans for an American Elsevier were worked on up to 1940.

M.D. Frank (1913–1995) established the second line of activity in science publishing in the Netherlands. After finishing secondary school and having worked at a book store in Amsterdam, he was sent by his father to learn the publishing trade in companies in Germany, France and the UK. In Leipzig, in 1934, he worked as a trainee at Aka. He got to know the key people at this company, including the Jolowicz family, their son-in-law K. Jacoby (1892–1968) who was co-founder together with Walter Jolowicz (who changed his surname to Johnson and later worked at Academic Press in New York), the physicist P. Rosbaud (1896–1963; a war hero who joined Butterworth in the UK after the war. He was the first scientific director of Pergamon Press, in 1951) and the chemistry consultant E. Proskauer (1903–1991; co-founder —with M. Dekker of Dekker & Nordemann — of Interscience in New York in 1940, and later vice-president of Wiley after they bought Interscience in 1961). In Leipzig Frank also worked in a bookstore and attended the Handelshochschule there. In Paris he trained with a bookstore and the publisher Gallimard, and briefly worked in London with a publishing house before returning to the Netherlands in 1936.

The Royal Netherlands Academy of Arts and Sciences had a vacancy in its newly established North-Holland Publishing Company and Frank was the successful applicant. The small company (its working capital was 500 Dutch guilders, but it did not need more as all its production costs were borne by the Academy) was founded on 13 August 1931. Naturally, the print runs of the titles published here were small but, in 1937, a law was passed which obliged all small self-employed businessmen to pass a test of proficiency in book-keeping, etc. before they would be allowed to set up shop. Frank was fortunate enough to become acquainted with the man who had the idea of preparing a set of simple textbooks for this purpose, which resulted in a series of study books which sold over a million copies until well after the war. Frank became deputy director of the company in 1939 and owner in 1963.

Before the war, Frank had established contacts with the research management of the Philips Laboratories, and through the Academy he maintained contact with leading scientists, but they did not result in publications. (In 1937, Frank had drafted a long-term plan for the company, outlining its future specialisation in science publishing in both English and German.) Ironically, North-Holland would not have survived the war years had it not been for its textbooks aimed at small businessmen.

Activities after the Second World War

Both Elsevier and North-Holland survived the war. Elsevier had an important list of Dutch publications, the encyclopaedia and general literature which sold extremely well. Even old stocks were sold out: in wartime, there was little else people could spend their money on. As far as North-Holland was concerned, the Academy publications and doctoral theses were not, of course, best-sellers, but the above mentioned textbooks did extremely well. However, starting a line of scientific publications after the war was no easy matter. Foreign currency, for example, was scarce, as were funds for foreign travel or supplies from abroad. (Klautz offered Churchill's literary agent in New York a guaranteed royalty of US$ 100,000 for Churchill's war memoirs without the prior consent of the Dutch Central Bank and only got approval for this after he threatened that he would write to Churchill to explain that he had had to withdraw his offer as Holland refused to honour its liberator by having his memoirs published in Dutch.)

Klautz' experience with foreign language publications had led to several printing houses acquiring considerable skill in typesetting complicated scientific material. The Dutch graphics industry benefited from this for many years. Other factors contributing to the favourable business climate were low labour costs following the war and the availability of immigrant scientists willing to support publishers by advising how to establish the necessary networks for book and journal publishing.

While Elsevier's focus between 1945 and 1955 was mainly on chemistry and related technologies, North-Holland's was on physics and mathematics. Klautz hired the brilliant chief-editor, the chemist W. Gaade (earlier employed by the Rubber Foundation in Delft) in 1946 and later that year hired the bookseller H.P.M. Bergmans to manage the science publications within the diversifying company.

With the start of its primary research journal *Biochimica et Biophysica Acta* (*BBA*) in 1947, Elsevier took its first decisive step in the Dutch science publishing scene after the war. The journal grew steadily, and published two volumes in 1950, thereby doubling in price. *BBA* was to become the largest primary journal in the world (in 1979 44 volumes were published).

To give a historical perspective to Elsevier's first journal, *BBA*, [4]: "It all started when the fugitive Carl Oppenheimer was forbidden by the German occupation in 1941 to continue editing his journal *Enzymologia* and asked [the Dutch professor H.G.K.] Westenbrink to carry on in his place. This he did, together with his old friend [the Danish professor K.] Linderstroem-Lang. After the War, it proved impossible to come to terms with the publishers about the manner in which the journal ought to be continued in the eyes of the editors [Oppenheimer had died in the meantime]. So Lang and Westenbrink decided to found a new journal, foreseeing that there would soon be a great demand for journals."

The initiative to start a new journal in the early post-war period often came from scientists. That you did not need a society behind the launching of a new scientific journal was one of the first important realisations of young science publishers. Another important step was the launch of a programme of multilingual dictionaries. Elsevier published its first scientific catalogue in 1948. Entitled *Elsevier's Scientific Publications*, it contained introductions to each work including many reviews of the *Encyclopedia of Organic Chemistry*, and came to 56 pages, describing 23 published works and 21 works in preparation. Among the journals listed, apart from *BBA*, was *Analytica Chimica Acta*, another future Elsevier success story. North-Holland had a later start. Its 1949 catalogue lists two of its 'own' book titles — but in the 1950's it too developed an impressive list.

Repeated efforts by Elsevier and Klautz to establish a US subsidiary, first in 1939/40 and, later, in 1945/51 and 1951/61, illustrate the difficulties European companies had at the time in getting a foothold in the US market. The other road, taken by Frank for North-Holland, was to put all North American book distribution in the hands of an established US company (in his case, Wiley, through their acquired subsidiary Interscience). In 1946, as a newly appointed full director of North-Holland, Frank had visited the US and re-established contacts he had made in Leipzig 12 years earlier.

In 1946 Elsevier's science branch had six employees, and reached a turnover of NLG 1 million in 1953 (US\$ 263,000). North-Holland reached this turnover level in 1958. In 1949 North-Holland employed under four people, and ten by 1955. (Up to the merger in 1970, the privately owned North-Holland always had fewer employees than the science part of Elsevier.) Up until the 1960's, the scientific branch of Elsevier was a public company in its own right, probably so as not to risk the rest of the Elsevier activities in case it ran into financial difficulties.

Stimulated by the Belgian physicist L. Rosenfeld, Frank had his first big successes in physics, first with Rosenfeld's book *Nuclear Forces* in 1948, and a few years later with an international journal in the nuclear field. Frank had struggled long and hard to establish this journal. His first attempts were in 1952, and he faced strong resistance from editors of existing national journals. To quote one of them [2]: "Das Leben der einzelnen Laender findet seinen Ausdruck in den einzelnen Zeitschriften, die jeweils ein characteristisches Gepraege zeigen." In 1955 two leading French phycisists declared that they were willing to join a European Board, and in January 1956 preparations began for the launch of North-Holland's research journal *Nuclear Physics* under the editorship of L. Rosenfeld. This coincided with the hiring of W.H. Wimmers, a physicist with a background in the Dutch oil industry in Indonesia, as physics editor.

Publishing scientific journals proved to be a commercial, as well as a scientific, success. Before the Second World War, publishing scientific journals was the task of learned societies, while scientific books were published by commercial publishers. Research in the US was funded by government or industry. The journals then charged the author a 'page charge' which was paid from his research grant. This system did not exist in Europe and when after the war science publishing became global, European authors had great difficulties in getting their contributions published in leading American scientific journals as they could not afford the high page charges.

There was an explosion in scientific research at that time, and with this the number of papers to be published also rose, so it became clear that a solution had to be found. The solution was found by commercial publishers who started 'open end' journals, which were journals that were not limited to one volume per year with a fixed number of pages, but were published in as many volumes, each with a fixed number of pages, as were needed to satisfy the demand for space. No page charges were levied but this was more than compensated for in the subscription price per volume.

In the years following the successful launch of *Nuclear Physics*, Frank and Wimmers established the most prestigious journal and handbook programme in physics worldwide, along with that of the American Institute of Physics. Their early journal titles included *Nuclear Instruments and Methods* (1957), *Nuclear Materials* (1959) and *Physics Letters* (1962). Frank also began activities in the areas of Logic and Mathematics soon after the war. In 1949 North-Holland published the proceedings of the 10th International Congress of Philosophy (held in Amsterdam in 1948), and at the same time established the editorial board of the book series *Studies in Logic and the Foundations of Mathematics*. The World Congress for Mathematicians in 1954 was held in Amsterdam, the proceedings of which were also published by Frank. In econometrics, a series of books was commenced under the editorship of J. Tinbergen in 1953.

The growth of science funding ("Big Science" years)
During the second half of the 1950's the growth in funding of the natural sciences worldwide, coupled with the growing number of institutes and scientists, as well as expanding librarians' budgets, began to have an impact on both publishers. The shock experienced in the US in 1957 when the Soviet Union launched its Sputnik clearly had an impact in Western Europe. This decade, however, was also a time when the majority of the war damage had been cleared away and towns were being rebuilt. Industrial and scientific activity had resumed in Europe, but many top scientists had moved to the US. Nationalistic feelings, as we noted earlier, still stood in the way of developing a broader European science publication activity. The number of new books and journals gradually began to grow, and both publishers branched out into new areas. They each experienced an almost 10-fold growth in turnover between the late 1950's and 1969, and their growth in profits was similarly impressive.

By the early 1960's the basic areas of science for these publishers — physics, chemistry and biochemistry — were the ones which had already seen a respectable growth. Elsevier had taken its first steps into biomedicine in the 1940's, and enjoyed success through the journal *Brain Research* in the late 1950's. Elsevier, more markedly than North-Holland, was moving away from publishing society-owned journals. Opportunities to start new journals were now offered by what was known as the 'twigging' effect in science, when sub-areas of major fields were receiving so much worldwide attention that the need arose for highly specialised journals in these subjects. As well as this, ventures into areas such as the earth sciences, pharmacology and other biomedical areas took place on a larger and, from 1960 onwards, planned scale.

Science is always in need of rapid information dissemination regarding new findings. The rather elaborate editorial and production process of traditional scientific journals which publish full length papers cannot achieve this. The American Institute of Physics solved this by starting a 'letters' journal containing brief and to-the-point communications — mainly from American authors — on very recent work. In order to offer the same facilities to European and other scientists, North-Holland also started a letters journal, called *Physics Letters*, in 1962, followed by *Chemical Physics Letters* in 1967. Editing and producing such journals had a profound impact on the way that journals were traditionally produced. Refereeing was done fast and on a yes/no basis, typically in a few weeks. Faxes and photocopiers were known technologies at the time but not generally available among scientists. In the late 1950's, carbon copies were still used in the refereeing process, all sent by post, and original copies saved for the production process. Figures, usually drawn by the authors by hand, often had to be redrawn at the publisher's office. Proof-reading was also done at the publisher's office. As commented on below, innovations in typographic technology during the 1960's helped to pave the way for the letter journals' breakthrough. Frank and his colleagues took a strong interest in the modernisation of typesetting, at the same time demanding high typographic quality in the North-Holland publications. (A North-Holland mathematics book from the mid-1950's was among books used by Don Knuth in his design of a new letter font for TeX in the 1970's.)

In 1962 Frank invited E. van Tongeren from *Excerpta Medica* (see Ch. 16) to develop a publishing programme in the hitherto underdeveloped field of bioscience. The major venture in medicine at that time was the *Handbook of Clinical Neurology* (based on the pre-war German *Handbuch der Neurologie*). Van Tongeren initiated several periodicals, such as the *European Journal of Pharmacology* (in 1967) and the letters journal in biochemistry, FEBS *Letters* (in 1968), the editors of which were appointed by the board of the European Federation of Biochemical Societies.

In Elsevier, junior editors in the areas of earth and biomedical sciences as well as technology had been hired around 1960. The company at this time employed around 40 persons. Of them, the geologist A.A. Manten was to be the first who systematically developed a new area in a planned fashion, but the chemistry programme, under W. Gaade, continued to be the core activity of the company. The Elsevier list had 14 chemistry and 13 earth science journals by 1969, most of which were a result of the expansion activities after 1960. North-Holland began to expand its editorial staff only in the second half of the decade. W.H. Wimmers was responsible for the expansion of the physics list in the 1960's, which included, apart from the above mentioned journals, *Crystal Growth*, *Optics Communications* and *Surface Science*.

The growth of science and technology research and the increasing capabilities of publishers led to a significant increase in the number of publications. The usual production process was hot-metal typesetting and impact printing. Offset printing had been making an inroad into general publishing in the 1950's, and in the early 1960's it was experimented with for producing the fast turnaround 'letters' journals. Typesetting using mechanical typewriters, each carrying different letter-types, had been used at *Excerpta Medica* by Van Tongeren since 1953 and at North-Holland since 1962. Shortly afterwards, electrical typewriters were introduced, followed in the early 1970's by IBM Composer machines with high quality fonts. This development led to the formation of sizable in-house typesetting activities within Elsevier and North-Holland before 1970, and developed, in the case of North-Holland, into a separate typesetting company in 1969. Initially, considerable savings were achieved in typesetting costs, as labour costs were relatively low in the Netherlands up to the late 1970's. The traditional typesetting/printing companies that had specialised in scientific works since after the war were, with a few exceptions, disappearing by that time.

The growth of international science publishing since the war had been market-driven. The need to obtain sufficient and timely information among scientists and librarians was so strong that publishers' really did not need to market their publications. However, Elsevier traditionally had a more developed sales/promotion activity, and an international sales network, including its own subsidiaries in the UK and the US. As part of a corporate structure, Elsevier had a more rigid organisational framework than North-Holland. From 1955, the Elsevier holding company had been managed by R.E.M. van den Brink, an economist who played a key role in the formation of the potential world-leading publisher and the group's development up to his departure in 1987. The merger between Elsevier and North-Holland took place on 1 January 1970.

Mergers

The Elsevier/North-Holland merger was no more than a year old when in 1971 the Elsevier holding acquired the medical abstracting service and databank *Excerpta Medica*. The resulting publishing group, which changed names on occasion through its 30-year history, would from now on be called simply "Elsevier", while the names of companies it acquired would be kept as imprints. In 1970, the total group turnover was around US$ 15 million, which was large in comparison with most of its competitors at the time, but small compared with the group's turnover of 2000, which was around US$ 1 billion. Was this growth planned or expected? Of the pioneers, only M.D. Frank was still at Elsevier, and he retired in 1972 at the age of 58. J.P. Klautz had been forced into retirement in 1955 because of his too ambitious plans for activities in the US, W. Gaade died unexpectedly in 1970 and H.P.M. Bergmans had retired in 1971.

Frank had been amazed at and even worried by Elsevier's growth and rapid development during the 1960's and felt pessimistic about the possibility of maintaining this growth, especially when taking into account the tendency of scientific libraries to form networks and the resulting decrease of subscriptions to the valuable, but at the same time expensive, core journals. However, this growth was indeed maintained, and this is proven by Elsevier's results. Clearly, for the Elsevier business as a whole, the science group was only one of several activity areas, albeit by far its most profitable. The uncertainty of long-term growth projections may have contributed to management's tendency in the 1970's to see the science group as a 'cash cow', a company in a mature state of exploitation.

Elsevier's strong growth can be illustrated by the following results: when totalling the subscription price of each journal published by the Elsevier/North-Holland group in 1973, the subscription price was 37,500 guilders (US\$ 13,500), but this had increased in 1977 to 79,900 guilders (US\$ 32,500). Even more spectacular was the group's contribution to Elsevier revenues. The science group's share in Elsevier's total turnover was 25% in 1976, but its contribution to the group's profits had grown to 67.5%, so that the group was able to finance its activities in other fields from the science group. In 1976 the group completed its first long-term plan, for the period until 1980. This was a cautious plan, which nevertheless predicted a doubling of its turnover. Efforts to consolidate and increase traditional publishing programmes in the natural sciences turned out to be successful, and this was followed by the establishment of a separate biomedical operating company.

At the same time, efforts were made to begin or develop lists in the areas of agri-sciences, engineering, mathematics, computer science and economics. A social science programme was sold to the emerging Kluwer group in the 1970's, while a small but successful psychology/cognitive science and linguistics programme was published under the North-Holland imprint. It can be concluded that Elsevier's developments from 1970 to 1990 showed much continuity: the growth was autonomous, and no significant mergers were carried out before that with Pergamon Press in 1991. Periodic reorganisations were mainly cosmetic in nature. Pergamon (see Ch. 7) came from a similar publishing tradition as its Dutch partners, and this was a merger of equals in many respects.

The basic organisational units of Elsevier became (first in the form of operating companies and later as divisions), (i) Biomedical, (ii) Chemistry, (iii) Physics and (iv) Information Technology (IT) & Business, in which (iii) and (iv) were kept as a single operating company until 1982 under the name North-Holland. The largest and (in the period up to 1990) most profitable divisions were those based on the basic science programmes of a generation earlier: (ii) and (iii) and the biochemistry-based kernel of (i). Within these units were profit centres, e.g. geosciences and agriculture were grouped under (ii), and mathematics and economics under (iv). In each profit centre were long-term commitments with external scientists as editors of journals and book series. Specialist in-house staff kept in contact with these editors, often for very long time spans, in order that continuity of association could be maintained. At the time of the merger, promotion/marketing activities were reorganised into a centralised sales department, but soon decentralised and reattached to their respective publishing units. Publishing activities in subsidiaries in the science areas were mostly derived from the editorial groups in

Amsterdam. In New York during this period, textbooks and society journals were added for the US market.

Each unit contributed to company growth in the period 1971–1990. The group turnover grew roughly 10-fold, from around NLG 50 million to 550 million (US$ 15 million to US$ 300 million). The profit margin required by Elsevier was set at 20% after tax, which few sectors of industry could reasonably sustain. To achieve this, new activities were discouraged, and experimentation in new technologies or media kept small (see the following section.)

Elsevier's pre-eminence among commercial science publishers was maintained in the traditional basic science areas, and established in the post-1970 period in a number of new areas. The time involved in establishing a presence and later a full publishing programme in a new area of science — including technology and medicine — could be several years. Often this depended on the expanding funding for research, education and libraries in an emerging discipline. For example, the area of logic/computer science was first encountered in the late 1940's by North-Holland; there was a surge of urgency in the subject after the first World Congress of Information Processing in Paris 1959, followed by the first journals in the subject around 1970, and a large book and journal programme in the 1980's. The turnover of sector (iv) above in the period 1970–1990 grew from NLG 1 million to 100 million (US$ 275,000 to US$ 54 million).

In the Netherlands there were also other science publishers after the war. In the 1960's a mainly physics programme was established by D. Reidel Publishing Company in Dordrecht. Other players included Dr. W. Junk, P. Noordhoff and M. Nijhoff, who were all to become part of a group that began in the 1970's and which resulted in the establishment of Kluwer Academic Publishers. Publishers like Reidel, trained by Frank — who in turn had had his training at Aka — were termed by Frank 'grandchildren of Aka.' In addition, in the 1980's, former Elsevier and North-Holland staff members formed their own companies, such as IOS Press.

On two occasions attempts were made to merge Elsevier Science and the Kluwer Academic groups. The first, in 1987, resulted in a merger by the latter with another Dutch group, Wolters/Noordhoff, to become the Wolters/Kluwer group. The second, in 1998, was meant to be a fusion between Reed/Elsevier and Wolters/Kluwer, but failed amid suggestions that this merger would form a cartel.

Expansion and innovation

With expansion continuing in the 1970's, new staff was being added to further develop existing project lines, and search for new opportunities where appropriate. Over 200 new journals were established by the group in the 1970's, followed by a similar number in the 1980's. Of the older titles, many became strategic ('core') journals in their (sub)fields. Journals begun before 1970 were usually well established and continued to grow in size each year. The numbers of subscribers per journal were comparatively high before 1970, and the earlier journals had in general peaked as to number of subscriptions shortly after that year. Growth in volume and subscription prices tended to be faster than the relative decline in income from lost subscriptions. This had the result that the turnover of most journals begun before 1970 grew until 1990, sometimes later.

In the early 1970's new journals were welcomed by the market, and it was not unusual for a new journal to have 400 or more library subscriptions after the first year of publication. By the early 1980's — only 10 years later — new journal titles were considerably less welcome. To reach 200 institutional subscriptions after the first year was considered satisfactory. The total number of Elsevier journals by 2000, including post-1990 mergers, exceeded 1200.

Book publishing also expanded (in the number of new titles per year) in the 1970's, especially with the appearance of 'camera-ready' manuscripts, which were produced through offset printing. With increasing specialisation and a larger worldwide supply of new book titles, the number of copies sold per title also started to decline around 1970. Elsevier published under 100 new books in 1970, more than 500 in 1980, and 700 in 1985. In the early 1990's this number was reduced, only to increase again after 1995.

Expanding volume and lower sales inspired continuous efforts to reduce costs. As we have seen, typesetting of journals through the use of typewriters was introduced in the 1960's.

For books, by the 1970's, the author-typed manuscript was becoming a serious alternative to traditional typesetting. Main innovative activities focused on typesetting, and the gradual introduction of computers in this process. In-house typesetting had gradually increased in popularity since the 1960's, as mentioned earlier. By 1980, computer typesetting had appeared and three systems were mainly used in Elsevier. The choice of two proprietary systems instead of TeX (which was favoured by mathematicians and physicists) dominated the in-house typesetting scene for quite some time. Developments in in-house typesetting systems, one MS-DOS-based and originally used for biomedical works, led to internal standards for manuscript handling which were in place by the 1990's. Internal typesetting was on the whole abandoned after 1995, at which point most typesetting work had been transferred out of Europe (to India and the Philippines, among other countries) in order to save money. The initial price advantage of in-house typesetting, obtained through the use of low cost typewriters and with comparatively low labour costs in the 1960's, had been lost by the mid-1980's.

Essential internal stimulation for computerising internal typesetting activities came from *Excerpta Medica*, which had been modernising its handling of journal abstracts. This influence also extended to the notion that full articles could be viewed as database records in electronic journals. This remained purely a theoretical concept until the technology became readily available to authors in the 1990's. (see also Ch. 16.)

Trends journals

Among innovations in the 1970's, we should mention the move towards more general (scientific magazine) journals. Elsevier already published variations on the standard primary journal, such as letters or review journals (in addition to abstracting journals, which were mainly in the field of medicine.) The first in the 'trends' series of journals was *Trends in Biochemical Sciences* (*TiBS*). The past President of the journal's sponsor, IUBMB (the International Union of Biochemistry and Molecular Biology), Professor W.J. Whelan, said of the journal's beginning:

> *TiBS* began after I became the General Secretary of the International Union of Biochemistry [IUB, the precursor of IUBMB], in 1973... Together with the IUB Treasurer, Bill Slater, we sought out Bart van Tongeren of Elsevier/North-Holland. During an informal exchange of ideas, I suggested a mini-review journal. Bart and his colleagues had been considering a news magazine. We combined the two together, with the reviews as the meat within the sandwich of news. Thus was *TiBS* born. The sales strategy was to price the personal copy low enough to make it easily affordable. The result was and has been an outstanding success. What may not be generally known is that there was strong opposition within Elsevier/North-Holland to publishing *TiBS*. Indeed, my Elsevier counterpart told me that but for the enthusiasm of the IUB for *TiBS*, it might never have appeared. On my side, the first appearance of *TiBS* brought me an attack from a biochemistry department head who said I had sold myself for the price of a free dinner. Such is the welcome extended to innovations.

With the purchases of the British journal *The Lancet* and the portal *BioMedNet* in the 1990's, Elsevier's trends journals are now published out of an office in London.

Adonis

New product discussion in the second half of the 1970's focused mainly on document delivery and the potential danger of people photocopying articles from the British Library and other organisations at the time. It was decided to form a consortium of publishers who would store and deliver single articles to paying customers. On the way towards implementing this, which took a decade, many new information technologies were looked at. Archives using database technology, rather than paper archives, were put in place. The consortium, which included Springer, initially managed Adonis. In 1997 it was absorbed back into the Elsevier structure and is currently under the Science Direct umbrella.

There were also attempts to link the EMBASE secondary service (see Ch. 16) with part of the primary journal package of the biomedical division. An experimental 'journals-online' database, including 25,000 pages from BBA and *Brain Research* proved to be before its time. Expensive and inadequate communication lines made the service impractical.

Compact journals

At North-Holland the first steps towards establishing the journal *Computer Networks* (see Ch. 17) were taken in 1974. Internal company experiences with databases and automating *Excerpta Medica*, combined with computer conferencing, led to the concept of 'compact journals' where news, announcements of forthcoming articles or books, conference items, and readers' letters, formed the main items. Database and navigation concepts were tested, and dedicated software was developed. The IFIP *Compact Journal* (co-sponsored by IFIP (the International Federation of Information Processing), Dutch and German government grants, and participating institutes and companies) was developed between 1977 and 1980, and had its first public demonstration at the IFIP and MEDINFO congresses in Tokyo in 1980. The costs of the leased phone lines for the week's demonstration exceeded US$ 10,000. With high phone line costs and no personal computers at that time, the project was disbanded in 1983 — some 15 years before it would have become viable. One of its files, a database of conference announcements, survived until recently in the form of EventLine.

Other innovative ideas, including preprint abstracts and synopsis publishing, were trialled between 1970 and 1990, but the book and journal business remained intact. It would only be in the 1990's that successful steps could be taken towards electronic publishing.

Growth through acquisitions

As Elsevier moved into the 1990's, it had 600 journals, an impressive profit margin, and after the Kluwer takeover debacle in 1987 it still owned one-third of the stock of its competitor, the Wolters-Kluwer group. Attempts to form a strategic liaison with the British Pearson group had led no further than a 7% share in their stock. Taking these factors into account, Elsevier had an extremely strong financial position, should the opportunity for another company acquisition or merger present itself.

The first opportunity of the decade was when Elsevier was offered to take over the Maxwell Multimedia Group, which at that time consisted of five companies. For various reasons this offer was turned down, and six years later Elsevier paid much more to buy only one of those companies, Molecular Design. But Elsevier chairman Pierre Vinken had realised the precarious position of the Maxwell empire, and Elsevier instead bid for Pergamon Press. In record speed, during the first quarter of 1991, Elsevier purchased Pergamon Press — and the investments they had made in the other groups in the 1980's proved very useful.

In 1992 Elsevier found a UK partner, Reed, which was a conglomeration of companies including a small science activity (Butterworths) and a large US branch, which included Bowker. The new partnership of Reed-Elsevier went on an acquisitions tour to expand into areas outside science publishing. The merger with Pergamon Press meant that the Elsevier science group now had around 1000 journal titles and an expanded book programme. There were few other expansion moves before the year 2000, but one of these included a French journal publisher, Gauthier-Villars, which signalled an end to commercial science journal publishing in France, and JAI Press (in 1998) from Jolowicz' grandson Herbert Johnson. A second attempt to merge with Kluwer, and discussions to that end with the Wolters-Kluwer group, were aborted in the Spring of 1998.

After the half-hearted and premature attempts to develop an electronic alternative to paper-based primary publishing in the 1980's, a series of production reorganisations took place before 1990. These continued throughout the following decade, along with a number of cost-saving measures. More or less simultaneously with these reorganisations, Elsevier began to accept 'compuscripts', machine-readable manuscripts, from authors, in order to convert them to SGML (see Ch. 17). The project in which this took place was called Computer-Aided Production (CAP). The progress of the CAP project was hindered by the above-mentioned reorganisations. There were also technical difficulties, especially in the processing of material with many mathematical formulae or complicated tables. One of the original goals of the CAP project was to convert the text of all articles to SGML as early as possible in the production process, and thus produce professionally typeset pages from the SGML files. This goal was never fully achieved, for various reasons. On the whole, however, the CAP project did result in large quantities of journal material in digital form, which was stored in an internal 'documents warehouse'.

All this was necessary preparation for a move Elsevier made in 1986. In this year Elsevier announced a new service, Science Direct, through which all their journals, and possibly also those of their competitors, would be made available in electronic form. This service depended very much on Elsevier's work on computer-aided production methods and the internal warehousing of documents. Science Direct commenced in 1998 and by 2001 included around 1200 journals.

Elsevier customers can also choose to use Science Direct On Site: special software developed for Elsevier, which can be run on a customer's website and which is fed with material coming from Elsevier. It also operates portals and electronic journals outside Science Direct, such as *BioMedNet* and *ChemWeb* (purchased in 1998), *The Lancet* and several electronic products developed in the Amsterdam office.

Issues concerned with user interface led in 2000 to the purchase of the library software company Endeavour Information Systems, which had successfully installed its Voyager library system in a large number of academic and research libraries worldwide. The decade ended with the announcement in October 2000 that Reed-Elsevier had bought the Harcourt group from the US media conglomerate Harcourt General. The Harcourt group includes Academic Press and the leading US medical publisher, Saunders. This takeover would (if it is approved by antitrust authorities) make the extended Elsevier group, with 1600 journals and a large book programme, the clear leader in its field, with an estimated 25% of the world market for advanced scientific/medical information.

References

[1]   Bakels, F. (1980) unpublished notes on Elsevier history.

[2]   Frank, M.D. (1974) *Leon Rosenfeld, Author, Editor and Friend.* Amsterdam, North-Holland, ix–xi.

[3]   Klautz, J.P. (1986) *In de ban van mijn schaduw.* (in Dutch) Huizen, RPL.

[4]   Steyn-Parve, E.P (1964) Hendrik G.K. Westenbrink 1901–1964. *Biochimica et Biophysica Acta* (without bibliographic annotation).

[5]   Van Leeuwen, J.K.W. (1980) The decisive years for science publishing in the Netherlands after the Second World War. In: *Development of Science Publishing in Europe.* A.J. Meadows (Ed.) Amsterdam, Elsevier, 251–268.

[6]   Van Tongeren, E. et al. (1972) *Toekomstbespiegelingen bij een afscheid.* (volume to mark the retirement of M.D. Frank; in Dutch) Amsterdam, North-Holland.

[7]   Vermeulen, R. & de Wit, P. (2000) *Onder uitgevers.* (in Dutch) Nijmegen, SUN.

[8]   Wiley, W.B. et al. (1973) *Eric S. Proskauer.* (volume to mark his seventieth birthday) New York, John Wiley & Sons.

A Century of Science Publishing
E.H. Fredriksson (Ed.)
IOS Press, 2001

Chapter 7

Robert Maxwell:
Forty-Four Years as Publisher

Robert N. Miranda
Cognizant Communication Corporation, Elmsford, NY, USA

It is next to impossible in a short chapter to link and weave into a cohesive whole the life, activities, and relationships of Robert Maxwell, a man with an extraordinary public and private persona, who intertwined public and private companies throughout his lifetime into a giant jigsaw puzzle. The question has often been asked: was he a visionary or an opportunist? I believe he was a little of both.

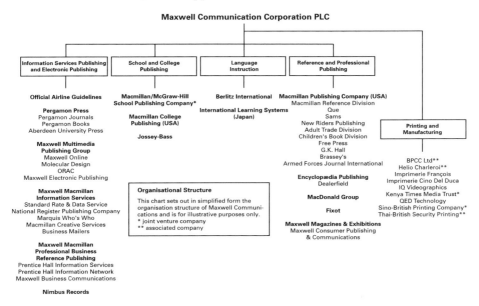

Figure 1. Maxwell Communications Guide to Companies, Products & Service, May 1991.

Maxwell's colorful life has been the subject of many books and articles, a brief bibliography for which is included at the end of this chapter. What I have chosen

to do is to show how his ability to charm, cajole, and impress people into supporting his many and varied ventures led to the building of what some considered the
tenth largest media company in the world [1, p. 1]. The one fact that remains as
tangible history is that Pergamon Press was the company that helped launch Bob
Maxwell's career in publishing that culminated in the chairmanship of a conglomerate that eventually included more than 100 companies (Figure 1).

In May 1991, Elsevier acquired Pergamon Press for $817,000,000. The pur-
chase price included some 418 journals, over 3,000 books in print, affiliations with
over 100 professional societies and associations, and publications on behalf of more
than 150 organizations and governments. Publication and sales and marketing
offices were located in England, the United States, Canada, Australia, Japan, Brazil,
Germany, USSR, South Africa, Israel, India, Pakistan, China, Hong Kong, Korea,
The Netherlands, Egypt, Singapore, Taiwan, Philippines, Ireland, and Scotland.
The publications covered all fields of Engineering, Material Sciences, Life &
Medical Sciences, Physical Sciences, and Social & Behavioral Sciences.

This impressive list encapsulates the results of Robert Maxwell's forty-four
years as the founder and publisher of Pergamon Press. This in itself should justify
his place in a Century of Science Publishing. To my knowledge, no other person
had greater insight into where scientific communications was headed, and no other
person knew better how to exploit this insight.

It is well documented that Robert Maxwell was born in Czechoslovakia as Jan
Ludvik Hoch and that he had a limited education. Throughout his lifetime he was
known as: Robert Ian Maxwell, Robert Maxwell, Captain Maxwell, Captain Bob,
Bob Maxwell, and just Bob. Numerous adventures [2, p. 2], well worth reading,
preceded his contributions to the publishing industry, which began at the end of
World War II.

When he arrived in England in 1940 as a volunteer with the French foreign
legion from France he was only sixteen and he enlisted in the British Army [2,
p. 14]. He was courageous and valiant in battle, for which he was commissioned in
the field and awarded the military cross. By the end of World War II he was a
Captain — a title he used throughout his life.

In post-war Germany, having skills in numerous languages, he was appointed
to the Berlin Information Control Unit with an assignment to the Control
Commission for Germany. This commission was under the Director of the Press
and Publicity Branch of the British Information Service. Within the scope of this
authority in this post he helped to reestablish a newspaper, *De-Berliner*, renamed
Der Telegraf [2, p. 24] in the British sector of occupied Berlin. This involved dealing with editors, publishers, and suppliers and using a great deal of ingenuity in

order to keep the newspaper in print at a time when materials were in short supply. It was then that he met the well-respected publisher Ferdinand Springer, who was struggling to continue his publishing business.

> It was a time when we had no telephone, no petrol, no paper, no spare parts for printing machines or any other vital matters which were so essential to restart production in an establishment such as Springer Verlag. It was Captain Maxwell who always knew how to cope in those days, who solved the most difficult problems and without any doubt the main merit for opening the way (from 1947 to 1949) for rebuilding of the publishing house must go to him. [3, Ferdinand Springer, p. 2].

In 1946 the British Government established a high-level scientific committee to discuss the feasibility of a British publishing house to deal with scientific matters. The committee recommended that the established publishing firm of Butterworths should undertake such a venture. In 1949, Butterworth-Springer started publishing journals and books in the sciences. Paul Rosbaud, a former Springer editor, joined the company in the capacity of scientific editor [3, p. 2].

At that time Maxwell had also recognized the existence of a wealth of information in Germany that had not been published or distributed to the outside world. Although research in Germany had continued throughout World War II and was well ahead of research in England and the rest of the world, little had been disseminated outside of Germany. After leaving the armed services in 1947, Maxwell began to distribute scientific publications for Springer and other leading German publishers through a company he formed called European Periodicals, Publicity and Advertising Company (EPPAC). In 1948, this company was integrated into Lange, Maxwell & Springer. This was Maxwell's first contribution to the distribution of scientific information — first in Britain and then in the rest of the world.

In 1950, the joint venture between Butterworth and Springer was having financial difficulties. In 1951, Maxwell made an offer to purchase the joint venture. The name Pergamon Press was then selected for the acquired joint venture. Paul Rosbaud, the former Springer editor, joined the newly formed company as Scientific Director. There is considerable disagreement as to how, why, and who selected the name Pergamon Press and the logo. But rather than try to sort out what is folklore and what is fact [3, pp. 3 & 575; 4, p. 240; 7], suffice it to say it is a name and logo respected worldwide.

In 1951 Pergamon started with a small list of books: *Progress in Biophysics and Molecular Biology*, edited by J.A.V. Butler and J.J. Randall; *Progress in Nuclear Physics*, edited by O.R. Frisch; *Progress in Metal Physics*, edited by Bruce Chalmers;

Introduction to Statistics, edited by M.H. Quenouille; *Metallurgical Thermochemistry*, edited by O. Kubaschewski and E.L. Evans. As of today, all of these publications continue to be published, although there is some variation in the titles based on the changing technologies. The base for the core of the company was also an established journal originally published by Springer, *Spectrochimica Acta*, edited by Dr. Alois Gatterer through volume 3. Rosbaud earlier had started this journal in conjunction with the Vatican Observatory where Dr. Gatterer was Director of the Astrophysical Laboratory. There were two more similar journals: *Journal of Atmospheric and Terrestrial Physics*, editor Sir Edward Appleton, and *Geochimica et Cosmochimica Acta*, edited by Correns, Ingerson, Nockolds, Paneth, Wagner and Wickman. It was Wickman who had indicated that the coin found at Herakleia became the colophon for the first issue in 1951 and was carried forward in 1951 as the colophon for Pergamon Press [3, p. 575].

During this time Maxwell was also becoming involved in the acquisition of Simpkin Marshall, an almost defunct British book distribution cooperative. This venture went poorly and was later closed down due primarily to nonsupport by British publishers with regard to consignment accounts and payments [1, p. 139]. The one positive outcome of this venture, if one can be found, was the purchase of The British Book Center, which became Maxwell's first base of operations in the United States. From this base Pergamon Press Inc., Maxwell Scientific International, and other ventures were developed in the United States.

Prior to the 1950's, communications in the sciences were mainly through learned societies and their in-house journals. With the rapid growth of science after World War II, the long delays that would occur in publication cycles of these society publications left room for the development of small, specialized publications in evolving fields where such societies did not exist. Admittedly, there was skepticism and mistrust that commercial enterprises could take up the slack. There was further concern that such commercial ventures would not allow the editorial freedom necessary for the editors to do their job. One of the most frequent comments regarding Maxwell in the early days was his willingness to publish highly segmented journals and to allow the editors freedom to select their boards and select the number and quality of papers required for each issue. Maxwell recognized early in his career as a publisher that he was more an innovator and marketer than a scientific editor. The growth of Pergamon during the 1950's was unique as the company continued to innovate and develop new scientific sectors and develop a new style of rapid communications.

It was also in the 1950's that the US National Science Foundation (NSF) took the initiative to support cover-to-cover translations of selected leading Soviet periodicals. In 1957, Prof. George Herrman [3, p. 127] and Bob Maxwell agreed to work on a cover-to-cover translation of the Soviet journal *Prikladnaia Maihematika Mekhanika* (*Journal of Applied Mathematics and Mechanics*). Funding was secured through a grant to the American Society of Mechanical Engineers. This was the first of many journals translated by Pergamon, and other publishers soon followed suit. In 1963, when the NSF withdrew its support, Pergamon continued with its dedication to the journal translation program, many of which are still being published as cover-to-cover translations. Some twenty years later Maxwell entered into a similar arrangement a translation of the *Chinese Astronomy Journal* [3, p. 493]. As an expansion of such a venture, in 1985 Pergamon established the first Western publisher liaison office in China, and was the first Western publisher to enter into a joint venture with China [3, p. 18].

As Maxwell's base of publishing continued to grow, he recognized the importance of giving recognition to the loyal editors and the contributors. In order to fulfill this goal, he established awards, medals, and grants to individuals, societies, and universities. Some, if not all, of these awards are still being given today. I list some representative sampling to illustrate the broad base covered. The Pergamon Geothermal Energy Award for the best paper published in the *Journal of Geothermics*. The Danckwerts-Maxwell prize endowed at the University of Cambridge to encourage research in the Department of Chemical Engineering and to support the Danckwerts Memorial Lectures. These lectures are in recognition of P.V. Danckwerts' work and are given by invited lecturers in accordance with the aims and scope of the journal *Chemical Engineering Science*. Because of his long-time affiliation with the publication of *Acta Metallurgica*, Maxwell donated annually the Acta Metallurgica Gold Medal for individuals who have demonstrated ability and leadership in materials research selected by the Board of Governors. He also was instrumental in the establishment of a number of new societies; in some cases he offered the funding and sometimes allowed the Pergamon publication to be owned by the society, as was the case with *Photochemistry and Photobiology*, and *Journal of Neurochemistry*. The editor of *International Journal of Engineering Sciences*, Professor Eringen, recalls that without the help of Bob Maxwell and the donation of the services of his law firm in 1963, the Society of Engineering Science and the journal may never have evolved [3, p. 260]. In addition, Maxwell was continually asked by his editors to fund Ph.D. candidates in support of their research. It would be interesting to be able to track these Ph.D.s to see where they are and what they are doing now.

The one thing that was of primary importance to Maxwell was the respect he had for the academicians affiliated with Pergamon. Even when he was involved with other matters of business, if an editor of one of his journals called he would put aside what he was doing and take the call. Many of us remember the type of request that he would receive from his editors concerning research that needed funding or the plight of a family member who may have been in trouble [3, p. 649]. When medical assistance was required for the famous Russian physicist Landau [3, p. 100], Maxwell chartered a plane and supplied the necessary penicillin that was required but unavailable to Landau. Based on these relationships, the company often took on pet projects of editors, most of which were costly indulgences for the company. One example that comes to mind is when the editor-in-chief of *Planetary and Space Science* asked Maxwell if he would publish his wife's book, *Talking About Cakes* [3, p. 38]. Without ever looking at the manuscript, Maxwell accepted it and the book did win a bronze medal at the Hamburg Book Fair. Most of such projects he agreed to do, however, did not show such positive results.

In the early 1960's, higher education was expanding. It was at that time that Maxwell launched the Pergamon International Library (PIL). The PIL accomplished its announced goal of publishing 1000 books and textbooks in the sciences in numerous languages covering technology, social sciences, and the humanities by 1970. Although there were many successful books and series published in the PIL, what immediately comes to mind is the Pergamon International Chess Series program — still considered among the top books on chess. During this period, Maxwell entered into a sales agreement with Macmillan (U.S.) for distribution of all Pergamon books in the United States, which further assured the widest possible distribution of Pergamon book titles. In 1964 the Macmillan agreement ended and Pergamon Press Inc. became the distributor for all books and journals in the Western Hemisphere. Pergamon Press Inc. was originally affiliated with Maxwell Scientific International, an independent Maxwell company, but was acquired by Pergamon Press Ltd. (PPL) in 1964 and became a public company in the United States in 1968, with PPL owning 70% of the shares.

It was in 1966, with the establishment of the journal *Materials Research Bulletin* under the editorship of Dr. Heinz Henisch, that camera-ready offset was first used to launch a journal [3, p. 121]. Although ascetically poor, this form of presentation was so cost-effective that it made it possible to publish material that was important only to a small number of scientists in a specific discipline. The use of this type of publishing soon evolved into the printing of major scientific meetings and proceedings. Camera-ready copy was also the forerunner to what became known decades later as desktop publishing. Pergamon was one of the first to experiment with desktop publishing when in 1987 it launched its first such project out of the editorial office of Robert Rubin [3, p. 366] for its journal *Psychoneuro-*

endocrinology using the new technology in its quest for more rapid reviews and publication. Although the use of such rapid publication methods saved time and money, the future use of this production would cause problems for conversions to database publishing, another area where Robert Maxwell had been a pioneer.

In 1963 Pergamon began publication of *Information Storage and Retrieval* [3, p. 99], including *Machine Translation*. This was the beginning of Maxwell's involvement with data storage. Within three years, the title was renamed *Information Processing and Management*. In 1965, as part of developing the use of information technology within Pergamon, its 1965 Annual Report reflected this goal:

> Scientists and engineers are at present unable to digest the volume of new knowledge becoming available and agree that this problem of information explosion needs to be solved urgently. So desperate is the problem that it now becoming far cheaper for certain research workers to go back into the laboratory and repeat the work, if necessary to re-invent things, rather than laboriously and time-wasting to struggle with the floods of professional journals, books, magazine articles, Ph.D. theses, etc.

Following this lead Maxwell sought an affiliation in 1969 with Leasco, a computer-based company located in the United States. This chapter in Pergamon's history was one of the most difficult ones for Maxwell and Pergamon Press because Leasco tried to wrest the company away from Maxwell (for full details see [1, pp. 297–334]). It took close to five years and the support of the editors-in-chief of the major Pergamon journals, who indicated to Leasco that if Maxwell were not involved in the business they would take their journals elsewhere, to resolve the matter. During this hectic time Maxwell maintained his position as Chairman of Pergamon Press Inc., successfully representing the minority stockholders by obtaining court orders to prevent PPL from voting their 70% holdings.

After regaining full control, Maxwell continued the expansion of the journal line by establishing the innovative Computer Series of journals — sixteen journals covering computer use in all fields of the sciences. Prior to that time few articles related to computer use in research were appearing, as there were few guidelines for such submissions. The type of research that was being reported was mostly in relation to information processing.

Pergamon Press was the first publishing organization to align itself with the concept of database management in relation to the publishing of information. Maxwell had a discussion with Brian Blunden [3, p. 44], who defined to Maxwell the concept of database publishing. It is believed that this discussion led to the acquisition of Infoline in 1982. Infoline later became known as Orbit Infoline, after Orbit's acquisition in 1986. The database companies were ultimately merged under the banner of Maxwell Online. With this goal of merging of technical information, Maxwell agreed to fund the concept by agreeing to fund the International Electronic Publishing Research Centre. "Without the commitment and foresight of men like Robert Maxwell & Gordon Graham, no such development would have been possible" [3, pp. 44,55].

In continued recognition of the joining of publishing with electronic companies, Pergamon acquired and began to mechanize the International Abstracts of Biological Sciences (IABS), continuing now as Current Awareness in Biological Sciences (CABS). IABS at that time was being designed to compete with Biological Abstracts (BIOSIS).

With the experience of integrated use of the new technologies and the industry acquisitions that Maxwell was making, Pergamon launched the first of its many major encyclopedic works in an electronic format. *The International Encyclopedia of Education*, which received the Dartmouth Award by the American Library Association, was announced in 1980 and completed in 1985 with 1,448 articles, five million words from over 1,300 contributors, printed in hard copy as well as compact disc (CD-ROM). Once such a work had been compiled, spin-off projects and updates became a regular staple of the company.

Continuing to seek new and faster ways to publish, in 1989 another experiment was begun with the creation of a new camera-ready journal, Cancer Communication. This publication was designed to receive all papers electronically. They were then sent to two or more reviewers either electronically or via fax. All fifty of the reviewers were given faxes and were paid a fee for two-day turnaround. The goal was to publish papers received through review to publication within six weeks instead of the traditional six months. The experiment as a prototype was successful but was cost prohibitive. But what it did accomplish was to establish a link to the company's database operation of Pergamon Orbit Infoline, which would begin to receive documents on a faster turnaround time. The journal is now in its twelfth volume with its new title *Oncology Research. An International Journal.*

It has often been stated that individual readership of a journal is limited. In order to create additional reasons for journal issues to be reviewed, Maxwell agreed to adding new and timely information within the refereed journal. Journal editors were polled and software review editors were appointed. This was a time when software was being developed in laboratories around the world and had no outlet for bringing the developed software to the attention of others working in similar fields. In-house support staff was established to locate and handle the software submitted, to find reviewers, and to determine in which publication the submitted reviews should appear.

A further enhancement was added to Pergamon journals by using the services of Pergamon Orbit Infoline's worldwide patent database. The editors were asked to select a profile of their readers' interest and for each issue a series of new patents that fit their contributors' profile would be generated. This new patent service not only generated more readership for the journals, it also generated requests for the company's database services.

With the rapid expansion of computers as a source of manuscript preparation, Maxwell agreed to the development of a software program to assist contributors with manuscript preparation. In 1986, Manuscript Manager was announced to deal with American Psychological Association (APA) and Council of Biology Editors (CBE) styles. Both associations endorsed the software program and promoted it to their members. Thousands of copies were sold. Development was discontinued when management was turned over to Macmillan after the remainder of Pergamon that was not sold to Elsevier was merged into their management structure in 1991.

Maxwell moved Pergamon Press to further profitability by first recognizing that with strong manuscript flow it was best to establish a clear term for subscriptions. In 1960 he established the calendar year as a subscription base. The subscription would be based on the volume announced for that year. Doing this also created an opportunity to announce new volumes within the same year; through this method the company was able to invoice its customers twice or three times within in one year. Other publishers soon picked up this creative billing cycle.

Because Pergamon was primarily a UK-based company, invoices were originally generated in British pound. As the pound began to decline as one of the primary currencies, Maxwell changed billing to other currencies. Invoices were issued for the United States and the Western Hemisphere in dollars, for Japan in yen, and for Europe and the rest of the world in Deutsch mark. By this simple move, with production being paid for in pounds and income arriving in stronger currencies, the company's profits increased substantially. What was of particular interest in the rate adjustments by currency was that the United States market was paying rates 20% below the rest of the world. This policy had to be modified later when the German Library Association filed a complaint to the European Commission [8, p. 20].

Maxwell's involvement in the daily operation of the company, especially in the early days, was legendary. He began his day with a review of the daily mail. "The mailroom is the heart of the business", was a favorite Maxwell axiom. When he was at the office in Oxford or New York he would be in the mailroom before staff arrived and would affix notes or call personnel to the mailroom to ask for explanations on a particular complaint. Each department head was expected to respond as to how an order or request was handled. Each of his officers was required to be in the mailroom daily to review the mail. He would regularly review and revise company form letters. His hands-on approach was often more than disconcerting to his staff, but it forced them to focus and not become complacent about their jobs.

He approved all promotion pieces and coined an acronym on which all promotion should be based. This acronym is still widely used throughout the industry by former Pergamon employees: KAMP-BC [Know (your product). Audience (who will buy the product?) Media (how do you reach your audience?) Promise (every promotion must have a built-in promise) Benefit (it's not enough to promise) Clarity (assume your audience knows nothing)].

No matter where Maxwell was in the world, if you required an answer a call could be made and he would give you a yes or no immediately; there was no delay in making decisions and in making an immediate commitment within or outside of the company.

As one of his many endeavors, Maxwell won a seat in Parliament in 1964 [1, p. 221]. Although he accomplished a great deal during his six-year term, I think the following quote from a report he prepared best exemplifies his visionary approach to science. The report was prepared on Science, Government and Industry, in which he concluded:

> Government and science are now completely joined together in an indispensable partnership. Government is dependent on science as an essential resource for national security and welfare while science cannot flourish without government support.

With this statement he helped to establish that governments everywhere must offer more support and funds to universities and industry to expand research for the national good.

During Maxwell's time in Parliament his daily involvement with Pergamon became less of a factor. He had created the momentum and honed the working ethic, and the company continued to grow. Still any one of his staff could give details of his arriving in the office, gathering up staff in the mail room, rewriting form letters, and immediately involving himself in some ongoing negotiation, for which in most cases he had given prior approval. Sometimes there were also mass and individual firings during these sessions.

This style of jumping in and out of the daily business calls to mind one representative negotiation in which Maxwell and I became involved. When he found out that I was going to have a meeting with the Franklin Institute Board on renewal of their journal contract, he pointed out that many members of the Board were leading scientists. In order to make his point he rattled off what he had accomplished for some of these scientists: Proceeding (AGARD) Aeronautical Research development, First and Second Conference on Peaceful Use of Atomic Energy; Annals of the International Geophysical Year, etc. He then said, "These boys are too big for you to handle but come along and learn something".

At the meeting he quickly reviewed our own proposed terms, which he immediately dismissed. After a long reminiscing session, Bob proceeded to give away the proverbial store, agreeing to everything that the board put on the table. This was not uncommon when Maxwell dealt with editors of the journals; he was not as generous when dealing with the less profitable book editors. As we left the meeting, I remember him putting his arm around my shoulder and saying, "I hope your were paying attention and learned something in there". I said, "Yes! If I had negotiated a contract like that I would be fired". He slapped me on the back and said, "Right, now you put it right." This was so typical of his style. It was fortunate for him that the long-term members of his staff were able to "put things right". We were, after all, largely responsible for the profitability of the company.

The research community has in many ways shown its appreciation and recognition for Maxwell's efforts. His contributions to international science have been recognized with many awards and degrees from industry and academia. He received Honorary D.Sc. from Moscow University, and from Polytechnic Institute, New York, and was named a Kennedy fellow at Harvard. In 1987 he became a member of the United States Information Agency's International Council, advising the President, the Secretary of State, and the National Security Council on perceptions of the United States abroad. He received the Duke of Edinburgh's 1983 prize for the best nonfiction work in the English language *Seaspeak*. This project was fully funded by Maxwell. In order to assure its success, he waived all copyright for its use worldwide [3, p. 239]. "The contribution made by Robert Maxwell to marine communications, and thereby to safety at sea, has been immense. It is highly probable that this contribution could not have come from any other source." A particular honor was bestowed on Robert Maxwell when they chose to use his profile on the cover of *Current Argument on Early Man*, which was part of the series of books published on behalf of the Swedish Academy of Science's Nobel Symposium Science, Technology and Society in the time of Alfred Nobel.

With the sale of Pergamon Press in 1991, Maxwell had disposed of his crown jewels. It was at a time when many companies were suffering from the long recession. Maxwell had overextended himself by massive, and sometimes ill-advised purchases (such as Macmillan, Inc.), and the most valued piece of his empire was Pergamon Press. I recall that after the sale I was asked to travel along with his daughter, Ghislaine, to introduce the editors to Elsevier's new team in meetings across the United States. The purpose was to assure that the sale would not affect their editorships. At that time Maxwell had bought and become the publisher of the *Daily News* in New York City. It was during his reorganization of the News that I spent time with him calling Pergamon editors. He wanted to stay in touch and also to advise editors about the electronic rights that he was involved in and how he would work with them during the transition. He didn't want to let go. This was a trying time for him and it seemed to me that there was more to this sale than just the money. In my opinion this sale was more to protect his legacy because there were other assets that could have been sold. I have come to this conclusion based on numerous conversations with him, in which he said, "When I go to my maker or baker there will be nothing left," and "My children will not receive a penny from my life's work". Both of these statements did come true. Decades earlier, during the five-year Leasco matter I had traveled heavily with Bob to line up support, and this reminded me of much the same plight.

In November 1991 Maxwell was found drowned off his private yacht, The Lady Ghislaine. There will probably never be an answer to what occurred. It was Maxwell's request to his family that he be buried in Israel, and this was accomplished [4, pp. 1–7]. There has been much discussion on how or why Maxwell received a national burial in Israel. A eulogy was offered by the President of Israel and prayers offered by Chaim Herzog, Chief Rabbi of Haifa, by many other dignitaries, and also by his son Philip [4, pp. 34–37]. In addition to being born a Jew, his involvement in the 1948 Israeli war for independence was little known and never discussed [6, pp. 197–218]. One had to be at the funeral to fully appreciate the words that were spoken in recognition of his life.

During Robert Maxwell's tenure as founder and publisher of Pergamon Press he was instrumental in publishing over 7,000 monographs and reference works and in launching some 700 journals, 418 of which continue to be published with the imprint of Pergamon Press within the Elsevier publishing group [9, pp. 139–140].

I believe that of all the tributes that Bob Maxwell has received, this quote from Arnold Field best captures how Maxwell would have liked to be remembered.

> I do believe, however, that he possessed a genuine desire to publish works on scientific and professional subjects which I am certain would otherwise remain just dusty manuscripts. Selective he must be, astute to the market potential he must be, but those of us who have had the privilege of being published, are grateful for the fact that he also prepared to place on record for public knowledge and present and future research, books on subjects which would otherwise remain within the domain of restricted groups. [3, p.104]

Bibliography

[1]   Haines, J. (1988) *Maxwell.* Macdonald, UK.

[2]   Bower, T. (1988) *Maxwell the Outsider.* Viking Penquin, UK.

[3]   Maxwell, R. (1988) *Robert Maxwell & Pergamon Press.* Pergamon Press Ltd., Oxford

[4]   Maxwell, E. (1994) *A Mind of My Own.* Harper Collins, New York

[5]   Kramis, A. (1963) *The Griffin.* Houghton Mifflin Co., Boston.

[6]   Loftus, J. and Aaron, M. (1994) *The Secret War Against the Jews.* St. Martin Press, New York.

[7]   Cahn, R.W. (1994) The Origin of Pergamon Press: Rosbaud and Maxwell. *European Review* **2**, 37–41.

[8]   Cox, B. (1998) Circulation Autumn: Some Thoughts on Forty Fulfillment Years. *Against the Grain* **10**, 18–22.

[9]   Cox, B. (1998) The Pergamon Phenomenon, 1951–1991. *Logos* **9**, 135–140.

A Century of Science Publishing
E.H. Fredriksson (Ed.)
IOS Press, 2001

Chapter 8

Learned Societies Adapt to New Publishing Realities

A Review of the Role Played by U.S. Societies

Robert H. Marks
Publishing Consultant, USA

The dramatic development of radar and the atomic bomb during World War II was the direct result of a massive basic and applied research effort by the scientific and engineering community. This set the stage for future substantial increases in financial support of research programs by industry and the U.S. government.

Scientists and scientific societies have always recognized the prime importance of publishing the results of scientific research. The basic principle is that research is not complete until the results are peer-reviewed and published. Each research project builds on the published results in the archive. This also avoids the delays and added expense of "reinventing the wheel".

However, learned societies have always been concerned about the cost of publishing a large and growing amount of research results for a relatively small audience in each of the scientific disciplines. The proposed solution to this problem was the invention and introduction of the publication charge system. In essence, this system called for the payment of a publication charge by the organization conducting the research. This payment, on behalf of the author, was designed to cover the cost of the producing the first copy of each article. It was charged as a set amount per page for a given journal and varied with the length of each article. This payment covered the cost of editorial management (including peer-review), editorial mechanics (including copy editing) and composition of text, illustrations and tables. The remaining cost of printing, paper and distribution would come from individuals and libraries who subscribe to each journal. The publication charge rate was only $2.00 a page when the plan was first introduced in 1930 by the American Physical Society. In later years many of these rates reached levels well in excess of $100 per page.

Increased funding of research and development led to the graduation and employment of increasing numbers of Ph.D. scientists who then joined scientific societies operating in their chosen fields of research. It also resulted in the formation of many new societies covering specialized areas that were not adequately covered by the established learned societies. These developments produced a tremendous increase in the size and scope of all society programs including employment services, scientific meetings and conferences, publishing research journals, magazines and books and even providing information about the benefits of research to the general public.

All of these developments posed a wide variety of challenges for society publishing programs. Society members expected prompt publication of their papers, low subscription rates, wide circulation of the research results and low cost membership dues.

Exponential growth in the number of submitted research papers led to long publication delays. In addition, income from publication charges and subscriptions failed to keep pace with rapidly escalating publication costs. Subsequent increases in the level of publication charges persuaded many authors to publish with commercial publishers who did not levy page charges. Even though publication charges were paid by the authors organization, the expense was normally charged to the authors research budget. Without this expense the author had funds for other research purposes. However, without page charge income the subscription prices for commercial journals had to be much higher than society journals with page charge support. This increased each organization's expense for library subscriptions. With decreased levels of page charge income support, society subscription rates also had to increase. All of these increases led to regular annual declines in the number of journal subscriptions bought by libraries.

During this period most society publication programs were running at substantial losses. The shortfall in income had to be made up by increasing membership dues and attendance fees for society conferences and meetings. In the early 1970's some societies recognized that they needed professional management for their publishing programs to take full advantage of new technology, streamline their operation and regularly produce a substantial net income. It was recognized that additional income was needed to carry out the long term goals of the society without substantially increasing membership dues. At this point in time most society publishing programs were managed by scientists who were very familiar with the scientific content, and at the same time handicapped by their limited publishing experience and expertise.

At the American Institute of Physics, with new publishing management in place, the first challenge was to reduce publication time by streamlining the production process and increasing the page budget so that accepted papers would not be delayed because of page budget limitations. There was a substantial saving in time and cost by eliminating the author galley step. Each author only received page proofs of the complete article with all illustrations and tables in place. Authors that had the habit of rewriting their papers when they received galleys were quick to see that they should only change errors of fact and interpretation. This change dramatically reduced production time as well as the composition cost incurred for authors alterations.

The most expensive step in production was monotype composition. The monotype process was required to accommodate type setting the wide range of special characters needed for scientific text and to compose complex mathematical equations. Composition cost during this time period was in the range of $45 to $50 per page.

To decrease cost and shorten production time, *Physical Review Letters*, published weekly, pioneered the use of electric typewriters for in-house composition. A set of some 200 special typewriter keys, for individual manual insertion in the typewriter, made it possible to compose unjustified scientific text containing special characters and complex mathematical equations. The typewriters were operated by typists with no special composition skills compared to the highly skilled monotype operators at printing plants. The cost of typewriter composition was about $18 per page including authors alterations.

Typewriter composition was rapidly introduced on practically all of the physics journals published by the American Institute of Physics. A fan mechanism developed for the electric typewriter contained practically all the special character keys needed for composition. This device increased the output efficiency of each typist. They also became very adept at composing complex mathematics with the special keys and adroit use of the typewriter roller to accurately position the various component parts of each mathematical equation.

The next improvement was the introduction of computer photocomposition for the "heads" and "tails" of articles using Datapoint terminals. Each article heading contained bibliographic information including title, abstract, authors and indexing and classification terms. The tails included complete references to articles cited. This computer software was still unable to compose the complete scientific text and mathematics so typewriter composition continued to be used for the main text of each paper. The computer tape from the heads and tails system efficiently produced annual subject and author indexes for each journal. It also provided income from the sale of this information to secondary service publishers as input for their abstract journals and bibliographic data bases.

Computerized photocomposition of the main text became a reality with the introduction of the Atex system at the American Institute of Physics in the early 1980's. The electric typewriter and Datapoint terminals were replaced by computer keyboards and video screens that quickly and accurately composed complex scientific text and built up mathematics. In addition, the appearance of each page dramatically improved and the information content of each page increased.

The next advance came from Kurzweil equipment that scanned each author manuscript and sent the captured keystrokes directly to the Atex system. This reduced keyboarding time and expense. All keyboard operators had to do was correct any scanning errors and add mathematics at appropriate locations. One major drawback of the Atex system was its inability to compose complete pages with illustrations in place. It produced galleys which had to be manually pasted up into complete pages for plate making and printing.

The Xyvision composition system, currently used by both the American Institute of Physics and the American Chemical Society, produces complete digitized pages with illustrations and tables in position, for mounting on the internet and production of the printed publication. In addition, digitized text from the author can be input directly into the computer system, copy edited on line, and then sent directly into the Xyvision system. This development speeds up production and greatly reduces costs.

The 1990's have been characterized by learned societies growing use of strategic planning with the primary goal of developing successful publishing programs that produce a net income to help support overall society activities. Another important goal is achieving a completely digitized publishing program to meet the demands of members for fast, low-cost, world-wide access to scientific information on the internet.

Publication time and cost has been further reduced by efficient computerized editorial management systems for manuscript receipt, peer review and acceptance. Improved communication between authors, editors and editorial staff is a time saving byproduct benefit of these new systems.

Secondary service data base products are almost completely electronic although there are still some die-hard paper subscribers. Many data base producers are using direct computer tape input from primary publishers. Electronic full text of more and more journals is available on the internet with links to abstract data bases and the full text of other computerized journals. Simplified, easy to learn interfaces are being developed so that individual scientists can directly access data bases and the full text of electronic journals without using an expert intermediary.

All societies are now facing up to the challenge of setting realistic value based prices for magazines, journals and books. Scientific journal publication charges and subscription prices have traditionally been set to support publication of the complete peer-reviewed archive. The subscription system allocates the considerable cost of publishing the complete archive among all subscribers to the journal. The sale of individual articles that happen to be of current interest to scientists and other users will not provide the income needed to replace the current subscription system. In fact, it will lead to much higher subscription prices for the others who continue to subscribe. The single article sales approach also doesn't recognize the value received when a search of the complete archive does not locate any published research in the area of interest.

The successful research journal is one that attracts papers from the best authors and quickly publishes all submitted articles that pass the test of peer-review and belong in the editorial scope of the journal. Scientific papers and articles are not and should not be evaluated and accepted for publication on the basis of their potential single article sales or readership. This approach stands in sharp contrast to book publishing where editors do not publish all peer-reviewed, high- quality science submitted. In addition to scientific quality books are evaluated on their potential sales to individuals, libraries and educational institutions. The same philosophy applies to magazine publishing.

Currently, with some exceptions, there is greatly reduced reliance on publication charge income. Page charges have either been greatly reduced or eliminated for most existing and new journals. Additional income is needed to keep abreast of new technology and cover the growth of traditional and other rapidly expanding niche areas of science in existing and new publications. Today's competitive climate also calls for substantial financial resources to support comprehensive marketing and promotion programs for existing journals and for the introduction of an increasing variety of new niche publications.

A Century of Science Publishing
E.H. Fredriksson (Ed.)
IOS Press, 2001

Chapter 9

German Post-WWII Developments and Changes in the Language of Science

Ekkehard Hundt
Akademische Verlagsgesellschaft Aka, Berlin, Germany

After the Second World War German universities and scientific research recovered only very slowly. In West Germany, many scientists left for the USA and other Western countries. A prominent example of this "brain drain" is the physicist Rudolf Mößbauer. He discovered a special interaction of gamma rays with atomic nuclei ("Mößbauer-Effekt") in 1957 in München. In 1961 he received the Nobel Price for his discovery, but in the same year he started to work in the California Institute of Technology in Pasadena. When he returned to München in 1964 he insisted that the Physics Faculty had to be reorganised. As a by-product of this reorganisation, the physics section of the Technical University of München in Garching was renamed into "Physik Department" (explicitly with the English word "department", and not with its German equivalent "Abteilung"). Even now, in 2000, there is still a debate whether this is an acceptable name for a German institution.

Corresponding to the slow recovery of universities, scientific publishing started from a very low level. The division into two German states was an additional handicap for the development of the publishing industry. Many traditional publishing houses had independent east and west German successors who could not contact each other for political reasons. Many owners of publishing houses in East Germany (many of them in Leipzig) had been dispossessed, and some of the companies were continued as VEB ("Volkseigener Betrieb"), while the owners re-established their companies in West Germany. In a table of publishing companies from 1960 the following "dual" companies are listed [1]:

Johann Ambrosius Barth	München 1949	Leipzig 1780	Medicine, Sciences
Bibliographisches Institut AG	Mannheim 1953	Leipzig 1874	Dictionaries
Breitkopf & Härtel	Wiesbaden 1947	Leipzig 1719	Music
F.A. Brockhaus	Wiesbaden 1945	Leipzig 1817	Dictionaries

Gustav Fischer Verlag KG	Stuttgart 1948	Jena 1878	Medicine, Sciences
Otto Harrassowitz	Wiesbaden 1947	Leipzig 1872	Orientalistics, Literature
S. Hirzel Verlag KG	Stuttgart 1947	Leipzig 1853	Medicine, Sciences
Insel-Verlag Anton Kippenberg	Wiesbaden 1945	Leipzig 1899	Literature
Max Niemeyer Verlag	Tübingen 1950	Halle 1870	Germanistics, Philosophy
Julius Perthes	Darmstadt	Gotha 1785	Geography
C.F. Peters	Frankfurt/M 1950	Leipzig 1800	Music
Philipp Reclam jun.	Stuttgart 1947	Leipzig 1828	Literature
Dr. Dietrich Steinkopff	Frankfurt/M 1948	Dresden 1908	Medicine
B.G. Teubner Verlagsges. mbH	Stuttgart 1953	Leipzig 1811	Mathematics, Sciences
Georg Thieme Verlag	Stuttgart 1946	Leipzig 1886	Medicine

(This list is not comprehensive; I know of at least one pair of companies that is missing: Akademische Verlagsgesellschaft Geest & Portig KG, Leipzig, and Akademische Verlagsgesellschaft, Frankfurt/Main.)

In both parts of Germany, academic publishing started with university textbooks in German, mainly new editions of pre-war books. The East German publishers flourished with translations of Russian books (that were heavily subsidised). One famous example is the *Lehrbuch der Theoretischen Physik* in 7 volumes by L.D. Landau and E.M. Lifschitz, published in German by Akademie-Verlag, Berlin 1966. In West Germany, translations from English textbooks were also done, but on a much smaller scale. Most traditional academic publishers kept to developing German language textbooks by German authors. Only one publisher (Springer Verlag) started early with English language journals and books, and founded an affiliate in New York 1964. The aim was not only to distribute English language books and journals published in Germany but also the development of a genuine international product by American and international authors.

Though the university textbooks were written in German, the research level literature (journals, conference proceedings, monographs) was mainly in English. So even long before the introduction of the "Impact Factors" (which are heavily biased in favour of American journals) German researchers tended to publish their results in the English language, and they had to rely on Springer or foreign publishers. So in 1972 it was natural that I published my own thesis in English, and the obvious medium was the Springer journal *Astronomy and Astrophysics*. That journal was founded in 1969, as a merger of five national journals (*Annales d'Astrophysique, Bulletin of the Astronomical Institutes of the Netherlands, Bulletin Astronomique, Journal des Observateurs, Zeitschrift für Astrophysik*). This merger ended the strange situation that a journal with the German title *Zeitschrift für Astrophysik* contained nearly 100% English language articles.

Late in the Sixties it had become obvious that scientific education and research in Western Germany were behind, and the turbulent upheaval associated with the "68 generation" coincided with demonstrations against the "Bildungs-katastrophe". (I don't know whether this was just a coincidence or whether these two developments were factually inter-related. If I remember correctly, the impression that academia was neglected by politics was at least one of the components of the severe frustration that discharged at that time.) In order to end this "Bildungs-katastrophe", many new universities were founded (24 new universities, and 12 special high schools on top of 29 existing universities). The number of students rose dramatically within a few years, and also the percentage of school graduates with "Abitur" (qualification for studying) within the corresponding age group, as the following table shows [2].

	Students		Qualified
	beginners	total	for studying (%)
1960	79,400	291,000	5.5
1965	65,700	384,000	7.5
1970	125,700	510,000	10.8
1975	166,600	840,000	20.1
1980	174,000	978,000	22.8

When I started in the publishing business in 1973, I had expected that the market for university textbooks would increase dramatically along with student numbers. But the contrary was the case: the sales figures of academic books had shown a marked drop in 1968.

I had left university and started in the publishing business in 1973. The company was "Bibliographisches Institut" which published mainly dictionaries, reference books, atlases, and had just started a big encyclopedia. Only a small fraction of the company's resources was devoted to academic books: the BI-Hochschultaschenbücher (university pocketbooks). First experiences with small, low-cost academic books had been made before the war with Meyers kleine Handbücher, and the new series had been started in 1958 with Werner Heisenberg's Physikalische Prinzipien der Quantentheorie. The series continued with small reference books, and "additional reading", but also included an increasing number of compact introductory texts. The usage of these books spread rapidly among students and thus attracted more and more authors. The sales figures rose correspondingly. This very agreeable development slowed down around 1968/69, and only in 1972 was the situation obvious, and the section devoted to academic publishing was restructured subsequently (and I was then hired to help in this restructuring process).

What were the reasons for the adverse development of sales figures despite growing student numbers? Fortunately there is a written account which speculates on some of the reasons in the relevant chapter of the commemorative publication for the 150 years anniversary of "Bibliographisches Institut" in 1976 [3]. Apart from a few wrong assumptions, this analysis reflects some general aspects of academia and publishing in these critical years: One of the internal mistakes was that too many books had been included with a limited market that did not fit into a pocketbook series — it is never easy to reject an important author. But at the same time, due to reformed teaching models, more and more lecturers chose to (or were forced to) distribute their lecture notes free of charge to the students. At the same time, free photocopying in university libraries propagated. As authors made a point of low selling prices, several publishers started paperback series (*Heidelberger Taschenbücher* by Springer, *Teubner Studientexte*, a joint venture of Vieweg with rororo Pocketbooks). So the sales potential for textbooks in the already limited German language market diminished rapidly. Falling print runs imply rising unit costs, and, to absorb these, cheaper typesetting methods were used. *BI-Hochschultaschenbücher* moved from proper Monotype typesetting to the IBM Composer, and later to just reproducing the authors' typewritten pages (with handwritten Greek letters and mathematical symbols). This production development again reinforced the impression that there is no big difference between a proper book and your professor's (free) lecture notes.

Looking back now, more than 25 years later, I believe the increase in student numbers itself had an influence on the book market. My hypothesis: Before the rapid increase in numbers, most students had an academic interest in their field of study in Humboldt's sense, and tried to read about many different aspects of certain ideas and results in order to get a deeper understanding. Many of the "new" students were attracted by improved career chances and saw their studies as a professional training. They would strictly adhere to their own professor's lecture notes in order to pass their examination, and would avoid being distracted and losing time by worrying about different aspects of their subject. I think this new situation — when learning focuses on grades with minimal effort rather than on the acquisition of knowledge — is an additional explanation for the fact that the use of literature did not grow with the number of students. But I think there will always remain a small but constant "hard core" of students with a deeper interest in their subject.

In 1972, as a response to the mentioned difficulties, BI-Wissenschaftsverlag was founded, the new university branch of Bibliographisches Institut that was no longer dependent on pocketbooks. To become a full scale academic publisher, one of our next steps was to publish in English. We were not alone with this decision; around the same time many traditional German publishers started to publish higher level books in English that would previously have been published in German. This decision was obviously based on the assumption that this step would increase the potential market while more or less maintaining the previous local market, at least a major proportion of it. A 1975 survey [4] among German academics, students, and business executives confirms: English language academic literature is accepted by 60% of researchers, 54% of students (and only 23% of business executives); among academics, acceptance is highest in the arts (58%), lowest in medicine (40%), and has a medium value in economy and sociology (38%) and sciences (47%). Many readers prefer German translations but 22% of researchers, 20% of students, and 29% of executives would read the English original even if the German translation is available; among academics, the proportion is again highest in the arts (32%), and lowest in medicine (9%). To add some personal recollections to these statistics: I remember that even as early as 1965 our mathematics professor had based his lecture on an English text (Ahlfors, Complex Analysis, McGraw Hill International Student Edition), mentioning that we would have to learn and read English in any case during our further studies. In 1969 we had enjoyed reading the English original of *The Feynman Lectures on Physics* (Addison-Wesley), and in my subsidiary subject, Watson's *Molecular Biology of the Gene* (Benjamin) was indispensable.

Around 1984, our company moved into English language publishing; as first steps we started a new international journal (*Expositiones Mathematicae*), published English or mixed language conference volumes, and included English language articles in our *Jahrbuch Überblicke Mathematik* (and gave it the English subtitle *Mathematical Surveys*). Only then did we discover the obvious fact that the English language is a necessary but not a sufficient condition to sell books internationally. In order to obtain some knowledge and assistance in marketing books worldwide, we joined the "International Group of Scientific, Technical & Medical Publishers" (STM). We were not alone; the stm information booklet lists quite a few publishing houses from the German speaking countries (German or Swiss subsidiaries of international groups are not included). Springer Verlag is one of the founding members (not surprisingly), and many companies joined in 1969–1970, immediately after the founding of the group, then there was a second accumulation in 1977–1983; (a tabular overview is shown on the next page).

Various attempts to start individual international book marketing culminated in the early eighties in the idea of a joint effort. The Boston affiliate of Birkhäuser Verlag (in person of Alice and Klaus Peters) offered German publishers help in entering the American market. This offer included joint distribution and marketing, advice for adjusting the advertising material, but also for re-designing the books themselves (and even for re-orienting the publishing strategy). Parallel to this support of stm publishing, they founded Suhrkamp/Insel USA, and started publishing translations of important German works. Goethe and the collected poems of Heinrich Heine are but two examples. We learnt much from this cooperation, and — with hindsight — it might have developed into a successful German book marketing institution. But unfortunately, this ended in the mid-eighties, when Birkhäuser Verlag, including its Boston subsidiary, was bought by Springer Verlag. So a number of German stm publishing houses lost their guidance in America. The only comfort in this situation was that at least Alice and Klaus Peters did not have a big problem; they received an immediate offer from William Jovanovich to build a new office in Cambridge (MA) to handle the program in the mathematical sciences for Academic Press, and to publish trade books within Harcourt Brace Jovanovich. Today, they have their own independent publishing house (AK Peters, Ltd.).

German, Austrian and Swiss Members of the STM Group (1986)
and their first year of membership

Verlagsgruppe Bertelsmann (on behalf of Vieweg)	1970
Bibliographisches Institut	1977
Birkhäuser Verlag	1969
Gustav Fischer Verlag	1978
Walter de Gruyter & Co	1969
Carl Hanser Verlag	1974
Otto Harrassowitz	1984
Hans Huber Verlag	1969
R. Oldenbourg Verlag	1969
Paul Parey	1973
K.G. Saur Verlag	1983
F.K. Schattauer Verlag	1970
Schwabe & Co	1977
J. Schweitzer Verlag	1985
Springer Verlag	1968
B.G. Teubner	1977
Georg Thieme Verlag	1969
Urban & Schwarzenberg	1969
VDI-Verlag	1977

So in the end, Springer Verlag remained the first and only German scientific publishing house which moved successfully into international English language publishing. In the late eighties the attempts of German publishers to become international had stopped. In a reversal of that trend, international publishers started to establish their own subsidiaries in Germany and/or acquired German publishing houses on a larger scale. I thank Rolf Pakendorf (Pearson Education, München) for the following account of this movement from the view of an insider:

> As prosperity increased in Germany after the War and after the reforms of the sixties in the university sector student numbers increased dramatically — instead of 10% of all children born in a particular year enrolling in university, the number rose to 25% by the late seventies. The approximately 1 million German students suddenly constituted an attractive market for US textbook publishers. The first to follow the siren song of large enrolments was McGraw-Hill Book Co.
>
> McGraw-Hill, at that time the largest and most international of textbook publishers, started a distribution company in Düsseldorf in 1974. Jolanda von Hagen, who started and ran Springer's New York office took over the management of McGraw-Hill's German operation in 1976. She initiated a German publishing programme at the college level which was expanded in the eighties to cover the professional market in the fields of computer science and business and marketing. In the late eighties McGraw-Hill branched out into medical publishing with the translation of Harrison's Principles of Internal Medicine. The fact that a major US house was on their doorstep encouraged a number of German academics to offer their (English) monographs to McGraw-Hill, thus exacerbating the dire situation of German STM publishers.
>
> McGraw-Hill was followed by Addison-Wesley in 1984. Addison-Wesley Germany was conceived of as a publishing operation. The company concentrated on publishing books in computer science for professionals and was so successful they soon ventured into a fully fledged university textbook publishing programme (which they abandoned after a few years, because of the difficulty of the marketplace). The textbook publishing activities led to funneling of (English) monographs to the Addison-Wesley offices in the UK and the US.
>
> Basil Blackwell established a German subsidiary in the late eighties. Blackwell Germany acquired McGraw-Hill's German medical list when the latter company abandoned its German operation in the early nineties. Blackwell's German subsidiary concentrates on publishing STM books in German, but obviously English monographs are referred to Oxford.

There are more examples for the establishment of international publishers in Germany. Just to mention a few: as early as 1966 Pergamon Press acquired Vieweg

Verlag in Braunschweig (which became part of the Bertelsmann group in 1974 and moved to Wiesbaden), and in 1996 the Japanese publisher Ohmsha and the Dutch publisher IOS Press re-established Akademische Verlagsgesellschaft in Berlin.

But most such moves cannot be described in few words. To give an example of the more complicated nature: In 1992 the Thomson group established itself in Germany, and founded the subsidiary ITP (International Thomson Publishing) in Bonn which was originally intended to publish textbooks but later moved into computer applications. In 1993 Thomson acquired the medical book program from VCH, Weinheim, and incorporated it into Chapman & Hall. Later VCH became part of John Wiley. In 1998 Thomson disengaged from the German market, and sold ITP to Verlag Moderne Industrie (who made it MITP), the German part of Chapman & Hall was sold to Thieme, and the international parts of the Science publishing to Wolters Kluwer. In 2000 Thomson reengaged in Germany by buying K.G. Saur Verlag from Reed Elsevier, and incorporated Saur into its Gale Group. This is an indication of the accelerating merger, acquisition and reorganisation process which is typical for international businesses, and which eventually had its impact on academic publishing in Germany. In this context the two major German publishing groups with relation to academic publishing should be mentioned: Holtzbrink and Bertelsmann.

Here I have to thank Andreas Deutsch from Spektrum Akademischer Verlag for his valuable material that was the basis of the following paragraphs. This is not only an account of the Holtzbrinck story but also gives an excellent view of the development of academic publishing in the 1990's.

> In the academic and stm field the Holtzbrinck group comprises Spektrum Akademischer Verlag, Gustav Fischer Verlag, Urban und Schwarzenberg, Schaeffer-Poeschel, Metzler, Handelsblatt and shares of VDI Verlag. The academic aspect of the Holtzbrinck story begins in 1978, when the journal *Scientific American* founded its German daughter journal *Spektrum der Wissenschaft*, at the suggestion of Prof. Helmut Grünewald of VCH, Weinheim. The German journal started as a joint venture of Scientific American and VCH, and the first issues were published 1978 in Weinheim, in 1980 the journal became a 100% daughter of Scientific American, and moved to Heidelberg. In the first years the German journal was more or less a one-to-one translation of Scientific American, but from 1983 it was also used by German scientists for their own articles and short contributions. Meanwhile, Spektrum der Wissenschaft had started to publish books, beginning with collections of articles from the journal in the series *Verständliche Wissenschaft*, and since 1982 a new book series, lavishly made-up, about different scientific subjects independent of the journal articles. According to their high academic value, understandable writing, and high quality make-up, the books had printruns that were unusu-

ally high in relation to usual academic publications. In 1986 the whole company Scientific American with all its American and international daughter companies (including W.H. Freeman, Scientific American Medicine, and the Heidelberg daughter) was acquired by the publishing group Georg von Holtzbrinck in Stuttgart.

In 1991 the book publishing was separated from the journal, and *Spektrum Akademischer Verlag* was founded with the intention to start a full scientific publishing program. An English language book program was started, together with Freeman in Oxford. But the planned strategic cooperation with Freeman failed after some time due to a re-orientation of Freeman towards pure College publishing. Since an international distribution was missing, even after the acquisition of Macmillan (and Nature) the publishing house had to concentrate on the German language. Meanwhile, after internal growth, but also due to the take-over of BI-Wissenschaftsverlag and the biology program of Gustav Fischer, Spektrum is the market leader in the German scientific textbook market, above Springer. As a second pillar, besides the textbooks, a series of scientific dictionaries and reference books was established. The publisher included electronic media at an early stage so that most of the program is available in digital form. In spite of all this effort it is nearly impossible to continue a German language program on a library level, because of the restriction to the German language market. The publisher continues his — small but successful — scientific non-fiction program, in continuation of the early tradition of Spektrum der Wissenschaft.

Gustav Fischer Verlag was acquired by the Holtzbrinck group in 1991, to strengthen the stm-field that was until then covered by Metzler, Schäffer-Poeschel, and Spektrum. The biological titles of Gustav Fischer were taken over by Spektrum, and the medical field of Gustav Fischer was stengthenend by the subsequent merger with Urban & Schwarzenberg. Metzler concentrated on the humane disciplines with textbooks and reference books in the same way as Spektrum did in the sciences. Schaeffer-Poeschel was originally seen as one of the professional publishers, together with Spektrum and Metzler, but later it was integrated within Handelsblatt. Holtzbrinck's share in VDI-Verlag is also related to Handelsblatt, and the book program was sold to Springer.

In general, all these measures of concentration and consolidation were undertaken in view of a massive drop in student numbers in the natural sciences. The beginners in Chemistry dropped by 65% from 1991 to 1995, in other scientific fields the decrease was around 30%. A similar development took place in Medicine and Engineering. In view of this sharp drop in student numbers the present lack of technical specialists in many fields ("Bildungslücke") does not come as a surprise for those who had watched the 1995 development carefully. Parallel to the drop of student numbers the library budgets were cut drastically. All this caused a crisis atmosphere that also had an effect in private purchasing of academic books. Publishers had to concentrate on their core fields, and the costly development of new key titles or entering new fields of business was impossible for most publishers, not only the small ones. Final result was a reduction publishing activities in many places, and a new wave of sales and mergers.

The last turn of this account gives an excellent trigger for the surprise of the century. Given that Springer was one of the first successful commercial publishing houses, the first to move to America, was the founding member of the stm Group, remained the market leader in many scientific fields, had acquired Steinkopff, Physica, Birkhäuser, Urban & Vogel, had subsidiaries in London, Tokyo, Paris, Hongkong, Barcelona, Milan, and Singapore, was one of the first to establish a strong electronic publishing strategy — who could have imagined that this company would become the object of acquisition. On November 11, 1998 it became public: Springer had been sold to Bertelsmann, and the new company "Bertelsmann Springer Science + Business Media" would be born.

This leads us to the Bertelsmann story, and here I have to thank Sabine Schaub, leader of Springer's PR department, for valuable material. The name of the new company is an indication that scientific and professional publishing are put together, so the relevant story starts with the foundation of "Bertelsmann Fachzeitschriften" (professional journals), especially *DBZ Deutsche Bauzeitschrift* in 1953. A selection of the next expansions and acquisitions are given in tabular form:

1970	Heinrich Vogel	Traffic
1973	Münchener Medizin Verlag	Medicine
1974	Vieweg	Mathematics, Sciences
1977	ibau	Building
1978	Gabler	Economy
1979	Heinze	Building

That the activities of former Bertelsmann and Springer companies were coordinated was to be expected. As the three publishers Vieweg, Gabler, and Westdeutscher Verlag, all in Wiesbaden, had been grouped as "Bertelsmann Fachverlage" for a long time, they were of course integrated into the new group. Also the merger of Münchner Medizin Verlag and Urban & Vogel came as no surprise. The next sensation was the acquisition of Teubner by the new group in July 1999. In February 2000 the German "Financial Times" was started in co-operation with the Pearson group. More moves are to be expected, and they will no longer be associated with surprise or sensation. Though Bertelsmann is by far the biggest publisher in Germany, this is not the case internationally. The following table [5] shows the 10 biggest professional publishing companies in the world and their turnovers (1997, in Million DM):

1	Reed Elsevier	9.5
2	Thomson Corporation	6.7
3	Wolters Kluwer	4.6
4	McGraw Hill	2.7
5	Havas	1.8
6	VNU	1.5
7	Bertelsmann/Springer	1.3
8	Wiley & Son	0.8
9	Harcourt General	0.8
10	Weka	0.8

For the 1970's and 1980's we had touched on the question of the language of science, and whether German academic publishers could move into international publishing or if foreign publishers would take over. The success stories of ever and faster growing international publishing groups make this question more or less obsolete. A big international group would know how to act locally, independent of the location of its headquarters or the mother language of its CEO. We have seen from the Holtzbrinck group that international distribution of English language books can be a problem even within an international group. It is reported that within Springer Verlag the decisions about marketing of English language material in the U.S.A. were always made in New York, and never in Heidelberg.

Directly after the German unification and the fall of the iron courtain some people expected (hoped or feared?) that the German language would regain some of its old potential in science. But this expectation was not fulfilled. Scientific research literature had been published in English since the war, and nothing changed after 1990. There is also an obvious tendency for German participants of German conferences in Germany give their contributions in English. The most recent idea is that university students should receive their regular lectures in the English language — because they will have to do their research in English anyhow. On top of that everyday German is flooded with English expressions, and serious efforts have been started to save the German language from extinction. At least we will have to face the threat that German shares the fate of "small" languages.

As far as the everyday use of language is concerned, this development could certainly be deplored. From the view of a scientific publisher nothing has changed.

On the one hand, the steady tendency towards the English language in scientific research and teaching cannot be reversed. On the other hand the export potential of English research literature from Germany is very limited. So it remains a challenge for German scientific publishers to find their individual niches for publishing in German.

References

[1]   Der neue Brockhaus, 3. Aufl. 1960.

[2]   Turner, G. (1981) Studentenberg und Akademikerlücke. *UMSCHAU* **81**(Heftz 7) S. 209.

[3]   Sarkowski, H. *Das Bibliographsche Institut. Verlagsgeschichte und Bibliographie 1826–1976.*

[4]   Zur Situation der wissenschaftlichen Literatur in der BRD. Juli 1975.

[5]   Börsenblatt des deutschen Buchhandels, 27. Nov. 1998.

A Century of Science Publishing
E.H. Fredriksson (Ed.)
IOS Press, 2001

Chapter 10

Akademie-Verlag Berlin. Academy Publishing Tradition in Eastern Europe

Hans Kruschwitz
Akademische Verlagsgesellschaft Aka, Berlin, Germany

In the time after WWII up to the break-down of the communist system in Eastern Europe the academy presses of the Eastern European countries enjoyed a great significance in their respective countries. The history and role of the "German Academy of Science in Berlin" is touched upon, as well as the international context within which the Academy found itself. The founding of Akademie-Verlag took place in 1946. The early history and publication milestones are described. The number of journals grew from the first business year's 5 to 60 in 1989. Humanities publications and carefully prepared new editions of classical works received international recognition. International cooperation and sales systems are described in the final part.

During the time between WWII and the break-up of the communist system in Eastern Europe, the Academy publishers of the Eastern European countries assumed a remarkable importance for the development and dissemination of the scientific book and the scientific journal in their respective countries.

In this chapter, Akademie-Verlag, Berlin will be described as an example. Along with the Russian Academy publisher "Nauka", Moscow, Akademie-Verlag achieved the largest international circulation. The title already gives an indication: the history of the publishing house is inextricable from that of the Academy, or, more precisely: with the history of the "Deutsche Akademie der Wissenschaften in Berlin".

On July 1, 1946, Berlin was still not divided, but as a result of the War was a highly damaged four-sector city. The Academy was reopened on the basis of Order Nr. 187 of the Soviet Military Administration. This was the successor of the former Prussian Academy of Sciences and it had scientists from all parts of Germany as its members.

The art and function of science academies adapt themselves to the given political and societal circumstances. The contents and scope of tasks clearly depend on the kind of society in which they operate, the structure and organisation of the total scientific and research potential of the countries in question, as well as upon the science policy of their governments. This can be seen in the history of the various academies in the past as well as in our time, and was also the case of the Prussian Academy in the times of the Monarchy, the Weimar Republic and the "Third Reich".

Due to the universal importance of science and research for the economy, society and state governments are keen to support promising research projects and science based companies. Therefore, most countries have specialist ministries or institutions on a federal or central level, for science and education. These instances finance research projects of central importance to the state, and they make use of national research councils and other suitable bodies to obtain a professional selection, evaluation, steering and state financing to be able to undertake sponsored research. For example, Conseil National de la Recherche Scientifique in France, Consiglio Nationale delle Richerche in Italy, Deutsche Forschungsgemeinschaft in Germany and National Academy of Sciences in the US.

The Academies of science assume different positions in the system of state steering of science and research. In some countries they have responsibility regarding the area of basic research concerning distribution of funding as well as with international exchange. In socialist countries the Academies of science were given special planning and coordination functions for research in their countries — modeled upon the Academy of Science of the USSR.

With the reopening of the Berlin Academy in 1946 it lost the traditionally "pure" line of a learned society. The statutes of 31.10.1946 had already made it legal to set up and maintain research institutes for specific problem areas. Thereby it began to realize a request made in 1930 in a pro-memoriam by the Prussian Academy of Sciences.

In this way, with the statutes of 1946, the Academy took the step towards integration of research institutes. This laid the foundation for its later expansion to the central science and research institution, which it became in the perspective of the political division of post-War Germany and as a result of the societal development in the Soviet occupation zone and the G.D.R.

The basic change of the socio-economic structure of the national economics in the Soviet Occupation Zone created a science and research institution which was tailored for basic R&D in service of industrial R&D and production. The results of this institution would incorporate industry in applied research. The transformation of key industries into state-owned enterprises was thus supplemented by the formation of a state-directed science and research institution.

Historically the DAW in Berlin became a legacy of ideas of Leibniz, Wilhelm von Humboldt and Harnack. Under pressure and in recognition of the increasing division of Germany, it strove to become the science institution for the G.D.R. alone, though earlier scientists had aimed for a German Academy.

The fact that many results of research find their way to application (in society) through publication in books and journals had always caused scientific bodies to look for suitable publishing possibilities. It is therefore understandable that important academies realize their publication needs through the establishment of their own publishing houses. The lines of tradition are of different length here. If you look, for instance, at the publishing house of the Russian Academy of Science, Nauka, or at the Hungarian Academy-Publishing house, the years of foundation go back to the beginning of academy tradition in these countries.

For Akademie-Verlag, Berlin, this line started shortly after the re-opening of the academy. Earlier, the Berlin Academy had not published proceedings of its research in its own publishing house. Immediately after its re-opening the Academy made preparations for the establishment of its own publishing house.

It was therefore natural that a Publishing House of the AdW was established, and on 23 December 1946 the Akademie-Verlag Berlin GmbH was registered in the Chamber of Commerce. In the statutes we read: "the aim of the company is to publish scientific works and writings from the fields of the German Academy of Science of Berlin and other scientific institutions".

At the start of the company the Academy had a very direct influence on its production. Its work was dependent on approval by scientific council, which consisted of five members of the Academy and the company director. Without the unselfish assistance and support by established scientists of the Academy it would not have been possible for the company to establish its reputation in such a short time.

Until the founding of the Academy's own company it entrusted the publishing activities of its scientific endeavors to different publishers. Now these activities became concentrated in Akademie-Verlag.

In rapid succession and in parallel to the re-establishment of research and teaching, book series were added from Academy committees or newly founded institutes or sections. Serials and above all editions of the fields of academies, not only the Berlin Academy, annuals and monographs resulted in the programme's fast growth. Agreements with the Saxon Academy of Science in Leipzig, the Mining Academy Freiberg and later also the Agricultural Academy of Berlin and numerous university institutes contributed to this.

On the 250th anniversary of the founding of the Academy the first volume of the Leibniz collected works edition produced after the War was presented. Participating in this collection were the DAW in Berlin and later also the Leibniz archives in Hannover as well as the Leibniz research institute in Münster.

Leibniz, the founder of the Academy, was commemorated in the logo of the publishing house designed in 1957. The profile of the head surrounded with his maxim Theoria cum Praxi became the inexchangeable logo of the Akademie-Verlag.

The proximity to the Academy facilitated access for the company to leading scientists at home and abroad, which was a great advantage after the foundation of the G.D.R. in 1949 and the coming of the Cold War. The company soon became an appreciated and sought after partner by many scientists.

Intensive effort was expended on the scientific journals section from the start of publishing activities. In the first year of business, in 1947, five journals were commenced. Among these was the abstracting journal *Chemisches Zentralblatt*, the journal *Astronomische Nachrichten* and the Academy publication *Deutsche Literaturzeitung*.

Most significantly, as could be expected, came the dominance in physics and Medicine. "The other sciences layered themselves more and more along the page of the book", as Wilhelm Oswald remarked already in 1905. Also his observation 80 years ago about the growing trend towards journal publishing is extremely valid. "This is because today, much more than earlier, the individual — facing the flood of knowledge in his field — is in need of securing his discoveries through publication. This is easiest done in the form of a short journal article". What Oswald only barely could foresee was the rise of abstracting services to a necessary tool for scientists, giving them an overview of international literature on their specialty in the easiest possibly way.

As publisher of *Chemisches Zentralblatt* (since 1950 in collaboration with Verlag Chemie, Weinheim), the *Physikalische Berichte*, the *Technisches Zentralblatt* as well as the *Landwirtschaftliches Zentralblatt* the company assumed significant advantages in publishing capabilities of scientific documentation in the 1950's and 1960's.

The *Chemisches Zentralblatt* represented a complete tutorial for all branches of pure and applied chemistry. It was founded in 1830 by the psychophysicist G.T. Fechner and was published 1897–1945 by the German Chemical Society. After 1945 the DAW Berlin took over its publication, later (from 1950) assisted by the following institutions: the Academy of Sciences in Göttingen and the Society of German Chemists, and from 1954 the Chemical Society of the G.D.R.

The *Chemisches Zentralblatt* had become an indispensable tool for chemists active in research or industry, and provided the basis for all research in the field of chemistry. Also, patent offices used this means of documentation to establish priorities. The 230 pages thick weekly of the *C.Z.* gave information on the latest thoughts and investigations in the various sub-fields. It reported from 4,000 journals, and, moreover, the *C.Z.* with its annual 16,000 pages was also considered the information source for patent descriptions: it covered 36,000 patent documents annually.

In addition, book production from all over the world was covered through bibliographical references and reviews. Finally, every five years a general index was published. With this, the chemist had a reliable coverage of publications during a large span of time. The index contained yearly 4,800 printed pages.

Attempts to create an information source for the engineer and technician, which would provide the same source for all branches of technology as *C.Z.* did for chemistry, were realized through the founding of the *T.Z.* Similarly, the *L.Z.* contained abstracts of all works published worldwide in the areas of agriculture, forestry and veterinary medicine.

Characteristic for virtually all journals of the publishers was the fact that the responsibility for the contents was not only in the hands of an Editor-in-Chief or Editorial Board, but also shared through additional Advisory Boards. The trend towards internationalization was yearly carried to a higher level. A sign of this was that the original German titles of journals were changed into Latin or English ones. With these title changes the basis was laid for an internationalization of publishing activities. At the same time the transition towards a predominantly English publication language was implemented. The internationalization of the Boards contributed significantly to expand the geographic basis for submission of articles and to make the international character of the journals more visible. An important proof of value of a journal is its international sales. This developed very positively, also outside Europe, and thereby provided a significant financial support in the development of a science journal programme.

As mentioned earlier, while 5 journals appeared in the first year of business, the number had grown to more than 60 in 1989. More than 20% of the scientific and professional journals of the G.D.R. were published by A.V.

The humanities programme of the company was internationally acknowledged, in particular, the carefully edited works of the German classics. These editions mainly contained the printed versions of texts, which the authors had published during their lifetime. The published result came from philological research as well as critical comparisons of texts. Every edition also contained an index, thus contributing to the variety of work done in archives and libraries.

Besides the continuation of collected works by Wieland and Jean Paul were the works of Georg Forster, the secular edition of Heinrich Heine, the works of Ludwig Feuerbach and others. After acquisition of publishing rights, the basic handbook of Karl Goedeke "Foundation of the History of German Poetry" was enlarged and continued in a new series covering the period 1830–1890.

The publication of the works of Aristoteles in new German translation found an enthusiastic reception in the German language area. The linguistics programme was also a remarkable publishing achievement and in this one should mention the vocational and dialectical dictionaries. For instance, Poggendorff, Biographical-literary Dictionary of the Exact Sciences, …

In Germanic expert circles the *Dictionary of German Contemporary Language* in 6 volumes, published by the Institute of Philology of the Academy, was critically acclaimed.

Classical antiquity (history) has belonged for more than a century to the most actively developed areas of the Berlin Academy. Scholars like Theodor Mommsen, Hermann Diels, Adolf von Harnack and Ulrich von Wilamowitz-Moellendorff are closely connected with the history and development of this area. In 1955 the Institute for Greek-Roman Antiquity was founded, after which publications from this area assumed a significant part of the humanities programme. Authors were not the only members of the Institute, it included scholars from all over Germany and beyond. For instance, the series *CMG*, consisting of Greek Christian writers of the first Centuries, and "texts and research on the history of the early-Christian literature" has continued its activities, until today.

Besides journals and book series, the monograph had an appropriate place in every academic-publishing house. Companies tried continuously to keep high scientific standards for the publications of monographic work. This was a financial necessity, because printrun and price had to stand in harmony with printing costs and overheads.

A significant part of the monographs constituted translations from Russian into German. Knowledge of the Russian language in Western Europe was very poor and thus there were good opportunities for distributing monographs of Russian scholars with worldwide reputation. Scientists who had been educated at Soviet universites and Academy Institutes assisted the company in obtaining high quality scientific translation. In cooperation with Soviet authors and West German publishers, demands of the Western book markets were fulfilled. In this way translations of Gnedenko's text on probability theory and Landau/Lifschitz' on theoretical physics were compulsory readings in some of the German language universities.

The development of a book is a work-intensive process, in which author and editor both have their special roles. It is therefore of mutual benefit that the editor can already exercise influence in an early phase of the manuscript — given of course that he masters the publishing craft. The author expects the editor to have sufficient competence to turn a scientifically important manuscript as far as possible into a useful book. In reviews, the editorial quality of the works of AV was often praised. The downside of this was the large editorial time spent on each manuscript, which by necessity had a negative consequence in the price calculations.

In the 1960's the Academy as a scholarly community lost its bridge function in inter-German relations. The reason for this was that the USSR let loose its policy to create a neutral Germany and the G.D.R. leadership steered towards full statehood and international recognition. In 1972 the re-naming of the Academy into "AdW der D.D.R." and its natural legitimization as national Academy of the State G.D.R. followed.

This political development had significant influence on the programme of the company. Nevertheless, its publishing programme continued to have a remarkable significance in the scientific world.

The Academy publishers in eastern countries possessed their own graphics enterprises in counter distinction to other publishers. Also, the Academy of the G.D.R. had several printing plants which were primarily occupied with work for the Academy publishing house. This had a significant influence on quantity and graphical quality. Lacking new investment and spare parts, the machinery was soon insufficient to meet demands of the international book and journal market. Time between manuscript submission and date of publication became steadily longer and thereby reduced the competitiveness of the company's production. As a result of this situation the maximum number of published titles of 400 went back to less than 300.

The international book exchange, the export of co-publications as well as licensing had seen significant increases in the most recent decades. They became an important part of the publishing activity.

The scientist and author expects the publisher to secure not only national, but also international, access among expert groups and libraries for their research results, be it in book or journal article form.

Well established and functioning sales routines are a condition for successful trade in science publication. The most important condition for this is a well-developed promotional capability of the company for the current stock as well as for work in preparation — especially the specialized scientific title. Printed in a small edition, it is in need of worldwide distribution.

In the Eastern European trading area the company had close contacts with foreign trade companies, which possessed a state license for book imports. In particular, however, it had close relations with the Academy publishers of Eastern European Countries, which, like the Akademie-Verlag in Berlin, belonged to their Academies. This mutual support mainly concerned the organisation of book fairs in science centers and distribution of catalogues and brochures to selected addresses.

Sales efforts were naturally concentrated in the German speaking areas. By 1948, shortly after the founding of the Akademie-Verlag, the company had appointed an agent in Stuttgart to represent its commercial interests in what was then the German West Zone. In 1952 the "Berlin Agreement" between both German states was reached and exchange of goods became the subject of state regulations. In agreement with the publishing house the agent founded his own company with the specific aim of distributing the publications of Akademie-Verlag in the F.R.G. In this way rapid fulfillment of orders from the Stuttgart warehouse was secured. For worldwide distribution, and in particular for non-German publications, the company made use of publishers in West Europe, USA and Japan. To mention a few typical examples: AP, ES, Sansyusya, Birkhäuser. Total sales abroad, including F.R.G., amounted to almost two thirds of the company's turnover.

The rise and development of the Berlin Akademie-Verlag between 1947 and 1990 occurred in a historic period. This was characterized by the repercussions of WWII, the change of political relations in Europe with the political partition of Germany into two states, the Cold War between the Western Powers and the USSR, the period of relaxation of political tensions in Europe and, finally, the collapse of the Socialist Society order in Eastern Countries and the dissolution of the USSR.

The publishing programme of the Akademie-Verlag, with 14,000 titles, and 64 journals from 25 science areas in humanities, natural sciences, medicine and technology, is an impressive reflection of current science publishing history.

At the beginning of 1991 Akademie-Verlag was privatised and lost its position as the leading science publisher of an entire region.

References

[1] Dunken, G. (1958) *Die Deutsche Akademie der Wissenschaften zu Berlin in Vergangenheit und Gegenwart.* Akademie-Verlag, Berlin.

[2] Hartkopf, W. und Dunken, G. (1967) *Von der Brandenburgischen Sozietat der Wissenschaften zur Deutschen Akademie der Wissenschaften zu Berlin.* Akademie-Verlag, Berlin.

[3] *Wissenschaftliche Literatur für die weitere Gestaltung der entwickelten sozialistischen Gesellschaft.* (Symposium anlasslich des 35. Jahrestages des Akademie-Verlages, 1984) Akademie-Verlag, Berlin.

[4] Scheler, W. (2000) *Von der Deutschen Akademie der Wissenschaften zu Berlin zur Akademie der Wissenschaften der D.D.R.* Karl Dietz Verlag, Berlin.

A Century of Science Publishing
E.H. Fredriksson (Ed.)
IOS Press, 2001

Chapter 11

Scientists as Publishers:
The Company of Biologists Ltd.

Richard Skaer
Company Secretary, Cambridge, UK

What is the Company of Biologists?

The Company of Biologists is a Company Limited by Guarantee, owning, printing and publishing three, fortnightly, international journals. These journals publish primary research articles in the field of biology. Their combined extent amounts to approximately 13,000 pages a year. The Company has, at present, 14 Directors all of whom give their time free. Almost all of them are active professional biologists. It is they who bear the responsibility for making policy decisions about the Company. The Board of Directors, though it meets together formally only four times a year, is organised into advisory groups — such as the Charity Policy group, the Investments Group, the Future Directions Group. There is also an Executive Group that meets monthly, and is chaired by the Company chairman. Three other Directors are also members of this Group, as is the production manager, the accounts and sales manager, the investments manager and the Company Secretary. The Company accountant is normally also in attendance.

The Company uses 'awaydays' on particular topics of concern as occasions when Directors, managers and staff can, together, generate new ideas or new ways of shaping the strategies of the Company.

The Company has been a registered Charity since 1952, when it was incorporated under the Companies Act. It now provides financial support to three major biological Societies and various conferences in the field of its journals. It also offers Travelling Fellowships worldwide to junior research workers who need to travel to laboratories in other countries to learn new techniques. Such fellowships are highly competitive and are awarded by the Editors of the Journals.

History of The Company of Biologists Ltd.

The Company of Biologists Ltd was founded in 1925 through the efforts of one man, in order to rescue a new journal that was failing. The man was George

Parker Bidder, a biologist, an authority on sponges, and a businessman — a director of the Cannock Chase Colliery. Among his many activities was (in 1889) to buy and run a hotel, "Parkers", in Naples and to provide accommodation for visitors to the Stazione Zoologica at Naples. On another occasion when Bidder was commissioned by the Government to carry out a long-term survey of the North Sea — for which he was paid a grant to hire a boat, he characteristically bought a boat, completed the survey, sold the boat for more than he paid for it and used the surplus to endow the "Ray Lankester Investigatorship" at the Marine Station at Plymouth (Ray Lankester was his teacher). A favourite phrase of his was "It has often occurred to me to wonder…".

The journal was the ailing, two-year-old *British Journal of Experimental Biology* published by Oliver and Boyd in Edinburgh. The Journal's existence was crucial for the developing new subject of Experimental Biology. Sir James Gray in Cambridge, as an important developer of this new subject, was particularly concerned.

Bidder called on friends, including Julian Huxley, Lancelot Hogben, J.T. Saunders and F.A.E. Crew to be Directors, while others became shareholders and "Members" of the new Company. Funds were needed to purchase the journal from the owners. An indenture, signed by F.A.E. Crew, sold the journal to the new Company for £150 on 14th November 1926. The Shareholders paid £5 but were liable for a total of £10 should the Company go into liquidation. At the time of the first statutory meeting in January 1926 there were 38 'Members'. Bidder, as chairman, approved Gray as the Editor of the journal and moved the publication to Cambridge University Press where, renamed as *Journal of Experimental Biology*, it remained for more than 50 years. Within two years the journal broke even financially with a profit of £3-8s-5d and even during the war it continued to be produced despite shortages of paper. Bidder later, in March 1946, gave the Company the *Quarterly Journal of Microscopical Science*, complete with Editors paid up to 31st January 1947. This journal had a long history dating back to the 19th century, and a rather cramped and meagre format. The Company re-founded and redesigned it in 1966 as *Journal of Cell Science*.

In 1952, for tax reasons, the Company, despite certain misgivings from Bidder, became a registered charity and its Memorandum and Articles of Association stipulated that each journal should have one Editor, with whom the Company dealt, and that that Editor had full and complete responsibility for what scientific matter was accepted by the journal. In other words, the Company, though made up of biologists of distinction, specifically disenfranchised itself from interfering in what went into the journal. The Company appointed the Editor, set the price and extent of the journal and monitored its finances, but otherwise "The Editor" was in control.

The Company in 1953 accepted the gift of yet another journal, this time with the catchy title *Journal of Embryology and Experimental Morphology*. This journal had been run by an Editorial Board who appointed three editors, each serving for three years and each in turn becoming senior editor in their final year. This arrangement meant that there was no ready authority to make long-term changes. The Company's policy of one Editor (or Editor-in-Chief) appointed by the Board of the Company, was clearly incompatible with an Editorial Board who appointed the editors, each of short tenure. In 1978, in order to bring the journal into line with the other journals of the Company, Professor D.W.T. Crompton, Company Chairman, asked for and obtained the resignation of the entire Board of JEEM — as the journal had come to be called.

Thus all three journals moved to production at the Cambridge University Press. Apart from the Board of Directors and editorial staff the Company consisted of only three part-time staff, i.e. a Company Secretary, a Financial Secretary who handled all the investment plans and expenditure, and a secretary. In the early seventies the job of the Company Secretary was described as "one hour a week".

With the spectacular success of *Cell* under Dr Benjamin Lewin, which achieved publication times of three months, rather than the nine or so months that was offered by Cambridge University Press at that time, Editors began to press for faster publication. It was the clear thinking Editor of *Journal of Cell Science*, Dr. A.V. Grimstone, who pointed out to the Board that the reason for the slowness of publication of the Company's journals was the time that they spent, at each stage, waiting their turn to be processed. Since there were many processes, there were many delays. He proposed in a letter to the Board dated 11th July 1979 that the way out of this situation was to employ staff who would give the journals their exclusive attention, so there were no delays. The idea that the Company should have its own printing house shaped the thinking of the Board, but for a couple of years the journals were entrusted to a forward-looking printer in Scarborough, Tom Pindar.

It was he who suggested in 1980 that the best way to manage the journals was for the Company to use two trained typesetters in Cambridge, whom he selected. Starting in 1982 they worked full-time on what were, in effect, word-processors. They then sent their discs to Scarborough along with the artwork for proofing, and eventual printing. At this time the Company's journals at Cambridge University Press were all being printed using hot metal — the change to offset lithography would not be for a further year. The system with Pindars worked well, but again, as with most major printers, delays at the printing house, though much less than before, were significant, to the displeasure of the Editors.

One highly significant concession that Cambridge University Press had agreed to in September 1977, was to pay the subscription money for the journals, after one month's delay, to the Company. The Company achieved even better terms when we moved to the Biochemical Society for distribution in January 1984.

The standard offer that we had originally accepted from Cambridge University Press as logical, was to be paid, at the end of the year, what remained of the subscription money for that year after all expenses had been deducted. With the new arrangement, interest would be earned on the subscriptions and, with luck, some money would be earning interest for a large part of, or for the entire year. This significantly improved our financial position, and made it feasible for us to hire premises and to employ technical staff and to purchase equipment. It must be stressed here that the very significant investment skills of the Financial Secretary, Dr S.H.P. Maddrell, FRS gave the Company the confidence and the cash to make some impressive and successful leaps of faith.

It is important to remember the conditions in the early 1980's when, with the increasing pressure from two of the three Editors, the Company moved to Pindars. Many typesetting and printing firms were being bought by entrepreneurs and stripped of their assets, leaving excellent staff unemployed. This was exacerbated by many printing works going into liquidation as hot-metal was replaced by offset litho and computerised typesetting. As the Company took over more and more of the production of its journals, we were astonished at the pool of highly skilled staff, eager to work to the highest standards, that we could employ. Many of these still work for us.

Although the print unions, particularly the NGA and Sogat 88 in London were locked in restrictive practices, the East Anglian branch of the NGA was always extremely helpful to us — they really knew each of their members individually and could tell us of their particular skills.

One trigger for going beyond the simple preparation of disks for Pindars was the discovery that equipment that was repossessed by the bank when a local type-setting works went into receivership could be purchased for a 'derisory sum'. We therefore found ourselves the proud owners of an industry-standard typesetter — a Linotron 202 that we initially had no plans to use, but which, after a while seemed worth trying out. Our initial approach to the Linotron as a 'toy' was rapidly taken over by those who really knew how to drive it. For five years the equipment pro-duced all our journals, after which, in true Bidder style, we sold the Linotron for more than we paid for it!

Since October 1983 it was clear that, eventually at least, biologists would routinely send us word-processor discs, so we agreed to terms with our union, the National Graphical Association, that we would sign an agreement, known as the RAGA (Reproduction And Graphics Association) agreement under which union members were permitted to insert typesetting commands so as to set text directly from an authors disc, provided that all union members in the Company were paid at an enhanced rate.

We were also very fortunate that we had three journals that we owned. This meant that there was enough throughput (then 1000–1300 pages/journal/year) to justify setting up on our own, and we could make sure that there was a continuing dialogue between editorial staff and production staff to achieve greater and greater production efficiency without compromising the standards of either side.

As biologists, we knew that biologists worldwide, were already, in the early 1980's, using word-processors, particularly Apple Macs, so, we asked for disks to accompany the manuscripts. Everyone, including authors, applauded such a move — but it sometimes took substantial pressure and telephone calls to convince authors that we really did want the actual disk on which they had typed their article! Although biologists, predictably, used a wide range of word-processing and other programs — unlike physicists who, very early on, had standardised on TeX and LaTeX, our typesetting staff found and used an increasingly wide range of programs to convert most discs into a standard production program. Our staff also became increasingly experienced at unpicking the results of an author using a standard program in a highly unorthodox way. Thus an author's printout on a laboratory printer might look perfectly satisfactory — until it is reproduced from disk onto a film that shows the true thinness of the line, only to discover that the line specified is only a few wavelengths of light thick — the lab printer simply printed the line as thin as it could!

Despite these propitious conditions it was an astonishingly brave move on the part of the Board to authorize first, the purchase of a Heidelberg SORS single colour printing press. They then, when it was clear that the advice we were given to keep printing and typesetting departments completely separate was wrong, authorised us to go out and buy a factory on the outskirts of Cambridge. This was opened in October 1985 by Dr. Anna Bidder, the daughter of Dr. G.P. Bidder and herself a zoologist of great distinction, and was named the 'Bidder Building'. The merging of the complete production system into one continuous process on the advice of our production manager, combined with flexibility of working practices from our production staff has enabled us to remain efficient.

One early experiment that we tried while we were at Cambridge University Press, but that failed, was no ones fault but our own for not taking full account of human nature. As biologists, we knew that journals taken in a library disappeared "To the Binders" for long periods of time — a very substantial inconvenience to users and an expense to librarians. We therefore negotiated very good terms with the Press to put our journals directly into a proper case binding (with buckram), thus endearing ourselves to librarians. What we had not bargained for was that librarians, on receipt of case-bound monthly volumes, placed them directly onto the library shelves, rather than into the display rack of latest issues — so our journals became instantly invisible on delivery to libraries except to those that searched the shelves archivally!

The flipside of this experience was that we asked our printers to print the covers, with four-colour pictures, since they enjoyed the variety involved in running the covers four times through the huge single-colour press that we owned. They found that with just a small amount of overtime they could print four-colour sheets for the journals that could be tipped in by hand when the volumes were bound. In this way, we were able to offer (and still do!) free colour to our authors. Of course, free colour became so popular with authors, that tipping in a large number of plates became prohibitively expensive. The alternative was to purchase two, two-colour presses that print colour in-situ, though our editorial staff do try to place colour when possible so that it falls propitiously for printing as well as for relevance.

We also experimented at Cambridge University Press from 1982 onwards with the numbers of offprints offered free to authors. We innocently thought that 200 offprints were probably enough to satisfy everyone and if we offered these free to the senior author of each article, we suspected that everyone would be pleased and we could give a standard order to CUP for the numbers required. We felt that this should allow us to negotiate better terms for printing, with a fixed run-size. Alas! Human nature merely accepted the 200 free copies and then added to that the strange variable numbers that authors use in their offprint order forms. We nevertheless continued to offer 200 free offprints to authors for many years.

A more successful experiment initiated on 29th April 1983 was to pay referees if they returned their reports on articles within two weeks. The going rate was £15 or $25. It is apocryphal that the fee could, if the referee were local, be commuted to a bottle of whisky (option now discontinued), but the fee can be accumulated to buy an individual subscription to a Company journal or book. The effect was magical. Traditional laggards got their reports in on the dot, with pleas for clemency on account of the vagaries of the post. Although the sum offered has not been increased, it still has a major impact on the return of reports and hence on publication times. On the other hand, it is a major expense, with some 3,000 articles submitted each year and each article needing at least two referees, but it is clearly appreciated as a token by overworked referees.

When we moved into our Printing House, it seemed much too large for our needs. This was an inducement to us to undertake our own distribution and to use our spare space as warehousing for distribution. We were encouraged to go ahead with this scheme by the officers of the Society for General Microbiology who pointed out to us how straightforward it is, at least, conceptually. We realised that one doesn't actually need to know precisely which libraries worldwide are taking our journals, for agents act as intermediaries. We, and others, also found to our surprise just how often libraries, that we had innocently thought of as pretty permanent, do change their addresses (and their agents). It has been a huge bonus to us to do our own distribution now that we are able to consolidate more and more information about which libraries, where, take our journals. We are thus in a strong position to negotiate with consortia, for our software can coordinate geography, numbers of libraries, journals and agents.

Not all our enterprises, of course, have been successful. When, early on, we bought some desk-top publishing equipment that was recommended by an organisation that had not used it under daily production regimes, we were told by the manufacturers that our troubles with it must be due to electrical spikes on our mains supply or operator errors. We found neither to be the case. The manufacturers would not divulge the names of their customers who were "finding the equipment so satisfactory" but we chanced to meet one who confessed to being as worried as we were about the way the equipment behaved. It took a visit to the High Court, followed by calling in the sheriffs, to get our money back (with costs), even though that had been promised in the High Court. We try not to deal, now, with firms who make it a principle not to say who their customers are. For a horrific six months while this was going on we had to use print-farming around Cambridge to cope with the increasing overload from the three Editors (who by chance had all allowed extent almost to double over that fraught period).

The Company has certainly benefited from links with the two Universities in Cambridge, particularly in relation to obtaining advice from experts. Thus in our High Court case over desk-top publishing equipment, we had expert advisors available from the Computer Labs in Cambridge. Moreover, when we needed to set up our Web-site at the Bidder Building, that is located at the back of beyond, and had no prospect at that time of fibre-optic cable being available, Professor Schnurr of Anglia Polytechnic University convinced us (and was quite right) that we could use a 2Mb/sec microwave link into his University, and thence into the main University network SUPER JANET. We also obtained a superb Webmaster from the Department of Chemistry, Cambridge, who was used to modelling maps of the changes in atmospheric chemistry. The system that he set up almost runs itself automatically provided that the journals do not change their format or their requirements significantly.

Our experiences have confirmed Bidder's original view, that an editor is the key figure in the journal and can make or break a journal (unless the Board intervene before it is too late). We were informed by one of our most distinguished Directors that our uncomfortably-named journal JEEM (what is Experimental Morphology anyway?) could be poised with a window of opportunity, owing to one of its American competitors becoming staid, slow and pernickety. With free colour, a new name, a new Editor and a substantial redesign, JEEM has now become our flagship journal, *Development*. This was not only the skill of the Editor however, it was that the journal was in place as the subject took off, as the prescient Director had suggested. It caught a net-full of excited authors who all cited each others papers and happily used their free colour to good effect. Despite other prestigious journals in the field, *Development* is the most cited journal in *Development*.

Could others do the same in their field? Certainly, they could! We, however, were often very lucky both in the staff we were able to employ and in having an adequate sized portfolio of journals to justify 'going it alone'. Of course, others like *Cell* have done it with just one journal initially and again it seems to have been the Editor and their vision that made the difference. This may be a very narrow viewpoint, however.

Advantages of the present step-up

It has been Company policy to employ editors who are themselves active in the research area of each journal and it may well be that many potential authors feel flattered to know that the distinguished Dr. X or Professor X will see or decide on their manuscript. Of course, full time, professional editorial staff, skilled as production editors, staff editors or editorial assistants, are vital to the smooth running of the journals and each journal has a production editor based in the Bidder Building to deal with production queries or problems immediately. It is indeed a heady mix to have experts in all aspects of the journal production, sales, editorial, distribution and website, housed in the same premises. Thus when negotiating sales with library consortia, the full geographic implications of a consortium, the subscription history of the individual libraries, the web down-loadings of articles and the other journals of the Company that are subscribed to by the libraries are all taken into account, as well as knowledge of special issues of the journals and CD-ROMs that are available. Moreover it is the case that staff feel that their suggestions, expertise and particular enthusiasm or knowledge of opportunities can be immediately explored and implemented, if sensible or useful — an example would be the availability of free colour for authors.

The main justification for the present system is that it works and the journals are produced to an extremely high standard, on time and we are thus able to attract and disseminate important articles. It has also been Company policy to give the journals that we own absolute priority in production, so although we have produced material for other Societies, such as the SEB symposium series, *Journal of Molecular Endocrinology* for the Society for Endocrinology, and *BioEssays* for ICSU press, we have now exclusively, as originally envisaged by the former Editor of *Journal of Cell Science*, concentrated on our own journals. Thus time is not lost whilst articles wait their turn in a line made up of other journals that we do not own or control. The crucial feature of ownership is to be able to establish those rules for a journal that in our view are viable and are indeed an improvement on what went before.

Another major advantage of going "against the grain" and using our own production line and printers rather than simply print-farming for the best price, is the quality of production. Our staff know precisely the quality of production that is required by our authors. Our sales staff enjoy getting to know the librarians, who are the majority of our customers: forging a relationship that is usually better than is available through middlemen. All staff work to very high standards and take pride in their work. Separated from the pressures of shareholders, the Company has been able fully to develop its professionalism, and to operate according to the principles of best practice in its operations.

A Century of Science Publishing
E.H. Fredriksson (Ed.)
IOS Press, 2001

Chapter 12

Science Textbook Publishing in the U.S.

Yale Altman
Publishing Consultant, USA

The growth of textbook publishing in science and engineering during the past 50 years represents a significant segment of the publishing industry. This is especially true in the U.S., a country that dominates the rest of the world in the publication of and reliance on textbooks from the freshman through the graduate years. Until the advent of Sputnik in 1957, science and engineering textbook publishing rested in the hands of relatively few publishers, such as McGraw-Hill, John Wiley & Sons, Prentice-Hall, and Macmillan. Clearly, this scientific event motivated the changes in the science and engineering curriculum in the U.S. As a result, greater emphasis was placed on subjects dealing with pure and applied science. Enrollments in these areas increased dramatically over the next decade, new publishers entered the field, and the more established publishers expanded their lists in the sciences to meet these burgeoning enrollments.

In the late 50's and early 60's, it is significant to note that several small publishers, such as Addison-Wesley and W.H. Freeman, published key undergraduate and graduate textbooks in mathematics, physics, chemistry, and geoscience. These books became the standard texts in their respective disciplines. Sales of approximately 25,000 to 30,000 copies during the life of the first edition were not uncommon, and these numbers increased substantially with future editions as enrollments increased.

The success of these smaller companies can be attributed to the experience and creativity of their editorial directors who were instrumental in recognizing the future curriculum changes. These editors developed key contacts with many leading scientists and teachers at the major universities. The leading academics at the stronger science and engineering schools were influenced to publish with these companies due to their strong emphasis on editorial, production, and design. The textbooks received instant credibility and although a number of the titles were too sophisticated for many schools initially, eventually they became the standard textbooks for their respective courses. These smaller publishers became formidable competition for the larger, more established houses, and they set higher standards for textbooks.

Part of the creativity in developing a strong list of textbooks and attracting first class authors was the emphasis on quality illustrations and design, which improved the pedagogy of the textbooks. In mathematics and physics, Addison-Wesley Publishing Co. led the way with high quality, three-dimensional illustrations in most of their publications. This new emphasis on design and production proved to be a critical factor if publishers were to compete for the best authors. Eventually, the major publishers were forced to invest their resources in this aspect of the publishing process, with the end result being that many of today's publications routinely offer 2 and 4-color presentations. In fact, without color, especially in the biomedical sciences, it is virtually impossible to attract first class authors. More importantly, it is very difficult to be competitive and secure adoptions without this attractive pedagogical feature.

During this period, textbook publishing was in the midst of enormous growth at all levels, and the competition for authors was intense. It was not uncommon for at least 10 publishers to be interested in the same textbook in various fields. Clearly, the authors were the beneficiaries of this fierce battle. An author of a potentially best selling textbook could expect to receive strong support from a publisher. This included attractive royalty arrangements; elaborate editorial, production and design; and above all, an effective marketing campaign. From a financial standpoint, various approaches were used to entice authors. Some publishers offered guaranteed royalties over a three to five- year period; escalating royalties; profit sharing; and stock options from some privately held companies. In addition to the above, substantial nonrefundable grants were offered to authors of textbooks at all levels.

Production and design costs have escalated substantially for textbooks over the past 15 years. Virtually all primary textbooks in the sciences, medicine, and engineering include color illustrations. In many instances, these design services are provided through independent graphic art studios in collaboration with in-house support. The services of a developmental or professional science writer have become common for many undergraduate textbooks.

Finally, and most critically, more aggressive marketing and promotional efforts are required to sell textbooks. More creative and concentrated efforts are made to pinpoint the key people responsible for textbook adoption decisions. Sales representatives and/or telemarketing follow-up are essential aspects of a total marketing campaign. It should also be noted that it is traditional to sample a number of complimentary copies to those faculty members teaching a course in which the book might be adopted. It is not unusual for a publisher to send out 3,000 to 5,000 complimentary copies for a freshman course. The costs to the publisher in this endeavor involve major expenditures.

Textbook marketing outside North America was becoming an increasingly important factor for science publishers. Although US science textbooks enjoy their greatest overall sales potential in the US, foreign sales have become a significant area of consideration for those publishers with successful titles at the undergraduate and graduate levels. Despite differences in curricula, many areas of the world, especially the United Kingdom, are using selected US textbooks in their courses. A good undergraduate text from a US publisher could expect sales representing 10 to 15% of a publisher's total sale to come from abroad. For graduate textbooks, which are often used as reference books, sales overseas can reach 30% to 40% of the total sales.

Since the cost of US textbooks are too expensive for most students abroad, it is common for US publishers to offer discounts of 50% to 70% so that the foreign publisher can offer a lower selling price to their student market.

Virtually all of the large US publishers have offices throughout the world to handle editorial and sales. Companies that do not have their own offices abroad rely on distribution arrangements with foreign publishers, which can be very effective in marketing textbooks. Several publishers abroad have their own sales staff to call on professors, similar to the structure in the US. For many undergraduate science textbooks, it is not uncommon for a US publisher to print an additional 5,000 to 10,000 copies specifically for a guaranteed foreign sale upon publication. In a number of instances, a foreign publisher will reorder copies after the initial purchase is depleted.

Foreign translations are another significant source of revenue for US textbooks. In general, translations into Spanish, Portuguese, and Italian have proven to be financially rewarding for both the US and the foreign publisher. Bulk sales, translation rights, and/or certain kinds of licensing fees result in additional revenue that assists the US publisher in offsetting the initial production costs related to science textbooks. Furthermore, bulk sales in particular, which necessitate a larger initial print run, help the publisher lower the unit cost per book.

Aside from the financial benefits derived from an active overseas marketing and sales effort, it is most gratifying to authors when their books are used throughout the world. It certainly enhances the author-publisher relationship when an extra effort is made to disseminate textbooks to the international community.

By the late 1980's and early 1990's, significant problems confronted textbook publishers. The escalating costs of producing and marketing textbooks was taking its toll on profit margins, especially when the number of competing texts was adversely affecting the market share. Publishers of introductory textbooks, where the enrollments were the largest, could no longer expect a book to be profitable during the life of the first edition. The used book market also had a large negative effect on sales of these new books. After the first year of a new publication, up to 50% of the next year's sales potential was diminished due to the used book market. This figure was less for the more advanced textbooks that students were more apt to keep as references.

To minimize the erosion of sales from used books, publisher found it necessary to accelerate the timeframe between editions. Today, many introductory texts are on a three-year revision cycle, compared to a five-year cycle in the 1960's and 1970's. The rapidly changing areas of science (e.g., molecular biology) necessitated a more frequent updating schedule to stay competitive. Immunology textbooks, for example, often are revised every other year to stay current with new technologies and developments.

During the past few years, textbook acquisitions have become more discriminatory, and fewer publishers are competing for major titles, especially at the lower levels. The costs and risks involved, given the number of titles currently available, are too high for many publishers to handle, particularly the smaller companies.

In the mid 1990's, computer technology began to have a serious impact on the publishing industry. At this time, textbook publishers were developing CD-ROMs as well as other products to accompany their books. It has now become part of the package, referred to as 'ancillaries'. Without ancillaries such as CD-ROM, study guides, transparencies, slide sets, and instructor's manuals, textbooks would not be considered seriously for adoption.

Recent surveys have indicated that computer technology in college courses is definitely on the rise. Multimedia and the World Wide Web have become an integral part of course instruction. Despite the increased use of electronic publishing, all publishers are deeply concerned as to how to make this new medium profitable. Many traditional publishers simply do not have the resources to develop their own line of electronic products. As a result of this situation, some companies have been formed to develop stand-alone software to be used in conjunction with traditional textbooks.

During the 1990's the publishing landscape changed considerably due to mergers and acquisitions. Today, only a few major scientific publishers, such as McGraw-Hill and John Wiley & Sons, remain independent. Although this takeover activity by other companies created internal problems initially, several positive developments resulted. One of the primary benefits of these mergers is the infusion of greater financial resources to explore and invest in newer and developing technology. For example, electronic publishing has become a focal point for all publishers. A number of the media conglomerates that have acquired scientific publishing programs have vast networks of sales outlets that offer new opportunities for publishers to reach previously untapped markets. In addition to opportunities inherent with the size of these large companies, a new set of fiscal criteria has been introduced to publishers. Pressure to focus on the bottom-line has forced companies to realistically reexamine goals and assess sales expectations, particularly in the highly competitive and fragmented market that currently exists. Executives with strong financial backgrounds now play a dominant role within these new publishing conglomerates, compared to earlier years when business aspects often played a secondary role to signing a prestigious author.

Current consensus among publishers is that text publishing in the near future will produce smaller books used in conjunction with multimedia materials. The whole area of electronic publishing vis-à-vis the printed word is becoming exceedingly complex. Textbook publishing will change dramatically in the 21st century to accommodate this new technology. Access to the Internet and the monumental exchange of information over the Internet will force publishers to reevaluate the way textbooks are disseminated. The challenges ahead are daunting and only time will tell what lies ahead for textbook publishers. The relatively straightforward approach to publishing in the early years was simple compared to the myriad of options that have to be considered in today's rapidly changing marketplace.

A Century of Science Publishing
E.H. Fredriksson (Ed.)
IOS Press, 2001

Chapter 13

Publishing Science and Technology Books in India

Mohan Primlani[a] and Raj Mirchandani[b]
[a]Oxford & IBH Publishing Company, New Delhi, India
[b]Capital Books International, New Delhi, India

In the early years of independent India, the libraries procured only books published abroad. In fact it was desirable to have such imports so as to enhance the standard of education and of setting standards for Indian publishing.

At this stage all STM publishing at the academic level was by the Government through their various laboratories and research centers of the Council for Scientific and Industrial Research (CSIR). These works certainly were the first efforts in publishing technical books, particularly in the field of Agriculture. The Indian Council of Agriculture Research (ICAR) was helpful to the agricultural community by bringing out many books related to their field. It was one of the factors that set the ground for the Green Revolution by Indian agriculture scientists in the late 1960's. The green revolution truly changed the face of agricultural research and growth. The late 1960's not only saw the growth of agricultural research centers and universities but a lot of qualified academics, many of them having earned their post-graduation or doctoral degrees from the better known western universities, now involved deeply in research and teaching in India. Agricultural education and research were coming of age. Constant and systematic exposure to western research and channeling efforts to develop technological break-through compatible to Indian environment was slowly initiating the urge amongst Indian authors to write. The biggest flaw was however the lack of good distribution facilities known only to professional book publishers.

The initial exposure Indian publishers had of scientific and technological books from the West were of reprinting some of the popular American and European textbooks. Prentice Hall of India, Tata-McGraw Hill and Wiley Eastern created a strong presence in the Indian textbook market. And the important effect of their activities was the new relationship which was being developed between academics, who saw in themselves the potentiality to become authors, and the publishing houses. Moreover these publishers were, to a certain extent, making up for the lack of proper distributional arrangement which prevailed in the government agencies' system.

Recognising the need to provide a fillip to science writing, the University Grants Commission invited authors to write books in their field. They were provided subsidies for preparing manuscripts. This effort was supported by a scheme of the National Book Trust of India which gave grants to publishers for publishing these works and marketing them at low prices. This twin combination certainly did help in promoting a great deal of writing in science books both in English and the Indian languages.

Although the Government of India set up these schemes there was a great deal of criticism about the selection of works and their approval. The red tape in getting works approved for publication eventually lead to its total disarray. The review process of such works was defective, often leading to poor quality publishing. The private sector had done nothing worthwhile in science books for twenty five years after independence. Few original works were published and the total emphasis was on school textbooks and undergraduate works. Many of these were student manuals prepared for examinations.

With industrial growth and greater exposure to science and technology internationally, obviously something worthwhile had to happen. Initially it was in the field of university textbooks, names such as Sultan Chand, S. Chand & Sons, Allied Publishers, Popular Book Depot and Oxford & IBH among others were the ones to be established. Along with them foreign publishers such as Macmillan, Orient Longman, Oxford University Press, Cambridge University Press, etc. through their Indian subsidiaries provided their contribution to original works published in India. These textbooks provided the lead to higher learning and to advanced publishing.

The first efforts of publishing in STM for the postgraduate students was led by publishers such as Allies in Pune, Current Technical and Popular Book Depot in Bombay, and Oxford & IBH, Wiley Eastern, Tata McGraw Hill and Narosa in New Delhi. In the field of medicine there were names such as JP Medical, Current Technical, B. Jain and BI and others who fulfilled the needs of medical students in India. It must be understood that medicine and science is often pertinent to each country, even though the principles of such learning are universal.

Unfortunately the scientific temper did not reach the higher levels of excellence required in the rapidly progressing world. These early books therefore did not achieve much recognition internationally. The concepts of editorial in science publishing did not find importance with the early publishers. There was never any dearth of capability and writing talent among Indians in this field. What was missing was the need to ensure high levels of accuracy and quality in order to find a place in the international community. In fact this was one of the reasons for the brain drain of the 1950's and 1960's. The finest scientists went to institutes abroad to study, teach or research and they often settled there. Their migration to those countries provided a wealth to them as a bounty. Even those who stayed in India would find publishers abroad for wider readership, recognition and better remuneration. There was never incentive in the country as books in India had to be sold at very low prices to find a market within the country.

In spite of all odds today we are witnessing as never done earlier not only higher researched written material but awareness to package the product. Improved higher education programmes in Africa and the Middle East have enormously opened the market for good Indian books in these regions. Indian publishers have realized that the potential export market is unbelievably large. The acceptability of the subject material coupled with the right pricing has made the export business viable and the effect has been better production quality and investment in capital expenditure. In the last few years many American and European publishers have also found it advantageous to print their books in India under the Export Processing Zone facilities set up under the Indian government's liberalization policy. Economics of scale have allowed many to ship the products from India to South Asian and Middle Eastern markets. This has indeed improved printing technology and many Indian authors who were very suspicious of not only the poor quality of production and the marketing of their research material are willingly working closely with Indian publishers.

It was in the 1970's that publishers in India realized the potential wealth in getting high quality works into western markets. The great difference between the retail price prevailing in India and those acceptable in the richer countries was an incentive to publish and export books for these markets. The publishing industry in India realized the need for quality production to reach wider horizons. The talent was high enough, but training was essential. No publishing institute existed to teach the fundamentals of editorial and production to capable young people. Soon some courses were developed. The University of Delhi established a paper for degree students. An institute of book publishing which was founded by O.P. Ghai provided the real beginnings of training personnel in publishing practices. It is to his credit that he drew upon the talent of the publishing industry itself to provide the faculty for teaching. Inspite of this, the entire overall situation is still not all together satisfactory. By and large the publishing community could not see the merit of hiring professionals to run publishing houses. Editorial needs, which is really the heart of publishing, never found a strong place in the industry. Even today this lacunae exists. Unless serious efforts are made to achieve the excellence required in today's world, there will be no real growth or improvement. So far only a few publishing houses incur the cost of professional editors to ensure an internationally demanded content. In STM only Tata McGraw Hill, Oxford & IBH, Narosa and a very limited number of other firms spend adequately on editorial inputs. Others even consider this cost and concept as unnecessary. Co-publishing programmes is also gaining tremendous credibility. Here again the Indian publisher is able to price the product keeping the low Indian purchasing ability in mind and producing the book for the American or European publisher for them to market the product internationally under their brand name. The attitude to think big and look beyond the subcontinent are the elements that are attracting internationally recognized Indian authors in science and technology to write for Indian publishers and this has lead to improved production facilities.

Asia has not seen a high level of eminence in science publishing. This is because of the need to compromise with the low purchasing power of the local population that this problem exists and continues to do so. Japan is the only country where books can be sold at prices comparable to those existing in Europe or America. But they have no publishing in the English language, whereas the earlier mentioned Indian publishers such as Oxford & IBH, Tata McGraw Hill, Wiley Eastern, Narosa, BI and JP etc. have realized the potential for science books in English being sold at prices much higher than the level of the local market.

The great software boom has helped Indian publishing to find a place in the rich western markets. With the use of these tools, better and better science books are being published. International seminars, conferences and workshops in science have also helped in providing good literature for the world market. As a result international scientists contribute willingly to books published in India. Thus monograph publishing has become internationally important.

Several Indian publishers are also using marketing networks abroad. These help in getting books to specialists in various academic fields.

Science publishing in the Indian languages remains at a basic level. Because of market limitations the works produced are mostly for lay readers. These works are confined to the different states within India. Hence the printruns are small. Also the writing is not so easy as there has been no development of a vocabulary for advanced science terminology.

With the participation of Indian publishers in important book fairs all over the worlds, the market for STM publishing is opening up. These fairs provide an exposure and a means to enhance sales. Within the next decade Indian publishing in science will be at the level of publishers in the west.

Even today some of the serious minded professional publishers are realizing the importance of creating the excellence which is required by way of editorial inputs and one can see a qualitative change in the product range. In Science, Technical & Medical publications Tata McGraw Hill, Oxford & IBH and Narosa are some of the few who are collaborating frequently with American and European publishers. These publishers are negotiating arrangements with their overseas contacts to publish their works for the international markets and for the domestic market on their own. This is allowing the Indian publishers to maintain quality at competitive prices and at the same time authors are getting enormous international exposure.

A Century of Science Publishing
E.H. Fredriksson (Ed.)
IOS Press, 2001

Chapter 14

The Move of U.S. Publishers Overseas

Peter Brown
Publishing Consultant, UK

The growth of science in the years after World War II followed an exponential curve. The War itself had proved a strong stimulus to science by virtue of the huge effort and resources invested in science to achieve both military aims, such as the Manhattan projects for making the atomic bomb, and radar, and non-military objectives such as the purification and manufacture of antibiotics. Concentration on such projects meant that the application of science to non-military objectives was very limited but once the constraints of wartime were lifted there was a wide expansion of the applications of science in all directions. For example, polythene, an ICI invention patented in 1931, had found its industrial application restricted to use as an electrical insulator in wartime but had a wide variety of other possible applications which were rapidly exploited once the end of the war came. On the basis of wartime restriction ICI were able to obtain a maximum extension of the term of their basic patent for polythene. Activities such as these contributed to the general optimism for science and technology and there was a big expansion in research in both the basic and applied sciences fuelled by an increase in the number of research establishments, government, academic and industrial.

A further huge fillip to investment in science arose as the result of the launching of the Russian Sputnik in 1957. The feeling was that the Western powers had been outwitted and left behind and this contributed to a strong belief that major further investment in science and technology was essential. In the UK the Robbins report led to the establishment of a whole group of new universities, each with a library which was a new customer on a large scale for books and journals and with science departments who would produce new authors and research papers, presaging good business for STM publishers.

Further factors were the decline of German and French as languages for the publication of science. Prior to 1939 German was a major language for the publishing of work in chemistry. The publication *Chemisches Zentralblatt* vied with *Chemical Abstracts* as a major publication of abstracts in chemistry, but it was affected badly by the war and never managed to re-establish itself subsequently, eventually ceasing publication. English became the lingua franca of science, much to the annoyance of De Gaulle, who insisted on French authors delivering their papers in French no matter what the occasion. I once was at a meeting where a French author spoke rapidly in French for 30 seconds, said: "That was my paper, I will now give an abstract in English", and spoke for a further 20 minutes. Despite De Gaulle the use of English has continued to grow and now classic German chemistry journals such as *Chemische Berichte* publish their papers in English.

In the wake of these factors the demand for new publications grew. Traditionally, journal publishing of research papers had always been in the hands of the learned societies (though, the most prestigious of them all, *Nature* had always been published by a commercial publisher). Each learned society was very much based on a single traditional scientific discipline (Institute of Physics, Physiological Society etc.). The demand for new journals occurred usually in one of two ways, either by sub-division of a broad disciplinary subject, or by covering a new inter-disciplinary subject which did not fall within the remit of a single learned society. As an example of the first one might consider the sub-division of chemistry, first into theoretical, analytical, physical, inorganic and organic chemistry, each with its own journal or journals, and then by further sub-division creating such journals as *Journal of Fluorine Chemistry* or *Journal of Mass Spectrometry*. As an example of the second, interdisciplinary, type, the field of the neurosciences is a good one. This field may involve anatomists, physiologists, biochemists, pharmacologists or psychologists and clearly at the outset no single disciplinary based society could cover the whole area, though a Society of Neuroscience has evolved since.

This background of change and potential expansion for English-language publications in science drew US publishers to look at establishing bases in Europe. It seemed logical to establish such bases in the UK, not least because of the growing predominance of English, and a number of US publishers established offices in London. In the early 1950's Academic Books was set up in London as a Sales Office under Fred Morgan and its success led to a publishing arm, Academic Press Ltd. being started under the direction of Charles Hutt.

Academic Press had been started in New York by Walter J. Johnson, a refugee from Nazi Germany who in common with other Jewish professional men had been forced to flee to the U.S.A. and to abandon the family publishing house of Akademie Verlag to their enemies. Johnson was joined by his brother-in-law, Kurt Jacoby, an exceptionally talented editor who was the architect of an impressive book list of monographs, edited treatises, series and serial publications ranging across the length and breadth of science. In particular series of up-to-date substantial reviews in specific fields such as protein chemistry were started in the 1940's, with the generic title "Advances in ..." and these became subscribed to annually by a wide range of libraries on a standing order basis. The need to gather together compendiums of techniques and methods in physics, chemistry and the biological sciences was also recognised by Jakoby and series such as *Methods in Enzymology*, edited by Colowick and Kaplan achieved wide currency and continue today, more than 300 volumes having been published and the scope extended greatly beyond that implied by the word 'Enzymology' in the title. Scientists responded to what they saw as an enlightened publishing policy and relationships were forged with the scientific community which lasted many years and which stood the company in good stead when new ventures were proposed. Advice and help were freely given and there was a willingness to take part. Some publishers today, when emphasis is laid on 'the bottom line' even in the short term, do not recognise the importance of retaining the goodwill of those who are both their contributors of raw material and their customers.

Jacoby also realised the opportunities that existed for commercial publishing houses to start new journals and a number of journals having a broad fundamental scope coupled with scientific validity such as *Journal of Colloid and Interface Science, Virology, Experimental Cell Research* and *Journal of Molecular Spectroscopy* began life and have continued to succeed.

Charles Hutt soon began making his own contributions to this international programme and from the London office he started *Journal of Molecular Biology*, for which he was able to persuade John Kendrew to become the editor, *Journal of Theoretical Biology* with Jim Danielli as editor (who owned a share in the journal) and *Journal of Sound and Vibration Research*. These were far-sighted projects which were still the mainstay of the London office of Academic Press thirty years later. In particular, *Journal of Molecular Biology* became the organ of choice for papers in a new field which took an outstandingly successful course. Kendrew, a Nobel Prizewinner as the first man to determine the three-dimensional structure of a protein, myoglobin, was a dominant figure and his strong personality played a role in establishing the reputation of the journal. It continued to lead the field for a number of years , but by the early 1980's had lost some of its lustre and ceased to seem the exciting journal that it had originally been. Kendrew's own research career was comparatively short (all his research papers were published within about fifteen years) and his interest remained in the physical structural side of molecular biology whereas the emphasis of excitement had shifted towards molecular genetics. Kendrew's main interest became scientific administration but he was reluctant to relinquish control of the journal which he saw as his baby. The effect was a loss of interest in the journal as a vehicle for publishing their work by those at the cutting edge of molecular biology. The situation was saved by Sydney Brenner, who loyally shouldered the difficult burden of changing the thrust of *JMB* with characteristic energy and who by vigorous use of his contacts throughout the world transformed the journal and recovered much of the ground that had been lost, eventually replacing Kendrew as Editor-in-Chief. *JMB* continues as one of the leaders in its field under its present editor Peter Wright.

Journal of Theoretical Biology also proved in its early days to be a source of interesting ideas and comment, particularly in biomathematics, the biophysical areas and in such topics as theoretical population biology. Jim Danielli, devisor with Hugh Davson of the Davson-Danielli theory of membranes, was an active and controversial figure who kept the journal lively and prominent. After Danielli's long illness and eventual death it has never found the same prominence.

Academic Press London built up an extensive book programme of monographs, serials such as *Advances in Physical Organic Chemistry* and series such as *Methods in Microbiology*. These were generally of high quality In 1969 Johnson sold out to Harcourt Brace, though at first this made little difference to the independence of the London office. By the early 1980's however pressures on library budgets, partly occasioned by the ever-rising cost of journals, had caused the market for specialist books to shrink and sales per title were falling markedly. The commissioning of books from London had continued to expand; as many as 200 titles per annum were being commissioned. The effect on profits was such as to cause the US parent management to intervene and the heyday of Academic Press in London was over. As this piece is being written the sale of Harcourt Publishing, as the group now is, to Elsevier is going through the legal processes. So what started with the reincarnation in New York of a German publishing house is now in European hands and might in some ways be considered to have come full circle.

In 1960 John Wiley & Sons Inc. set up a European office in London. Wiley had already by then been established for more than 150 years as a publishing house in Manhattan. They started with general interest books and fiction, publishing such authors as Conrad, Melville and Poe, but with the expansion of US universities in the 1870's went into engineering and developed a high reputation for their scientific-technical publications. Wiley had marketed their books in the UK and in Europe through Chapman & Hall as agents since 1895, but now decided that they wanted to run their own affairs in Europe.

Wiley's high reputation was justified; in my own original field of organic chemistry Wiley had made fundamental contributions to the science with the introduction of new types of publication which provided the chemist with tools that had never before been available. They can be said to have published the first graduate-level text with the two-volume text edited by Henry Gilman. *Organic Syntheses*, also edited by Gilman was an ongoing series which spelt out in detail exactly how to conduct preparations in the laboratory, so that they could be given to an assistant with confidence that the method described would work in his hands. *Organic Reactions* edited by Roger Adams was a series, originally appearing annually, which was invaluable in designing a synthesis. All of these and more made a big impact on the research chemist. They resulted from a close relationship between scientist and publisher which stimulated novel types of publication. Nor was this success confined to chemistry; physics and fields in engineering, mathematics, statistics and the life sciences were included.

Change was also coming to Wiley at home, as in 1961 they acquired Interscience Publishers. This company was another formed as a result of the immigration of the principals, Eric Proskauer and Maurits Dekker in response to events in Hitler's Third Reich. Dekker was part owner of Dekker & Nordemann, a large scientific book shop on the Continent. The Dutch publisher Elsevier decided to set up branches in London and New York and also to set up in New York Nordemann Publishing Co. to publish books which would be produced in the Netherlands but marketed outside. Before this operation could be finalised Hitler overran the Netherlands and Dekker and Proskauer found themselves cut off from their home base. Their only solution was to found a new company, Interscience and they went with vigour about the business of establishing relationships with leading scientists. Particularly fruitful relationships were with Herman Mark, whose polymer series dominated its field, and with Arnold Weissberger in organising a series of techniques of organic chemistry. But the most significant innovation to be introduced by Interscience to Wiley was the starting of new journals. In 1946 Interscience had started *Journal of Polymer Science*, building on the contacts that had been so successful in starting and expanding the book series. With its companion *Journal of Applied Polymer Science*, it remains predominant in its field. Until exposed to the influence of Proskauer Wiley do not appear to have considered seriously the possibility of setting up new journals.

Undoubtedly a big factor in this must have been the predominant position of the large US learned societies. The American Chemical Society and American Institute of Physics are both major institutions with mega dollar budgets who have been active in publishing high quality journals with the strong support of their members from their inception. Indeed, many learned societies in Europe as well as US regarded as their prerogative the publication of journals in their subject area. This could lead to abuse in cases where the author's findings were out of favour with those in charge of the Society and there are still scientists around to this day who bless the name of Robert Maxwell, because a journal that he founded gave them an opportunity to publish otherwise denied to them. The only endpoint of research is to publish the results and there is a finite cost to the process of publishing research results. This was recognised in the United States by building in to research grants from Federal sources funds for publication. This led to the 'page charge' system in which US society journals charge a rate per page for the publication of accepted papers. In return, the society subscription rate for such journals is maintained at a lower rate than would be possible on a strict commercial basis. Hence US society journals are available internationally at a subscription price per page published which is relatively cheap by commercial standards. When I explained this system to William Jovanovich, at that time President of HBJ, he took great exception to what he considered to be the subsidising of competitive publications by the US taxpayer. No such funding was available to European scientists and if Europeans wished to publish in a US journal operating a page-charge system they either had to pay out of their own funds or seek a waiver from the publisher of the charge. This was often given, but some loss of priority for the paper might result. Page charges have been the motivation for start-up of a new journal. European scientists became disgruntled when they lost priority on submitting papers to *Journal of Chemical Physics* and this encouraged North-Holland to start *Chemical Physics* as a journal for full-length papers.

So opportunities to start disciplinary based journals falling within the remit of a society had to contend with such factors and this may explain why it took the advent of Interscience into the fold before journals became important to Wiley. Polymer science was a good starting point for it bridged chemistry, physics and technology, though the ACS has not hesitated to include it subsequently into its scope.

Wiley moved its European office from London to Chichester after a short while and has published from there across the board in engineering, mathematics, statistics, computer science, the physical sciences, life sciences and medicine. One of the main attractions it could offer to European-based authors and editors was a ready outlet and its consolidated experience of marketing in North America.

A journal publishing programme was developed which sought to identify a niche or emerging area of research, secure an editor and board in leading or influential positions in the area, possibly seek the support of a society in the field to ensure manuscript submissions and to provide a subscriber base possibly with member subscriptions tied in to the annual dues of the society.

Though a measure of success was achieved over the years in founding new journals it has to be said that the main expansion of journals within Wiley has come from acquisition of other publishers lists. In the early 1980's Chichester acquired the journals of Heyden & Co, whose programme was based on the marketing of spectroscopic and other instrumental chemical data, whilst in 1989 the New York office acquired Alan R. Liss Inc. with an extensive journal programme in the life sciences. Then, in 1996 Wiley merged, through the Chichester office, with the German publisher VCH, whose chemistry programme fitted very well within the Wiley framework. It brought a cluster of prestigious journals, of which *Angewandte Chemie* offered a high penetration of the chemical research fraternity, and VCH provided also a substantial book list in chemistry.

The story of the two major US STM publishers considered above shows both similarities and differences between them. Both derive great strength from their geographical situation in the US and their access to the North American market, the largest market in the world by a long way for scientific publications. Both have established extensive relationships with the North American scientific community, the largest and best funded in the world and used this effectively in major publishing programmes. This strength has given power to their European publishing programmes as an asset attractive to European authors.

Wiley remains close to its US origins, with the Wiley family still owning 51% of the business, It has been very much a book-based business which came later to journals than AP. Its international position has become much stronger in recent years and it has diversified from books. Academic Press, within the Harcourt Group since 1969, was earlier into journals but then did not pursue journal expansion as aggressively as Elsevier did. It now seems that the AP business, which owed much to the European origins of its founders, has now come into European ownership. Both companies have made their impact internationally on STM publishing.

Tools and Trends

A Century of Science Publishing
E.H. Fredriksson (Ed.)
IOS Press, 2001

Chapter 15

Institute for Scientific Information

Tony Cawkell[a] *and Eugene Garfield*[b]
[a]CITECH Ltd., Iver Heath, UK
[b]Chairman Emeritus, ISI, Philadelphia, PA, USA

The history and development of ISI, is, to a large extent, mirrored in the history of Garfield.

International Encyclopedia of Information and Library Science.

The man

In his *Times* article about the characteristics of Americans, Linklater [11] asks: "What other country could carry out a survey in which a staggering 81% from richest to poorest concluded 'I am optimistic about my personal future' and in which three quarters of those polled went on to endorse that corny but still deeply held belief that 'in America if you work hard you can be anything you want to be'." The belief may be corny but Eugene Garfield's progress is a classical example of it.

The author byline indicates that this chapter has two authors — but that is not really correct. Introducing myself as the first author, an Englishman, I wrote this chapter from information gained from Eugene Garfield, from the impressions of others, and from experiences gained while working for ISI. It is not necessary to write a hagiographic biography about Dr. Garfield. It is perfectly obvious that it was he who propelled ISI to its unique position.

Garfield got a B.S. in chemistry at Columbia University in 1949 and worked with Professor Louis Hammett in 1950–1951. His first paper (as a joint author with Bernhard [2]) written when he was at Columbia, took three years to be published. In 1951 he joined the staff of the Johns Hopkins University Welch library's Medical Indexing Project under contract to what would become the National Library of Medicine but was then the army medical library. His reference from Professor Louis Hammett of Columbia was somewhat inaccurate. It said he is a "hard but not very original worker". It was here that Garfield realised the potential of machines for handling large files of information. He used an IBM 101 statistical punched-card sorting machine for searching punch cards which had been encoded with subject headings and standard IBM tabulating machines for the preparation of printed indexes. More general inspiration was drawn from H.G. Wells' idea of a "World Brain" [12].

He met a number of people while at the Welch Library who were well known in the profession but he did not have a library degree and was advised to get one if he intended to stay in the library field. He attended the Columbia library school and was subsequently awarded a Grolier fellowship, partly because of the excellent references — rather better than those he received when joining the Welch library — he received from the eminent librarians he had met at Johns Hopkins. He could not have afforded the fees without it. He obtained his M.S. in Library Science in 1954.

In 1961 he was awarded a Ph.D. at the University of Pennsylvania [7]. Garfield has always been interested in chemistry and was concerned that the indexes produced by *Chemical Abstracts* were up to five years late. Later, he entered into competition with the entrenched state-supported *Chemical Abstracts* by introducing *Index Chemicus* in 1960, later re-named *Currrent Abstracts of Chemistry and Index Chemicus*. It included the Wiswesser Line Notation for encoding substructures.

This product tells us something about Gene's motivation. He had a small number of industrial charter subscribers for *CAC&IC* but it lost money for twenty years so why wasn't it killed off? Its continuation was one reason why several executives left in the sixties as described later. Garfield says that "the key point was that I had invested a lot of ego in it and there was a very loyal staff of chemists" [10]. He also explained why he pursued citation more intensively than chemical indexing: "I suspect the choice was motivated by the usual desire of a scientist for recognition. Maybe mine was stronger than my need for money or power… I came from a socio-cultural-economic family background that cultivated a deep sense of justice… A lot of people are passed over in the formal reward system of science… SCI and the citation analysis became for me a vehicle to transform an informal system of recognition into an explicit reward system for science".

Garfield ran his company in such a way that he rarely found it necessary to dismiss people. He didn't mind if his staff adopted flexible working hours. Consequently the company steadily acquired hundreds of members in its "10-year club". Dozens of them stayed much longer. I will never forget the African American man who had the job of bringing up journals from the basement in Chestnut St. as required. He wore a large badge proclaiming himself "keeper of the archives". Soon after I joined the company I was doing a search and needed some journals. "Yes Sir" said he "It will only take ten minutes". It did. He returned bearing the journals and a huge smile. He had changed a menial task into a challenge.

Current Contents

It was while he was at the Welch library that Gene started reproducing the contents pages of journals as *Contents in Advance*, this first version being targeted at librarians and library schools, assisted by some students from Columbia. Four photographically reduced contents pages were reproduced on 9" x 11" sheets. The price was $6 per annum. When Gene went to library school it was continued by Anne McCann of Prometheus Press, but folded a few years later suffering the fate of all underfunded businesses. In the article cited above, Garfield quotes an estimate from the Small Business Administration that two thirds of all new businesses in the United States cease trading within the first five years.

He has described his early progress [9]. This article includes a photograph of him standing in front of the chicken coop near the house into which he moved in 1955.

Garfield called his firm Documation Inc., later changing the name to Eugene Garfield Associates. Nothing daunted by the failure of *Contents in Advance* Gene decided to start up a similar but more ambitious booklet called *Management's Documation Preview* later changed to *Current Contents of Management and Social Science*, using a Xerox platemaker and a small offset press. He kept a dehumidifier running so that the dampness from the floor of the coop would not impede the workings of the machinery.

The Bell Telephone Company heard about *Current Contents of Management and Social Sciences* when it was starting up. They ordered 500 copies of a customised edition named *Survey of Current Management Literature* which had a different cover. The financing of this relatively large order reveals the spirit of a true entrepreneur. Garfield went to the banks for a loan but they were not interested. He then heard about the Household Finance Corporation. Having grown up during the depression Garfield thought that "going to a finance company was like being in the hands of the devil". However, they lent him $500 — the State limit — and suggested that he tried a branch in another city for more. He did just that when he learned painfully that large companies are often slow to pay, and borrowed from several branches.

The size of the Bell Labs order meant that the new publication had to be commercially printed. A Washington-based printer and their public relations man offered to put up $5,000 to partner Garfield with the new publication. If it was a success they would put in more. They also provided him with an office in Washington. His new partners spent the $5,000 on a mailing shot to a list of the highest paid people in the United States. It was a disaster, generating a total of about 20 subscriptions — but they did provide a better name for the publication

— *Current Contents* (CC). Meanwhile a *Current Contents* service for one pharmaceutical company had been started and then expanded to others.

Universities and medical people later heard about CC and it gradually became successful. Current Comments — an editorial piece which appeared in the front of *Current Contents* issues — were eventually reproduced in the *Essays of an Information Scientist*. In volume 1 Garfield said: "It would be difficult to acknowledge everyone who has contributed to these essays in one way or another... though I take full responsibility for everything I publish I owe a great deal to the knowledge and help of my colleagues and friends".

Joshua Lederberg wrote the foreword to this same volume. Of Current Comments he said: "Gene has displayed his enthusiasm, his deep insight into the scientific process and sometimes a candor and artlessness in the expression of his feelings that may even offend some who have not also experienced his own scrupulous integrity at first hand".

The Science Citation Index

In March 1953 Garfield found himself single-handedly conducting a symposium at the Welch library after two of his colleagues became ill. He presented a paper later published in *American Documentation* [5]. The title of the symposium was "The first symposium on machine methods on scientific documentation". Among the three hundred people who attended it was a reporter who gave it national coverage. It was noticed by Dr. Gordon Allen, a geneticist at the National Institute of Health.

Gene is remembered "vigorously marketing his ideas" about CC at the Dorking conference — a landmark meeting described later in this chapter. He has been no less vigorous in talking about his ideas for an even better known publication — the *Science Citation Index* (SCI). His output in print discussing aspects of the SCI has been enormous. As it was a completely new indexing concept the library and science communities took a long time to be convinced.

Lederberg and Allen

Garfield's first article specifically about the SCI was published in *Science* [6] in the same year as his *American Documentation* article. It was this article which prompted a letter in 1958 from Joshua Lederberg — the year that he won the Nobel prize for discoveries about "Generic recombination and the organisation of the genetic material of bacteria". Lederberg explained why his letter took so long to compose: "for lack of a citation index I cannot tell what happened to your article in *Science*". Lederburg later coined the name *Science Citation Index*.

It was the recommendations of the two geneticists — Lederberg and Allen — which were so influential at the end of the fifties when Garfield was attempting to get grant support for SCI development.

Much later (June 1960) Allen sent a diagram showing citation connections between a collection of articles to Garfield. Allen explained that: "The arrows indicate the direction in which one would be led in a conventional literature search, starting at any point in the network. A citation index would permit one to trace the arrows in the opposite direction and hence to find all the articles no matter where on the network he started" [13]. Allen's diagram shows citation interconnections between articles arranged in chronological order with the most recent at the bottom. When many articles are included it is confusing to try and follow the routes taken by numerous lines crossing each other — a problem encountered in the early days of the *Science Citation Index* when its applications were often explained with the aid of diagrams of this kind.

Allen's diagram showed the citation connections between a set of biochemistry articles.

Garfield's reply was enthusiastic: "The material you sent was fabulous. Why didn't we think to do this before? I didn't have this in mind when I said I had some examples of the power of the Citation Index. I merely meant specific articles which could be traced through a CI. I once had the idea that some type of network could be used with Citation Indexes. I am now convinced more than ever, from your example, that his will be true" [13].

The Institute for Scientific Information and launching the SCI
The name Eugene Garfield Associates Inc., was changed to The Institute for Scientific Information in 1960. The reason for the adoption of this name was to create a more equal ground in competing with non-profit organisations. The perception of the scientific and library community was that of a government agency such as the Russian Institute for Scientific and Technical Information. The name needed to be right. Shakespeare elegantly makes the point. Juliet knew very well that as a Capulet her family was at odds with Romeo's — the Montagus. In the famous conversation from her balcony with Romeo in the street below she said "What's in a name? That which we call a rose by any other name would smell as sweet". The rose which was Eugene Garfield Associates altered its name, but not the nature of it's activities, to The Institute for Scientific Information.

The 1955 *Science* article shows that Garfield already had in mind applications which are widely used today. The idea for the SCI was inspired by *Shepard's Citations* which contains a listing of American court cases, each followed by a record of publications which have referred to it. In regard to scientific articles, Garfield wrote in his *Science* article: "This would be particularly useful in historical research when one is trying to evaluate the significance of a particular work and its impact on the literature and thinking of the period. Such an 'impact factor' may be much more indicative than an absolute count of the number of a scientist's publications." Later Garfield wrote [10] "Using citations for evaluating people is a very tricky business. But if you use the data carefully you can facilitate an intelligence gathering process that can allow for reasoned and thoughtful decisions".

After initially giving ISI a grant the National Institute of Health was forced by Congress to change its rules. Because of these tortuous politics money had to be transferred from the NIH, which could no longer provide grants for companies, to the National Science Foundation. NSF negotiated a contract with ISI for one thousand copies of a *Genetics Citation Index* (GCI) for which a multidisciplinary database was required and for which ISI received $150,000 over a three year period. The idea was supported by Lederberg and Allen. From that database containing data from 600 journals the 1961 SCI was also created. Having produced the necessary machine readable data Garfield had hoped for a grant to proceed with it but that was not provided.

The GCI was published in 1963. It was extracted from a database of 100,000 articles and 1.5 million cited references In spite of the absence of a grant to proceed with the complete 1961 SCI Garfield took the risk of publishing it. His principle assistant was Irving Sher, a biochemist and mathematician. He was backed by Phil Sopinsky who was in charge of data processing. Regular quarterly editions of the SCI were launched in 1964.

Although *Current Contents* was bringing in cash, expenditure was exceeding revenue at this time and Garfield had to borrow some money as described in the later section "The Company". He also cut out the patent citation index section from the SCI.

Most people in the information industry believed that the SCI would fail. Garfield proved them wrong.

Other activities

In 1957 Garfield visited the UK for the first time. He was short of cash and paid for a ticket to the UK using TWA's installment plan. He had been invited to attend the 1957 Dorking classification and retrieval conference. He met such luminaries as Robert Fairthorne, Cyril Cleverdon, S.R. Ranganathan and many others. One delegate remembers him as "a young man vigorously marketing his ideas of journal contents lists". Another "recalled the evening when Gene Garfield defended his proposals for a citation index against a group of very skeptical and outspoken critics including Cyril Cleverdon".

He took one day off, caught a train to London, and spent 15 hours seeing The Tower, The British Museum, House of Commons, etc. When he returned to Victoria station around midnight it was shut. He took a taxi back to Dorking as he had been asked to chair the next morning's session. "The audience gasped when I told them — I didn't mention that it used most of my remaining cash".

The extent of Garfield's enthusiasm, curiosity and depth of knowledge comes across very clearly in his Essays, published by ISI Press, and now available complete from his Web home page These essays are mainly reprints of his Current Comments articles which used to appear at the beginning of *Current Contents* issues. There were 15 volumes running from 1962 to 1993. After ISI had been sold to Thomson, in the foreword of the last volume I wrote: "The boring reality is that in today's business activities often require that entrepreneurs must give way to a formal business structure. Roald's fears will be realised — Gene will no longer entertain us with Current Comments or with the Essays in their present form. Few readers will be pleased with this news. (Roald Hoffman, Cornell University, wrote the foreword for volume 12)".

The Essays include such items as "Why medical research?", "More on cremation and other alternatives to traditional burial", "Noise R&D abatement could help employment problems of physicists", "What your air-conditioner may be giving you besides relief", "Of presidents, politics, and chicken pluckers" and "Jazz transcriptions will blow your mind". At one time, ISI Press did not publish books. Gene met V.V. Nalimov at a Moscow book fair and said he would like to publish one of his books. "But your Institute does not publish books" said Nalimov. "It does now" said Garfield.

Another of Dr. Garfield's ideas — *The Copywriter* — never took off. Perhaps it was ahead of its time — it required some of the miniaturisation and optoelectronic developments of the eighties associated with microcomputers to be successfully engineered. To some extent it was made unnecessary by the arrival of Xerox photocopiers. *The Copywriter* aroused the interest of Verner Clapp, President of the council for Library Resources (CLR) [8]. Gene met him when he was working at Johns Hopkins. It was hoped that it would be manufactured and sold by an appropriate company, its applications being an appropriate part of ISI's business but not its manufacture and service.

The idea was to use a small hand-held scanning head for sweeping across that part of a page required to be copied. It would resolve 4-point type. The copying machine and printer, contained in a separate box, was connected to the scanning head by a flexible cable. The copied strip of data emerged from the box on Teledeltos electrosensitive paper. Several patents were taken out. The idea was put into practice and two prototypes were made, the second embodying a number of improvements. The construction was carried out by a local electronics company near Philadelphia. Some years later the Japanese made a device for a similar purpose called the Copyjack.

When the design started to become dated Dr. Garfield asked me to re-design the electronics which I did. I also took out a US and a European patent filed in 1984 on behalf of ISI. It embodied a CCD scanning unit with the means of scanning the whole page, and selecting the wanted part of the page by windowing and storing it. The circuitry was based on the microcomputer components available in 1983. The re-design and new patents were pursued in case a suitable company became interested in manufacturing. However, the idea was not taken up.

The company
ISI have developed a number of information products including the CC range, the SCI and related products, CAC&IC and many others. The SCI database represents the company's most valuable asset because of the many ways its data can be processed to form a new product.

Garfield needed all his faith and perseverance over a period of several years to get the SCI off the ground. Until then he had been the independent publisher of the successful *Current Contents*. In the early days Gene's wife did the paste-up work in the chicken coop. Later an office in Spring Garden St., Philadelphia was rented across the street from Garfield's consulting client Smith Kline & French. More employees joined the firm. He had almost decided to undertake the preparation of the SCI without the support of either NSF or NIH. However after some arrangements were made between these organisations, a contract was signed in mid-1961 and ISI moved into a building on Chestnut St., Philadelphia near Independence Hall using rented office space.

In 1965 the company was almost forced to close down under the pressure of bringing the SCI to the market. Garfield sold 20% of the company as a convertible debenture for half a million dollars to a group of investors representing the ten top Wall Street firms, themselves represented by Walter Eberstadt — a decision which later had some serious consequences.

Shortly afterwards Garfield was faced with a kind of conspiracy. Four vice-presidents — The Director of Production, Director of R&D, The Treasurer and the Marketing Director believed that he was going to run the company into the ground. They got together and presented him with an ultimatum. Unless he killed the loss-making *Index Chemicus* they would resign. Gene believed it had a future and told them to go. They resigned in a body. When Eberstadt heard about it he thought that Gene was totally dependent on them and became very worried. I had just joined the company and knew little about its operations. As far as I could make out these resignations did not make the slightest difference. I think that this was in part because Garfield was still an entrepreneur at heart and had always played a role in key company functions. Evidently the people who resigned were replaceable without too much difficulty with the exception of Dr. Sher who returned a few years later and remained with ISI until his death a few years ago.

By 1978 ISI employed 470 people and covered 5,200 journals published in 31 different languages. All its products are published in English. In that year construction of a purpose designed building started in the University City Science Center, Philadelphia, close to the Universities of Pennsylvania and Drexel. It cost $6.5 million. A child care centre was housed in a separate building. An IBM 370-148 computer was used for data processing. Peter Aborn was appointed chairman of the new building project [1]. The architects were Venturi & Rauch and Denise Scott Brown. The company moved into it in late 1979. "Every aspect of the building's design was carefully weighed to combine the benefits of rigorous systems analysis and energy efficiency tempered with a good measure of human whimsicality and warmth" writes Aborn.

In 1988 Ted Cross and JPT holdings acquired over 50% of ISI's shares. In 1992 they and Garfield sold their shares to Thomson Business Information, a subsidiary of the Thomson Corporation. The growth of ISI had forced Gene out of his role as a pioneer and entrepreneur into the politics associated with running quite a large Company — not his métier. The old incentive-driven success had been replaced with less satisfying activities. Although the manner of the change of ownership was not as he would have planned it he was left a rich man. Among his present activities he is President of the American Society for Information Science, where he is considering its problems — in particular its steadily declining membership.

Garfield continues to publish *The Scientist* — a biweekly news journal and the first full text journal available free on the Web.

Publications in print are gradually giving way to electronic publications — the Web of Science is a very large database designed by ISI for online network users. It is used in 14 countries by national higher education consortia. It contains details of over 23 million source articles containing 300 million cited references extracted from the science, social science and arts & humanities journals covered in ISI's services.

By 1998 ISI employed 800 people and covered over 8,000 journals. It also owns offices in seven different countries.

Eugene Garfield sold ISI partly because of ill-health and partly because of management and executive staff problems in the early nineties. The pioneering child-care centre was shut down by JPT but was replaced by a non-profit centre operated by the same staff. Also closed were ISI Press and the Atlas of Science product. *The Scientist* was spun off to Garfield. JPT were not interest in the company — only its potential to make money. Short term considerations determined every decision to maximise value.

Garfield and ISI: reminiscences

I met Gene by accident in 1966 while waiting to meet a colleague in the foyer of a London hotel. I was scanning *Current Contents Engineering* when a camera flash went off and an American introduced himself as Dr. Eugene Garfield, its publisher. He said I was one of its few UK subscribers. Soon afterwards I found myself at the Philadelphia out-of-town airport, having been hired as ISI's man in Europe. My first visit to ISI was interesting. At the airport I was advised to take a limo to the Holiday Inn. Being unaware that there were Holiday Inns at all city centres I was delivered to the Holiday Inn at the city centre, Atlantic City. I changed to a seat beside the driver — an ex-US army black man who thought my mistake was very funny. He took me back to ISI's address in Philadelphia for nothing.

I soon realised that I was going to have an interesting time working for a most unusual company run by a remarkable man. Gene said "find yourself a desk and familiarise yourself with the products". I worked out a search described as "Use of the Science Citation Index for checking the progress of television signal compression", based on Cherry's work [4]. I wanted to discover how well the system, designed for science users, worked in engineering. I knew a little about information retrieval systems [3].

The next evening Garfield invited me and another member of the staff to eat out. We eat one course and then moved on to a second restaurant for ice cream — according to Gene "the best in town" There were 20 varieties with a countless choice of "toppings". From then on I worked in Europe, returning to ISI two or three times a year for discussions. Garfield liked to become involved with the fine detail.

I had a free hand to promote ISI's products in Europe. Before a visit to a university I checked the authors listed under the address of the university in the SCI's corporate index section, found out who was their most heavily cited author, and arranged a series of slides to describe the use of the SCI using his work as an example, having become a self-appointed, if superficial, expert on the subject area. The SCI seemed very expensive to potential UK customers so a special effort per customer was justified.

Eventually I established several people to act as representatives in different parts of Europe. I was appointed Vice President R&D of the company in 1974. Garfield naturally expected me to work in Philadelphia. When I said I wanted to work out of the UK, I was rather surprised that he agreed. My reason was that Gene's enthusiasm was too infectious. I did not believe that I would be able properly to divide my time between business and family.

References

[1]   Aborn, P. (1979, August) How ISI designed its new workspace: an inside story. *Bulletin of the American Society of Information Science* 5(6), 14–17.

[2]   Bernhard, S.A., Garfield E. and Hammett. L.P. (1954) Specific effects in acid catalysis by ion exchange resins. 3. Some observations of the effects of polyvalent. Citations. *Journal of the American Chemical Society* 76, 991–992.

[3]   Cawkell, A.E. (1962) Classification and retrieval of technical information. *Wireless World* 68(8–9) 352–356 and 432–434.

[4]   Cherry C., Kubba, M.H., Pearson, D.E., Barton M.P. (1963) An experimental study of the possible bandwidth compression of visual image signals. *Proc. IEEE* 51, 1507.

[5]   Garfield, E. (1955) The preparation of printed indexes by automatic punched-card techniques. *American Documentation* 6(2), 459–467.

[6]   Garfield, E. (1955, July 15) Citation indexes for science. *Science* 122(3159), 108–111.

[7]   Garfield, E. (1962) *Thesis: An algorithm for translating chemical names to molecular formulas.* Ph.D in structural linguistics. University of Pennsylvania.

[8]   Garfield, E. (1973, May 2) Current Comments: Introducing the Copywriter and ISI's subsidiary Selective Information Devices Inc. (SID). *Current Contents.* Reprinted in *Essays of an Information Scientist* Volume 1, 1962–1973.

[9]   Garfield, E. (1980, January 21) Current Comments: how it all began — with a loan from HFC. *Current Contents* 3, 359–362. Reprinted in Essays of an Information Scientist Volume 4, 1979–1980.

[10] Garfield E. (1983, July 25) How sweet it is — The ACS Patterson-Crane award. Reflections on the reward system of science. *Current Contents* 30, 229–236. Reprinted in Essays of an

Information Scientist Volume 6, 1983.

[11]   Linklater, M. (1996, March 15) Socialism and the American way. *The Times*.

[12]   Wells, H.G. (1938) *World Brain*. Doubleday Doran, New York.

[13]   Wouters, P. (1999) *The citation culture*. Thesis, faculty of science, University of Amsterdam.

Note. Essays of an Information Scientist are available on www.garfield.library.upenn.edu

A Century of Science Publishing
E.H. Fredriksson (Ed.)
IOS Press, 2001

Chapter 16

Medical Databases:
Medline versus Excerpta Medica

Robert R. Blanken[a] and Pierre J. Vinken[b]
[a]Former Executive Chief Editor, Excerpta Medica,
Amsterdam, The Netherlands
[b]Former Chairman of the Board, Elsevier and Reed-Elsevier,
London, UK and Amsterdam, The Netherlands

1. Prehistory: the situation up to and immediately after World War II

During the 19th and the first half of the 20th century, efforts to make the world's medical literature more accessible to the end-user were dominated by the German *Zentralblätter* in Europe and the various publications of the Surgeon General's Office/Army Medical Library/National Library of Medicine and the American Medical Association in the United States. Later, these were complemented (and to a certain extent copied) by the *Bulletin Signaletique* in France and the *Referativnye Zhurnaly* in the Soviet Union.

Credit for the first major attempt to index the world's medical literature must be given to John Shaw Billings, who was responsible for the creation of the *Index-Catalogue of the Library of the Surgeon General's Office*, first published in 1880. This monumental work, the first series of which was finally completed with volume XVI (W to Zythus) in 1895, ultimately contained subject entries for 168,537 books and 511,112 journal articles, and author entries for 176,364 books; its major handicap, however, was the lack of currency that inevitably resulted from its alphabetical setup. In 1879, the cumulative alphabetical catalogue was therefore complemented by the first volume of the *Index Medicus: a Monthly Classified Record of the Current Medical Literature of the World*. Financial problems, however, caused this first attempt to fail (temporarily) after 21 volumes, in 1899. Following a three-year intermezzo during which the *Bibliographia Medica* was published in Paris, publication of the *Index Medicus* in the U.S. was resumed in 1903 and continued until 1927.

Meanwhile, in 1916, following caustic criticism of both the *Index-Catalogue* and the *Index Medicus*, the American Medical Association started publishing the *Quarterly Cumulative Index to Current Medical Literature*, which was to appear in parallel with the *Index Medicus* for the next 43 years. The *Index-Catalogue* also continued into a second series (21 volumes, 1896–1915) and even a third (10 volumes, 1918-1932), thanks to the vigorous support of the Medical Library Association, but the setup and goals gradually changed and subject entries to the current literature were no longer included after 1925. In 1927, following prolonged negotiations, the *Index Medicus* and the *Quarterly Cumulative Index to Current Medical Literature* were merged to yield the *Quarterly Cumulative Index Medicus*; the cooperative effort ended, however, in 1931, after which the QCIM was continued by the American Medical Association.

Following a brief hiatus, the 'Friends of the Army Medical Library' together with the Medical Library Association started publishing the *Current List of Medical Literature*, a classified listing of the tables of contents of journals received in the library; monthly subject indexes were added in 1945, so that the *Current List* and the QCIM became more or less competing services, while the plans for future series of the *Index-Catalogue* were scrapped. Following its modification in 1950, the *Current List* contained a register section listing articles in serial numbered order under their journal titles, plus an author index and a subject index using standardized headings, clued to the descriptive bibliographic data by means of the serial numbers. These standardized subject headings became the basis for the later *Subject Heading Authority List* and still later *Medical Subject Headings* (MeSH). The American Medical Association finally discontinued publication of the QCIM in 1959, after which the Current List was transformed into the *Index Medicus* as we know it today.

An important characteristic of all of the above publications is that only bibliographic information was provided; although sometimes indexed in depth, the journal articles were not abstracted and no summaries were included. In Europe, the practice was quite different. The venerable, German-language *Zentralblätter* published abstracts of the current biomedical literature in a series of specialized, classified abstract bulletins intended for use by the medical specialist. In the pre-war days, when most scientific articles did not even contain a summary, let alone an abstract, this meant an intellectual abstracting effort that inevitably delayed the appearance of the bibliographic reference. The *Zentralblätter* were therefore used more for retrospective searches and the compilation of bibliographies than for current awareness, a concept that had not yet acquired the importance we give to it today.

An essentially similar service, in Russian, was provided by the Soviet government in the *Referativnye Zhurnaly*, also a series of specialized, classified abstract bulletins, not only in medicine but in all areas of science. Originally intended for domestic use in the USSR, and later disseminated (also in the form of tapes) to the 'satellite' countries of Eastern Europe, the *Referativnye Zhurnaly* attracted the serious attention of the West, and especially the U.S., after the launching of the first Sputnik. During the next decades, the U.S. government sponsored extensive translation programs of the abstracts in the *Referativnye Zhurnaly*. In Eastern Europe, however, preference was generally given to information from the West; in the medical area, this meant a preference for *Excerpta Medica* and (when available) *Index Medicus* above the comparable Soviet sources.

To a small group of German Jewish publishers who had been hidden in Amsterdam during World War II, it was clear that the key role of the *Zentralblätter* would not survive the defeat of Germany and the ascendance of English as the international language of science. The lack of abstracts in the *Current List* and QCIM meant that there was an urgent need and potential market for an English-language medical abstracting service. As a result, *Excerpta Medica* and its original series of 15 specialized abstract bulletins, with the slogan "By the medical specialist, for the medical specialist", was born.

The original basic concept of the series of semi-independent, specialized abstract bulletins or 'sections' bearing the joint name *Excerpta Medica* was very similar to that of the *Zentralblätter*. Each bulletin, with names such as 'Anatomy, Anthropology, Embryology and Histology', 'Physiology and Biochemistry', 'Endocrinology', 'Dermatology and Venereology' or 'Chest Diseases, Thoracic Surgery and Tuberculosis', had its own specialist editorial staff that was responsible for selection, classification and (ultimately) indexing, its own international editorial board of specialist advisors, and its own international staff of volunteer abstractors. The some 3000 journals then received regularly in Amsterdam were microfilmed with the collaboration of the Royal Netherlands Academy of Sciences and placed in a dated cabinet in the editorial offices of *Excerpta Medica* where they were screened by the specialist 'section editors' to select articles relevant to their abstract bulletins. Later on, historically speaking, this process was supplemented by a team of 'assignment editors' who wrote relevant section numbers in the table of contents, to be checked later by the section editor. After one week, the journals received on a particular day were taken out of the cabinet, torn apart into individual articles, and the articles were stapled to an indexing and abstracting form that also contained the section numbers, in presumed order of priority, to which the article had been assigned. The article then began on a sometimes-lengthy voyage through the hands of multiple section editors, each of whom added the necessary classification codes and index terms from his specialist point of view. The first editor who decided that the abstract should be published in his bulletin was responsible for creating the abstract, either by modifying the English summary, by selecting portions of the text, by sending a foreign-language summary out to be translated, or by sending the entire article to one of several thousand volunteer abstractors, many of whom were also members of the international editorial boards. Ultimately, the product of this work was checked by a native speaker of English, after which the abstract was ready for publication in all sections that had selected it. In the case of multidisciplinary articles, this sequential processing sometimes meant that more than a year elapsed between journal receipt and publication of the abstract. Nevertheless, *Excerpta Medica* soon acquired a large number of individual subscribers, as well as medical libraries.

Actually, during the first few years of *Excerpta Medica*'s existence, the monthly abstract bulletins did not contain a subject index; retrieval was by means of decimal classification systems, specific to each section, with a cumulative subject index published at the end of each year. Initially, the terminology used in these annual indexes was also subject-specific and thus varied from abstract bulletin to abstract bulletin; all this was to change radically after the appointment of Pierre Vinken (a neurosurgeon who ultimately became the Chairman of Elsevier after the latter acquired *Excerpta Medica* in 1971) as President and Chief Editor in the 1960's, marking the beginning of the efforts at professionalization that would continue unabated for the next 30 years. The philosophy underlying *Excerpta Medica*'s ultimate system of semi-controlled subject indexing was that the specialist editor should be left free to write down all those terms he considered necessary to represent the content of the article, at the level of specificity he deemed necessary, using the preferred terminology of his subject specialty, and that these suggested terms would be controlled afterwards ('à posteriori') against a growing 'thesaurus' (initially a separate one for each specialty) to eliminate synonyms and spelling errors. This was felt to be preferable to a forced choice of indexing terms from a pre-existing list, such as was the case at the National Library of Medicine, since it not only spared the valuable time of the medical specialist but also enabled a much more rapid response to specific new concepts (such as drugs) appearing in the medical literature. The indexing was precoordinate, with a preferred length of two or three words per index term. In order to prevent an all too rapid growth of the thesaurus, there were some limiting rules or guidelines. Thus, all terms were in the singular noun form, in American spelling, and in the natural word order rather than rotated; furthermore, a philosophical distinction was made between 'primary terms', under which a reader could be expected to look in a printed index (names of diseases, anatomical terms, drugs, etc.), and 'secondary terms' such as child, diagnosis, treatment, the names of experimental animals, routes of drug administration, etc. that are usually significant only when combined with a primary term; indexing terms in which a primary term and a secondary term are combined were generally forbidden. Only the primary terms were controlled, and in the printed subject index, only the primary terms created separate alphabetical entries, followed in each case by the other primary terms and then by the secondary terms. These secondary terms or 'secondary text' created a kind of 'mini-abstract' that frequently included quantitative information or more detailed findings or methods. An example of such a rotated index entry is shown in the box below.

brain infarction, carotid stenosis, hydrocephalus, radiodiagnosis, bilateral, 4-year-old child, 114
carotid stenosis, brain infarction, hydrocephalus, radiodiagnosis, bilateral, 4-year-old child, 114
hydrocephalus, brain infarction, carotid stenosis, radiodiagnosis, bilateral, 4-year-old child, 114

Although this approach to indexing had definite advantages over the use of a pre-existing thesaurus, there were practical problems that only really became apparent after automation and the integration of the separate thesauri into one 'Master List of Medical Terms' or 'Malimet'. First of all, as we shall see below, the thesaurus showed an irrepressible tendency to grow much too fast, with the addition of terms that were used extremely rarely, and secondly, the use of this increasing number of highly specific terms turned out to be relatively inconsistent, with similar articles often being indexed in different ways; although not disastrous in a printed subject index, this created difficult problems later in the training of users for on-line retrieval.

2. Automation, professionalization, and thesaurus development

Given the geometric increase in the volume of medical literature, together with the increasing cost of human labor and the need for more rapid access to biomedical and especially pharmacological information, it soon became clear to everyone that automation was the answer. It was expected that automation of the production systems for indexes and abstract journals would also create improved possibilities for information retrieval. In the United States, however, the initial experience with a punched-card system was disappointing in this respect.

In the 1940's and 1950's, the Welch Medical Indexing Project gave high priority to the development of machine methods for the production of the *Current List*, together with more theoretical work on coordinate indexing and the development of a 'Subject Heading Authority List' that was ultimately to result in the first MeSH. By 1960, a production system had been created consisting of Flexowriter composing machines for the index copy, IBM keypunches and sorters for alphabetizing the copy, and a Listomatic step-and-repeat camera for composing column-width film. It quickly became evident, however, that this was inadequate as a retrieval system. The fastest card sorter then available could handle only 1000 cards a minute; to search a 5-year file containing 750,000 subject cards would take some 12 hours. A far-reaching decision was therefore taken to invert the objectives, i.e. to design a retrieval system from which a publication system could later be derived. This ultimately led to the computer-based system now known as MEDLARS (Medical Literature Analysis and Retrieval System).

Early in 1964, a system based on a Honeywell 800-200 computer and GRACE (Graphic Arts Composing Equipment) for phototypesetting was able not only to produce *Index Medicus* but also to perform experimental retrospective searches in batch mode. By 1968, there were 12 search formulation centers in the U.S. and several in foreign countries, and searches were being performed on four computers outside the National Library of Medicine. Meanwhile, in the latter half of the 1960's, plans were being made for the on-line input of indexed material, and the first experiments were carried out with on-line retrieval. In 1971, MEDLINE (MED-LARS On-line) was officially started, and a new system based on two IBM 370/158 computers, coupled together as a multiprocessor system to operate as one, was delivered in January 1975.

At *Excerpta Medica* in Amsterdam, the problems were similar, but the efforts were concentrated initially on automating the production of the abstract journals and standardizing the indexing terminology, rather than on retrieval as such. Between the late 1940's and the middle 1960's, the volume of the *Excerpta Medica* operation had increased significantly. Thanks partly to subsidies and stimulated by pressure from both specialist subscribers and specialist editors, several new abstract journals came into existence and a number of larger 'sections' were split to yield more specific daughters. The volume of literature processed had also increased significantly, to about 250,000 articles (100,000 of them with abstracts) per year, derived from some 3500 journals yielding ca. 20,000 individual issues annually; all of these articles were indexed on the basis of a thesaurus that had in the meantime grown to about 400,000 terms (preferred terms and synonyms), and classified in a polyhierarchic system containing more than 3500 'pigeonholes' at four levels in 39 independent 'sections'. The need for cost reduction coupled to the desire to provide better and more rapid access to medical information led to the decision to transform the loosely connected series of manually published abstract bulletins into an integrated, uniformly indexed and classified, electronic database from which the abstract bulletins could be obtained as a by-product.

In 1965, Pierre Vinken contacted Frans van der Walle, the director of a small software development company named Rescona; this contact was to lead to the creation of Infonet, which was given the contract to create *Excerpta Medica*'s 'Mark I' system for the automated storage and retrieval of biomedical information.

At that time, computer technology was still in its infancy. Standard word-processing software and disk memories did not yet exist and the 'mainframe' processors had a power that is dwarfed by any present-day PC. Electronic phototypesetters had just started to become available. The choice of hardware eventually fell on two NCR 315-501 RMCs (Rod Memory Computers), 10 CRAM-V magnetic card storage systems, and an NCR 321 communications controller. The internal memory capacity of the configuration was 40k. The CRAM-files were equipped with large information cartridges, each containing 384 3.65x14-inch magnetic cards, each containing 144 recording tracks with a recording density of 936 bits/inch and a resultant capacity of 1500 six-bit characters; these cartridges had to be exchanged manually, since two were required for each year of *Excerpta Medica*, but this took less than a minute. Any card from a cartridge could be dropped into read/write position within 125 milliseconds. The developed software was revolutionary, being completely randomly organized and using a CRAM-card storage facility with direct addressing possibilities similar to those of present-day disk systems, together with NCR's 'FAMOUS' index-sequential software package that made the on-line update and recall of the thesaurus for each separate index term possible with response times measured in seconds, at a time when comparable information systems were still completely magnetic tape oriented with thesaurus update runs of some 24 hours (F. van der Walle, personal communication).

The *Excerpta Medica* production system also comprised 16 magnetic tape units and a paper-tape input unit that read 600 characters/second. Although all information for input was normally punched on paper tape, input was also possible via a Micro-Image Card Reader. The software included a systems supervisor that controlled the legitimacy of all input, as well as checking on the presence or absence of certain types of information; its most important component, for controlling indexing input, was based on Malimet and included a program that controlled the logical consistency of the relationships between Malimet preferred terms and synonyms. Finally, there was a publishing subsystem that provided for the compilation of the bibliographic information and abstracts in the database, assignment of abstract and page numbers, make-up of the final pages and compilation of the author and subject indexes for each abstract bulletin, resulting in a magnetic tape that was used to drive a Digiset photosetter.

Another and more intellectual aspect of the automation of *Excerpta Medica*'s production system was the creation of an integrated thesaurus to control the index terms to be input into the integrated database. As early as 1963, *Excerpta Medica's* Board of Chief Editors had decided to try to alleviate the existing chaos in medical terminology and the resultant inconsistencies in the subject indexes of the individual abstract bulletins. On the other hand, they had no desire to create an à priori thesaurus from which indexers would be forced to select terms. Taking the 1962 cumulative annual indexes as the starting point, the Chief Editors discussed the how and why of each entry and each cross-reference with the responsible indexers, which soon resulted in a number of small thesauri, one for each medical discipline. However, when an attempt was made to integrate these thesauri, it was found that many of the terms had several different meanings and that the cross-references were often mutually incompatible. Furthermore, the number of terms was so large that even punched cards and conventional IBM equipment did not suffice to control the thesaurus input. A computer program was therefore requested and obtained (see above).

At the end of this initial project, Malimet represented a file of about 25,000 preferred terms and 50,000 synonyms. With this as a starting point, the indexing entries suggested daily by the specialist indexers were checked against this growing authority file. Any term not recognized by the computer was printed out on a weekly 'error list', which was referred to a team of medical specialists who were experienced in the terminologies of all medical disciplines. Each term on these error lists had to be either 'translated' into an existing term or accepted as a new term in the thesaurus. Unfortunately, however, the error lists were so large as to be practically unmanageable in the time available, and to make matters worse, Malimet was not yet available on-line, so that the editing work of this team was based on periodic printouts or (later) microfiche versions that were quickly out of date. As a result, Malimet grew very rapidly and in a somewhat uncontrolled fashion, so that the number of preferred terms soon reached 125,000 and the number of synonyms perhaps twice that. Despite the guidelines referred to above, the transfer of the processing of the error lists to internal staff and the later availability of Malimet on-line, the growth of this à posteriori authority file continued at an alarming rate and a decreasing percentage of the preferred terms were frequently used.

Automation also made possible (or necessary) a number of other changes in *Excerpta Medica's* production system and retrieval facilities. Thus, the tables of contents of the individual abstract bulletins were cast into a consistent decimal form, if necessary, and integrated into EMclass, a polyhierarchic classification system with a maximum of four levels, the first of which was the section number. The subclassifications within each section remained independent and pragmatic, being designed to divide the literature into a large number of more or less equal piles rather than to provide a logical breakdown of the field. New subclassifications could be created at any time, although changes in the hierarchic structure were discouraged. In order to make a selected list of secondary concepts retrievable by projected future users of the database, these concepts were given numbers and compiled into the Item Index (later to be known as EMtags); these were terms representing, for example, the type of article, routes of drug administration, age groups, geographic concepts or the names of experimental animals, and were similar to the 'checktags' of Medline.

Since the bibliographic information ('reference' or 'citation') for all selected articles was now input first, before the abstract or any indexing, a new type of product also became possible: the literature index. Among the ca. 250,000 articles selected annually for the database, about 150,000 never received an abstract but would nevertheless be indexed and classified, often by multiple sections. It therefore became tempting to use some of these for saleable products (even before database tapes became a product), and the first such 'literature indexes' to be produced were the *Drug Literature Index* and *Adverse Reactions Titles*. Especially the *Drug Literature Index* (section 37 in the database) was an impressive product, including upwards of 50,000 articles per year, derived not only from the 3500 'normal' journals but also from some 200 specially selected chemical and pharmaceutical journals, and indexed in depth from both a medical, a pharmacological and a chemical point of view (with separate fields, for example, for trade names, manufacturer's names and the Wiswesser Line Notation). As DrugDoc, these two sections would come to represent an unusually valuable portion of the total database.

In the interest of getting the information into at least the literature indexes and the database more quickly, the routing of the articles and indexing forms was also streamlined. Now, instead of a single index form to be used by all the assigned sections, the system responded to the input of the bibliographic information by printing out separate forms for each section, which were attached to the article and sent along to the first editor (this always being the DrugDoc editors if relevant). When the article with its forms was returned (within a strictly controlled time period), the indexing for the first section was immediately keyboarded and sent for input while the article and the remaining forms went on to the second section. As a result of the input of indexing and classifications, the reference became available for printed publications such as the Drug Literature Index and for output onto database tapes. This process was repeated for each assigned section, until ultimately only the abstract form, on which the editors had indicated whether or not they wished to publish the abstract, was left. This abstract could very often be prepared by the internal abstracting department that had in the meantime been organized. This sequential input of indexing from the point of view of several assigned sections of course meant that the database user (tape subscriber) would receive the same item repeatedly, sometimes with only minor additions. As we will see later, this was a major objection, leading to various attempts to prevent or alleviate it.

3. 'Mark II', on-line access and the battle for currency

Early in the 1970's, the Directors and Chief Editors of *Excerpta Medica* became convinced that the long-term future lay in the sale of electronic information via database tapes, and that the existing production system and the hardware used for it were no longer the most suitable for the purpose. They therefore again turned to Infonet with the request to make an inventory of the problems and ideas in the minds of the *Excerpta Medica* staff and to come up with a concept for a new system. Meanwhile, in line with earlier attempts to professionalize and streamline the processing of biomedical information for the database, two full-time Executive Chief Editors had been appointed to help the Chief Editors (themselves part-time with responsibilities elsewhere) run the system. These two would play an active role in the next two decades in the attempts to accelerate the input of information and at the same time make it more readily retrievable, beginning with a key role in the consultations with Infonet on what would become the Mark II system. Following a detailed analysis of the bottlenecks and the possible solutions in terms of hardware and software, it was decided to abandon the NCR equipment and to replace it with a network of Digital minicomputers, linked together to provide the necessary speed and capacity; it was felt that this would provide greater flexibility, at lower cost, than the choice of a mainframe. The CRAM-cards were therefore replaced by disk drives and magnetic tapes, and the thesaurus control group was given improved access to Malimet. Very soon, the first experiments could also be organized on search formulation for the retrieval of information, as a result of which the quality control over the medical indexers was tightened up.

With a view toward accelerating the input of the abstracts, the role of the volunteer abstractors was gradually phased out; this was made possible by the fact that the overwhelming majority of the articles from important journals now had English-language summaries, combined with an increased contribution from in-house personnel. At the same time, various experiments were made with the input of bibliographic information and indexing at different stages, separately and combined. For many articles from important journals, a bibliographic reference and an abstract were input first, together with the assigned section numbers, providing rapid (albeit unindexed) information for on-line retrieval by means of free-text searches. In other cases, highly specialized articles from important journals were indexed and classified before input of the bibliographic information, so that everything could be input together. Tape subscribers, however, continued to complain about the multiple receipt of essentially the same information. This was aggravated by the increasingly multidisciplinary nature of the medical literature and by the subdivision of the abstract bulletins into increasingly specific daughters, so that the average number of sections to which an article was assigned tended to increase. Although these more specific abstract bulletins were attractive to the specialist individual subscriber, and the more specific classifications were useful for retrieval, the multiple receipt of the same information was an aggravation to librarians and database managers alike. To try and alleviate this, some arbitrary limitations were placed on the depth of assignment, particularly for articles from less important journals, and attempts were made to group the indexing input for several secondary sections. All of this made for a continuing process of change in the editorial procedures, guidelines and forms.

By the middle 1970's, *Excerpta Medica* was sending computer tapes weekly to a number of pharmaceutical companies and governmental agencies in foreign countries, and EMbase was accessible on-line via providers such as Dialog, DIMDI, DataStar, BRS, STN and JICST. Although the printed abstract bulletins were still the major source of revenue, on-line access was starting to represent an attractive alternative, particularly for the individual end-user. The attention of *Excerpta Medica*'s user training programs was therefore increasingly directed at retrieval from the database, and this in turn had an inevitable effect on editorial procedures and production streams. For example, the primary indexing terms on an article were further subdivided into A-terms and B-terms, depending on their relevance in that article, and only the A-terms were rotated in the printed indexes. The number of EMtags and classification subcategories was increased, and a continuing effort was made to reduce the time between journal receipt and input of indexed references.

4. EMbase versus Medline and the role of user aids

This period also witnessed the appearance of several articles in which retrieval from EMbase was compared with that from Medline. The general conclusion from these comparative studies was that the speed of input into the two databases was comparable, that EMbase often yielded more references, particularly in drug-related areas, but that the proper formulation of searches designed to yield comprehensive retrieval with a high degree of relevance was relatively difficult for EMbase. Users often complained about the inconsistent use of specific indexing terms, classifications and EMtags, and about the need to use several alternative formulations simultaneously in order to retrieve all relevant articles. This underlined the need for user training and for the development of user aids. After all, even though most individual users would probably start with a free-text search of the terms appearing in the titles and abstracts, and although the higher percentage of abstracts in EMbase, combined with the deep indexing using both primary and secondary terms, gave EMbase a certain advantage in this respect, there are many theoretical reasons for not relying entirely on free-text searching if either comprehensive or highly relevant retrieval is desired. Retrieval using the controlled vocabulary is to be recommended, but then one must know how to use it.

The first of the many new user aids produced in the 1980's was the Index to EMclass. The classification categories represented an effective tool for the retrieval of broader concepts (more effective than the very broad Malimet terms), but the polyhierarchic nature of the classification system made it difficult for the on-line user to find the relevant classifications. Similar subcategories could be found in several sections, but their use of course depended on the assignment of the article to those sections, and the point of view of the medical discipline involved was implied in the definition of the classification subcategory. Following many serious discussions with the Chief Editors and section editors, an index was finally produced in which the users were referred from all concepts present in the entire classification system to all relevant subcategories in all sections. This guide was received with enthusiasm by the users.

A list of EMtags and the List of Journals Abstracted (with CODEN-codes and classified according to both subject specialty and country of origin) were of course relatively easy to produce and distribute. In contrast to MeSH, however, which was available in printed form in every medical library, Malimet was only available on-line or on (rapidly outdated) microfiches. Moreover, although control over its growth had been improved considerably, there continued to be a problem with pre-coordinated terms that were inconsistently used. Analysis showed that of the approximately 150,000 preferred terms then in existence, only about 20,000 were used with any frequency. It was therefore decided to produce a user aid (MiniMalimet) containing the most frequently used terms, and to encourage the more consistent use of these terms by distributing the list to the indexers as well. This list, which was eventually incorporated into a comprehensive *Excerpta Medica Guide to the Classification and Indexing System,* was also received with enthusiasm by users, although less so by the indexers, who felt that their traditional freedom was being curtailed. Simultaneously, an effort was made to limit the addition of new terms to the names of specific concepts such as drugs, syndromes, plant or animal species, etc. and to prohibit the addition of new precoordinated concepts.

This, however, would prove not to be the end of the story. During the 1980's, despite trials with the publication of various new types of printed products and even new abstract bulletins such as 'Toxicology' or 'Forensic Sciences', it became increasingly clear that the printed products were being supplanted by on-line access and electronic spin-offs such as sections of EMbase on CD-ROM or magnetic tape, EMSCOPES, EMbase Alert, etc. Although EMbase continued to be appreciated and used, particularly for the retrieval of drug-related and other highly specific information, users regularly complained of the difficulty of search formulation and the lack of hierarchic structure in Malimet, which made the retrieval of broad concepts particularly difficult. In 1988, therefore, the decision was finally taken to introduce a limited amount of hierarchic structure into (Mini)Malimet and create what was to become EMTREE or EMTHES.

As might be imagined, this was not an easy operation. First of all, a decision had to be taken as to the kind of structure to be introduced. The easiest solution might possibly have been to simply switch to MeSH, especially since this would have satisfied user demands that it should be possible to run searches formulated for Medline against EMbase as well with a minimum of modification. However, this would have meant a radical break with the past, making the information in the existing years of the database more or less irretrievable. It was strongly felt that the existing Malimet terminology had to be preserved, also for the benefit of the indexers. Furthermore, there was a feeling that MeSH, burdened by a history of more than 30 years with little change, could be improved upon in the light of new insights. The compromise reached was to take over the basic superstructure of MeSH, i.e. the 15 categories or "facets" at the highest level, together with some of the first-level subdivisions, and to attach the 20,000 most frequently used Malimet terms, plus 10,000 additional drug names and some terms newly created for 'umbrella' concepts at higher levels in the tree structure, to it. Moreover, MeSH headings would be added as synonyms of the EMTREE preferred terms wherever possible. This gargantuan task was largely accomplished within one year, so that EMTREE could be announced in 1989.

In its present form, EMTREE consists of about 40,000 drug and biomedical preferred terms or 'descriptors', plus over 170,000 synonyms (about 12,000 of which are included in the printed thesaurus); the descriptors are organized into a cascading tree-like structure with a maximum of seven levels of subdivision (15 facets at the top, divided into 127 subfacets, etc.), represented by about 10,000 numerical codes. Of the 40,000 preferred terms, about 5000 are 'explosion terms' with directly equivalent codes that have more specific terms under them, while about 30,000 are specific terms that are posted under broader concepts. Indexers are expected to use the existing terms consistently, but may of course suggest 'candidate terms' (which are also appended to the reference in the database) that are reviewed regularly for inclusion in EMTREE. The inevitable changes in the hierarchic structure and terminology are carefully documented and announced annually. EMtags and EMclass are no longer used as such by the indexers, but can of course be used to search older EMbase files.

5. The present

At latest reports, EMbase continues to do well in its competition with Medline. The need for speed and economy, combined with the new editorial procedures associated with the use of EMTREE, have resulted in a further streamlining of the production process. All input is now on-line, section assignment and even the generation of many of the tables of contents for the printed products are now automated or combined with input of the bibliographic reference. In principle, bibliographic references ('citations') are input for all articles (about 400,000 per year) in all biomedical journals processed, without selection. Many of these references and abstracts are also obtained in machine-readable form, from Elsevier and associated publishers, and the role of the individual medical editors has been reduced to a minimum. The original concept of "By the medical specialist, for the medical specialist" with which *Excerpta Medica* began more than 50 years ago, has thus been sacrificed to a considerable extent in the interests of speed, economy, consistency and user friendliness.

These days, everyone's attention is on the Internet and the possibilities that this medium offers for the retrieval of information. EMbase is of course also available via the Internet, although not for free. Perhaps more importantly, an increasing number of original journals are also available via the Internet. An example in this direction is the ScienceDirect project of Elsevier Science, which offers Internet access on a subscription basis to a file that currently consists of more than 1.2 million articles. More on medical publishing via the Internet can be found in Ch. 19.

References

[1]   Adams, S. & McCarn, D.B. (1976) Chapter II: From Fasciculus to On-Line Terminal: One hundred years of medical indexing. In: *Communication in the Service of American Health — A Bicentennial Report from the National Library of Medicine.* Bethesda, MD: National Institutes of Health.

[2]   Anonymous. (1969) *NCR: a biomedical information storage, retrieval and dissemination system.* Amsterdam: Excerpta Medica & The National Cash Register Co.

[3]   Anonymous. (1974) *The Excerpta Medica biomedical information system: computer tapes and abstract journals.* Amsterdam: Excerpta Medica.

[4]   Blanken, R.R. (1989) Thesaurus. In: *Archiefbeheer in de praktijk.* Alphen aan den Rijn: Samsom Uitgeverij, Band 1 (3075), 1–17.

[5]   Garfield, E. (1980) Excerpta Medica — Abstracting the biomedical litreature for the medical specialist. *Current Contents,* **28**, 5–10.

[6]   Mehnert, R. National Library of Medicine. In: *Current Practice in Health Sciences Librarianship.* Vol. 7. Bunting, A. & McClure, L.W. (Eds.) Health Sciences Environment and Librarianship in Health Sciences Libraries. New York: Forbes, pp. 91–115.

[7]   Vinken, P.J. (1969) Het Excerpta Medica Foundation systeem van informatieverwerking met de computer. *Nederlands Tijdschrift voor Medische Studenten* 15(6), 276–281.

[8]   Vinken, P.J. & Blanken, R.R. (1969) *Illustrated lecture on the Excerpta Medica automated storage and retrieval system.* Amsterdam: Excerpta Medica.

[9]   Vinken, P.J. & Blanken, R.R. (1972) *Excerpta Medica. Encyclopedia of Library and Information Science.* Vol. 8. New York, pp. 262–282.

[10]   Vinken, P.J. & Van der Walle, F. (1968) *Excerpta Medica automated storage and retrieval program of biomedical information.* Amsterdam: Excerpta Medica Foundation.

[11]   Vinken, P.J., Van der Walle, F. & Warren, P.A. (1970) Design and operation of an advanced computer system for the storage, retrieval and dissemination of the world's biomedical information. In: *Proceedings of the Third International Congress of Medical Librarianship, Amsterdam, 1970.* pp. 149–154.

A Century of Science Publishing
E.H. Fredriksson (Ed.)
IOS Press, 2001

Chapter 17

Impact of Computers and Communications on Publishing

Nico Poppelier[a] and Einar H. Fredriksson[b]
[a]Penta Scope, Amersfoort, The Netherlands
[b]IOS Press, Amsterdam, The Netherlands

1. Introduction

The application of computers to publishing, and to science publishing in particular, can be traced back to the period immediately after the end of the Second World War. In a paper published in 1945, former vice-president of MIT Vannevar Bush described the use of new technology for the recording, organisation and consultation of information [1]. This paper proved to be a seminal one, since it can be regarded as the start of various streams of development. These developments eventually resulted in applications and technologies we find in our offices and in our homes today.

In the western world most people are nowadays familiar with Internet, in particular with the World Wide Web. However, the World Wide Web is very recent technology. It was developed in the early 1990's at CERN in Geneva by Tim Berners-Lee, Robert Cailliau and co-workers. Internet, and the Web in particular, continues to influence the field of science publishing. Another significant step forward for the dissemination of scientific knowledge, especially in the fields of mathematics, physics and computer science, was the development, by Stanford professor Donald Knuth, of the TeX system (see Ch. 18).

In the second half of the twentieth century the following three trends can be observed. Firstly, computers became smaller, cheaper, faster and more versatile. The result of this is that many people nowadays use computers for their daily work, and in some cases people cannot even do their work without computers. We also find computers in schools, in our homes, and even in places called "Internet cafes". Secondly, various means of telecommunication became more widespread and cheaper. As a result we now have regular telephone service, mobile telephone service, and global computer networking both with and without wires. Thirdly, various people developed innovative applications of computers, other than the processing of numeric data (number crunching). Most people in the western world are familiar with word-processing software and calculation tools such as spread-sheets, but not so long ago manuscripts were still written by hand or typed on a typewriter.

When you consider how these trends apply to the area of (science) publishing, many different areas of development come to mind. In this chapter we will discuss the following three areas.

1. Without the Internet as a (nearly) world-wide facility for computer networking, there would not be a World Wide Web. The development of the Internet will be summarised in section 2.

2. As computers became more powerful and more easily available, people began to apply them to the production and processing of documents. An important concept in this field is the 'markup' concept, which will be explained in section 3. A well-known application of markup techniques to the production of scientific documents, perhaps even the best known throughout the world, is Donald Knuth's TeX system, the history of which is described in Ch. 18. Parallel to the fast deployment of TeX within the scientific community in the 1980's and 1990's there was another important activity, namely the development of the international standard SGML, and its application to document models for science publishing. Web technologies such as HTML and XML were derived from SGML. This will be also described in section 3.

3. Most text documents have a linear character, i.e. they are read from start to end. Using computer technology it is possible, however, to create and use non-linear documents, i.e. documents that can be read in various ways. Various people have played a role in this area, but the three most important ones are: Vannevar Bush, Douglas Engelbart and Ted Nelson. Their work, which will be described in section 4, underlies the World Wide Web as a global hypertext system, but also other forms of hypertext or hyperdocuments. The work of Engelbart also underlies the graphical user interfaces of contemporary computers. We do not describe here the work on 'search engines', based on information-retrieval research, which play an important role in the disclosure of the World Wide Web, which contains a tremendous number of pages and keeps growing daily.

2. Development of the Internet

The first public demonstration of what is now known as the 'Internet' was during the International Council for Computer Communications (ICCC) conference in Washington DC in 1972. It was developed under the auspices of the US

Defence Advanced Research Projects Agency (DARPA), which itself had its roots in the reactions in the United States to the Soviet launch of the Sputnik satellite in 1957. New directions in DARPA under J.C.R. Licklider from 1962 lead to the establishment of ARPANET in 1969 under R. Kahn.

In Europe experiments in the United Kingdom and France had been done on similar lines since the mid 1960's. In the United Kingdom, Donald Davies of the National Physical Laboratory (NPL) had in 1965 coined the term 'package switching' for the technology underlying the new computer communications. During the first decade the new technology had only involved a handful experts on both sides of the Atlantic, and it was only after 1972 that applications work did commence which could be said to have any effect on scientific publishing or communications.

It is interesting to note that the engineering association IEEE, with a leading communications society branch, in 1971 found the idea of a conference on computer communications premature: "it would not attract even 100 persons..." Hence ICCC was born and the conference of 1972 was organised independently of IEEE. This conference attracted more than 1100 participants, and the Internet ideas got its first large-scale exposure there. In connection with the next conference, ICCC'74 in Stockholm, the idea of an international journal was born: *Computer Networks*.

The days of conception of the Internet followed the introduction of the concept of time-sharing in the late 1950's, and Licklider reported that he first heard of it during the world computer congress organised by UNESCO in 1959 in Paris. Time-sharing was introduced as a solution to the need for sharing computer resources in a time when computers were few and very expensive. Connecting them via networks was in many situations a more cost-effective way of usage. In the concept of Donald Davies, traditional message switching as seen in telegraphy, albeit slow, was an alternative to using the telephone network. Communication between computers was characterised by short periods of intensive information exchange , for which the concept of 'circuit switching' known from traditional telephony proved less suited. Package switching combined message switching with time sharing. The next step was to define end-to-end protocols whereby each package contains information about sender, destination and how many packages make up the complete message.

The concept of 'open-architecture networking', introduced by Kahn in 1972, showed the way to connect entire networks based on different architectures. This was done with what was called an 'internetworking architecture.' ARPANET provided the testbed for the development of interconnecting networks, and this led to the widely used Transmission Control Protocol/Internet Protocol (TCP/IP) in 1978.

Since the mid 1970's the systematic introduction of Internet-related protocols into many operating systems in the United States provided a main ingredient in the spreading of Internet, partly because TCP/IP had been given away free of charge. The experimental Internet started in 1977 with 100 host computers, mainly within the scientific world. File transfer, electronic mail and discussion groups were among the main applications at the time. The now familiar Domain Name System was developed a few years later, in 1983, in response to the continuous growth of the Internet and the associated administration.

The ARPANET had its demise after 20 years, but around 1990 the management structure of the Internet was still very similar to the structure set up during the DARPA time. Already by the mid 1980's, DARPA was no longer the major funding agency supporting the Internet. Various governmental bodies, both inside and outside the United States, shared in the funding, and there was also an increased interest from the commercial sector. The management structure of the 1980's consisted of an Internet Activities Board (IAB), and a structure of task forces, with each task force focussing on a particular area of technology. Later, the Internet Engineering Task Force (IETF) was introduced to co-ordinate the work of the individual task forces. A major activity was always the standards process, which differed significantly from that seen in the international standards bodies, the International Organization for Standardization (ISO) being a well-known example. The increased variety of requirements from the user community as well as the increasing pressure to make the standards process open and fair contributed to the formation of the Internet Society (ISOC) in 1991. In 1992 the IAB became the Internet Architecture Board, and further organisational change were implemented within the framework of the ISOC.

While the initial usage of Internet was mainly scientific or military, the introduction of personal computers and local-area networks, starting around twenty years ago, have broadened the user communities to include large segments of society. All areas of science, medicine and education have been profoundly affected by networking technologies. The first uses of this in scientific publishing was, outside the physics laboratories, in the scientific abstracting field.

In the late 1970's the use of telephone lines for international calls was very expensive, and the leasing of dedicated lines even more so. The slow growth of messaging between scientists in the 1980's is partly due to the high costs of communications and the relatively low number of personal computers fitted with modems at the time. Experiments with computer conferencing started around the mid 1970's, but didn't have a broad impact on science communications until 1990.

Around 1980, 'intermediate' technologies were introduced. One of these was videotex, which combined telephone technology with television receivers, using an auxiliary device to connect the both. Storage on initially central computers, outside the US managed by the national postal and telecommunications authorities, and payments through one or other form of subscription arrangements, proved generally difficult to sustain. For general public use, only the French system Minitel proved successful in its first generation. Minitel used a simple, cheap terminal for alphanumerical data. None of these technologies had an impact on the field of scientific communication, however.

The way the DARPA research community collaborated with the computer and communication industry in the mid 1980's included access to the vast experience and use of TCP/IP protocols. This lead to the Interop exhibition and conferences, starting in 1988, which in turn became a promotion vehicle for the acceptance of internetworking by leading industries. This also started to affect the STM publishing environment outside the earlier uses by organisations like *Excerpta Medica* and the National Library of Medicine (NLM). In the commercial sector only Maxwell's Data Group had attempted to make serious use of Internet before 1989. This was the year of birth of the World Wide Web [2]. It would take another five years before Internet, mainly through the rapid deployment of the Web, today one of its principal applications, could commence to make its fundamental impact on science communication and publishing in general.

The Internet is constantly changing and has been developing largely in parallel with traditional telecommunications and telephony on the one hand, and television on the other. The demarcation lines between telecommunications and computer industries are becoming more and more vague as the Internet develops. New services such as digital telephony and TV provided through Internet are currently being introduced. Traditional content companies, e.g. science publishers and media conglomerates, are becoming part of a broader media industry. However, in this industry information costs money, so new concepts of publishing must be developed. Recent development of new concepts and new technology, such as mobile devices and wireless Internet access, is driven by scientific and technological developments, but not with the scientific community as the prime user group in mind.

3. The markup concept

The application of markup techniques to the production of scientific and technical documents has a long history. An interesting account of the early period, until the early 1980's, can be found in Nievergelt [6]. No doubt, the single most well-known application in this area is TeX, the history of which is described in Ch.

18. Parallel to the fast deployment of TeX within the scientific community in the 1980's and 1990's there was another important activity, namely the development of the international standard SGML [7], and its application to document models for science publishing. Web technologies such as HTML and XML are derived from SGML (although in different ways).

Markup is the name given to the technique of adding readable instructions (codes) to a text document. These instructions can describe the meaning of a word or piece of text, or the formatting (presentation), or both. This concept was developed in the late 1960's and early 1970's. Early applications of the markup concept were PUB, developed at the Stanford Artificial Intelligence Laboratory starting in 1971, nroff, developed at the Bell Laboratories for the — then brand-new — Unix operating system in the first half of the 1970's, and Scribe, developed at Carnegie-Mellon University in the late 1970's. These systems influenced each other and also developments such as LaTeX, the widely used macro package for the TeX system, and of course SGML.

4. SGML: a condensed history

In the second half of the 1980's a new international standard called SGML began to draw attention. But the roots of SGML go back more than thirty years ago. In 1969, three employees of IBM, Charles Goldfarb, Edward Mosher and Raymond Lorie developed a new markup language, which they named GML after their initials. Later, they started to call it Generalized Markup Language. It was a means of allowing editing and formatting of text documents, and information retrieval on collections of text documents. GML was used in an IBM system called the Document Composition Facility.

In the late 1960's several people proposed to use the markup concept in a new way: instead of inserting codes that defined formatting, one should use codes that described the *structure* of documents. In 1967 William Tunnicliffe, chairman of the Composition Committee of the Graphics Communications Association (GCA) gave a talk on separating information content from presentation at the Canadian Government Printing Office. Around the same time, book designer Stanley Rice proposed the idea of a universal catalogue of codes for 'editorial structure'. Norman Scharpf, director of GCA, recognised the significance of these trends, and established a generic coding project in the Composition Committee, which developed the GenCode® concept.

Nearly ten years later, a committee of the American National Standards Institute (ANSI) began the development of a text description language based on GML and the GenCode® concept. The first working draft of this language appeared in

1983. Development later continued under the auspices of the International Standardisation Organisation (ISO). Finally, the standard describing this new language, which was baptised Standard Generalized Markup Language (SGML), was published in 1986 as ISO International Standard 8879. The SGML industry gained impetus because of the inclusion of SGML-based document models in the CALS series of standards, which was developed by the US Government. The deployment of CALS in various industry sectors also triggered the development of specialised SGML software, e.g. editors and document management systems.

5. SGML applied

SGML became a useful tool for science publishing with the development of a series of standards for electronic manuscripts by the Association of American Publishers (AAP). In fact, development of these standards had begun before 1983, before SGML became an international standard.

The series of standards created by AAP consisted of definitions of markup conventions, document type definition (DTD) in SGML parlance, for books, journals and articles, especially for science publishing. For that reason, the publications could not only contain text, but also tables and mathematical formulae.

Although this early development was far from perfect, the influence of it is still felt. Many of the document type definitions used by science publishers today, both in the US and in Europe, still show the AAP influence quite clearly. Among the creators and early adopters of the AAP standards were IEEE, the American Chemical Society, the American Institute of Physics, the American Mathematical Society and Elsevier.

The AAP series of standards was later extensively modified, and became known under the new label of ISO International Standard 12083.

The definitions of markup for mathematical formulae in both the AAP series and in ISO 12083 were very much oriented towards the notation of formulae, i.e. their appearance on a sheet of paper or a blackboard. This approach was criticised by several people. Eventually, the discussion of the definition of mathematical formulae in ISO 12083 contributed to the development of MathML (see below). One of the core standards of the World Wide Web, HTML, is an application of SGML. Although earlier versions of HTML were not rigorously defined as an SGML application, for later versions a DTD was developed.

6. XML: son of SGML

More than ten years of experience with SGML led to the development of XML in 1997, by a working group of the World Wide Web Consortium (W3C). This working group grew out of the consortium's Web-SGML activity, which was intended to bring the power of SGML, in other words complex document structures, to the Web. XML is a simplification of SGML especially intended for wide deployment on the World Wide Web, and is described in a text of merely thirty pages.

Within a few years after publication of the first working draft on XML, in 1997, it has become the core of a growing family of related standards that supplement and extend XML. For various fields of applications, suitable document type definitions are defined or are under development. HTML itself has been re-defined as an XML application called XHTML.

The publication of the XML Recommendation [8] by the W3C is undoubtedly an important milestone in the history of SGML. XML has the same strengths as SGML, but because of its simplicity it is also much easier to implement in software. Therefore, XML will have a significant impact on almost every branch of economic activity, including publishing, more than SGML ever did.

7. XML applied

One of the first applications of XML created within the World Wide Web Consortium was MathML, the Mathematical Markup Language [9].

Even though the World Wide Web was invented as a means of supporting scientific communication, by 1994 the best way of producing scientific documents was to insert images (pictures) of mathematical expressions into HTML documents. The W3C recognised the lack of support for mathematics. W3C staff member Dave Raggett published a working draft for HTML Math in 1994. Discussions on mathematics on the Web were held at the Web conferences of April 1995 (Darmstadt) and December 1995 (Boston). In the summer of 1996 a group of people interested in this subject area got together, and this group later became the W3C Math working group.

MathML was developed with the following goals in mind.

- It should encode mathematical material suitable for teaching and scientific communication.
- It should encode both the notation (appearance) and the semantics (meaning).
- It should facilitate conversions to and from other formats, with output formats including e.g. graphical displays, speech synthesisers, computer-algebra systems, TeX and braille.
- It should support efficient browsing of complicated and lengthy expressions.
- It should be extensible.

- It should simple for software to generate and process, and be suited for template-based and other editing techniques.

For MathML, several well documented and tested versions exist, the most recent one being version 2.0 [9]. MathML will continue to evolve. Various implementations of it exist already, and many more will appear. Eventually, most Web browsers, including the very popular ones, will support MathML. This will greatly improve and enhance the use of the Web as a vehicle for scientific communication, which was its primary goal. MathML will play an essential part in this, and is therefore without any doubt of great importance to science publishing.

8. Non-linear text

In 1945 Vannevar Bush wrote an article [1] that displayed great vision and would influence the work of many people. Bush was director of the US Office of Scientific Research and Development under President Roosevelt. Before that, he had been Vice-President of MIT and Dean of MIT's School of Engineering. In 1950 Bush became the first director of the National Science Foundation (NSF), an institute which he himself had proposed.

In his 1945 article Bush discussed possible ways in which scientific and technical developments that resulted from the war effort could benefit mankind. The first benefit of science and technology to mankind is, according to Bush, man's increased control of his material environment, e.g. food, clothes, shelter, and health-care.

Bush recognised that, as part of their work, researchers make written records of their findings, and that these written records steadily increase in volume. Already in 1945, Bush found the rate of increase of such records alarming. Therefore he asked himself how new technologies could help researchers make more and better use of the results of prior research. He suggested that new recording techniques such as photography would help. One of the techniques he had in mind was the microfilm, and he used the hypothetical example of the Encyclopaedia Britannica reduced to the volume of a matchbox.

Bush also believed that the future would bring advanced computing machines that would handle advanced mathematics. Nowadays we indeed use computers for complicated numerical calculations, as well as for algebraic manipulation of mathematical expressions, thanks to software packages such as Mathematica and Maple.

For Bush, the problem of consulting the growing mountain of information was perhaps the most staggering one. As a solution to this problem he proposed a new device, 'a sort of mechanised private file and library'. This is probably the most important part of his 1945 paper, and it is certainly the one most often cited. Bush gave this device the name 'Memex', short for Memory Extension. The memex was supposed to be a device for making and following links between documents. Writing about the memex, Bush in fact described hypertext, although that name would be used for the first time by Ted Nelson in the 1960's (see below). Although Bush was clearly thinking of microfiche in his article, he described the idea of the memex in more general terms, which makes his paper all the more impressive. Near the end of his article he writes "Presumably man's spirit should be elevated if he can better review his shady past and analyse more completely and objectively. He has built a civilisation so complex that he needs to mechanise his record more fully if he is to push his experiment to its logical conclusion and not merely become bogged down part way there by overtaxing his limited memory".

Bush believed scientific and technological advances would improve life on our planet. In the first section of his paper he mentions increased control over our environment. Nowadays many people believe man has exerted his control in the wrong way. In the last paragraph of his article Bush writes that the applications of science have made it possible for people to fight each other with cruel weapons, but that it may also allow them to grow, if they don't perish before learning how to use science for their own good.

Doug Engelbart was familiar with the 1945 article of Vannevar Bush: he had read it during his period of service in the US Navy. Engelbart began his career at Ames Research Laboratory, and later moved to the Stanford Research Institute (SRI). Partly due to Engelbart's influence, SRI became the second node on the ARPANET. After many years of thinking about ways of using computers that were regarded as unconventional at that time, he finally got funding to begin his own project. The first report he produced in this project was called 'Augmenting Human Intellect: A Conceptual Framework'. It is clear from his work that Engelbart was influenced by Bush, a fact he acknowledged in a letter to Bush shortly before publication of the abovementioned report. Roughly fifteen years after Vannevar Bush's seminal paper, Doug Engelbart and co-workers at SRI built a prototype system for collaborative work. Thanks to the improved technology Engelbart's team could build their system, which can be regarded as a form of 'memex'.

The system Engelbart's team developed was called NLS (oNLine System). It was a system for editing and browsing hypertext, as well as for sending and receiving electronic mail. It was also made available as a commercial system under the name Augment. Engelbart's work [4,5] had significant influence on the development of software tools for collaborative work, nowadays called 'groupware'. At the Fall Joint Computer Conference of 1968, Engelbart and his co-workers gave a 90-

minute demonstration of NLS. Using NLS, he and colleagues thirty miles away collaborated in a presentation that contained video teleconferencing, and hypertext links in text and graphics. In the demonstration they also used a pointing device that is regarded as the world's first mouse.

Engelbart had a vision of using computer to support the work of groups of people, by giving them means to communicate their ideas and share their knowledge. The phrase he used for this sort of work was 'CoDIAK': Concurrent Development, Integration and Application of Knowledge.

Engelbart observed that most human knowledge, from electronic mail and notes to heavy reports and books, are inherently hyperdocument objects: in other words that our knowledge consists of fragments of information that have various types of links or connections.

He also recognised the importance of explicitly structured documents. This would make it possible to select parts of documents, to view documents in different ways, depending on the application, and to link to parts of documents instead of to a document as a whole. Documents according to Engelbart were not restricted to being purely textual. In fact, it was essential for him that documents had mixed content, e.g. text, diagrams, mathematical equations, still or moving images, and sound, "all bundled within a common 'envelope' to be stored, transmitted, read (played) and printed as a coherent entity called a 'document'" [5].

Ted Nelson is known as the inventor of the word 'hypertext' and for his many papers about the hypertext system Xanadu. Nelson was interested in new ways of representing and connecting information, ways that went beyond the possibilities of traditional publishing on paper [3]. One of the metaphors he used was that of cutting and pasting — not in the way it is implemented in modern word-processors, but the way it was done before computers arrived on the publishing scene. When Nelson was working at the *New York Times* (his job was to fill up the pots of glue) he noticed how journalists would cut up articles into pieces, arrange them on a large surface in front of them, and would then paste it together the way they wanted it. Nelson became interested in using computers for arranging fragments of information and linking them together. In his second year of graduation at Harvard, he took a computer course in order to get a better understanding of the capabilities of computers. That was the start of the project that he later called Xanadu, a project that is unfinished, even today. For a presentation at the 1965 conference of the Association of Computing Machinery (ACM) he coined the word 'hypertext', which is a common word in the vocabulary of computer experts nowadays.

Later developments in hypertext include:

- HES (Hypertext Editing System), developed by Ted Nelson and Andy van Dam, at Brown University in Providence (RI) in the late 1960's, and used on the Apollo missions;
- FRESS (File Retrieval and Editing System), developed by Andy van Dam and students;
- Gopher, developed at the University of Minnesota;
- Hyper-G, developed at the University of Graze in Austria by Hermann Maurer and students.

In 1989, Tim Berners-Lee, while working at CERN in Geneva, wrote a proposal for the development of a new system that would allow easy dissemination of information, e.g. about experimental results or accelerator equipment, within CERN and the community of high-energy physics research.

Berners-Lee was familiar with the work of Bush, Engelbart and Nelson. In 1990 Berners-Lee, together with Robert Cailliau and other CERN staff, developed a prototype of his system on a NeXT computer, and called it World Wide Web. The new system found its way outside CERN, slowly at the start, but gradually picking up speed, especially with the launch of the graphical Web browser Mosaic in early 1993.

Systems such as NLS, HES, FRESS, Gopher and Hyper-G were in a way forerunners of the World Wide Web, but some offered features that the present Web does not have — not yet anyway. The World Wide Web can be regarded as the inevitable outcome of a simple addition: Internet technology meets the markup and hypertext concepts. In reality it was not as simple as this of course, and it took the vision and perseverance of people like Berners-Lee and Cailliau to make it happen [2].

9. Conclusion

In the early part of the Internet history, scientists formed the majority of the user community. Due to developments in computer science, e.g. hypertext and groupware, the widespread distribution of personal computers and affordable networking, Internet applications had a tremendous impact on all sectors of society, the World Wide Web being the most recent example. The developments seen in the past decade have changed the focus of Internet and of computers in general from science to commerce and administration. There seem to be no governmental bodies in position to control further developments of the Internet and computer or networking technology in general. For example, the World Wide Web is controlled by a consortium of 500 organisations and companies. By the year 2000, hundreds of millions of users have become stakeholders — beyond the control of national governments or international organisations. All participants in the science publishing circle have become stakeholders as well, from authors, editors, publishers, agents, booksellers and librarians, to the scientist-user.

References

[1]   Vannevar Bush (1945, July) As we may think. The Atlantic Monthly.

[2]   James Gillies & Robert Cailliau (2000) *How the Web was born.* Oxford University Press, Oxford.

[3]   Theodore H. Nelson (1980) Replacing the printed word: a complete literary system. In: *Information Processing 80.* S.H. Lavington, (Ed.) North-Holland Publishing Company, Amsterdam.

[4]   Douglas C. Engelbart (1990) Knowledge-Domain Interoperability and an Open Hyperdocument System. In: *Proceedings of the Conference on Computer-Supported Cooperative Work, Los Angeles CA, 7–10 October 1990.* 143–156.

[5]   Douglas C. Engelbart (1992) Toward High-Performance Organizations: A Strategic Role for Groupware. In: *Proceedings of the GroupWare'92 Conference, San Jose CA, 3–5 August 1992.* 77–100.

[6]   Jurg Nievergelt, Giovanni Coray, Jean-Daniel Nicoud & Alan C. Shaw (Eds.) (1982) *Document Preparation Systems.* North-Holland Publishing Company, Amsterdam.

[7]   Charles Goldfarb, et al. (Eds.) (1986) *Standard Generalized Markup Language (SGML), ISO International Standard* 8879:1986. International Organization for Standardization ISO, Geneva.

[8]   Tim Bray, Jean Paoli & C.M. Sperberg-McQueen (Eds.) (1998, February) *Extensible Markup Language (XML) 1.0.* World Wide Web Consortium.

[9]   David Carlisle, Patrick Ion, Robert Miner & Nico Poppelier (Eds.) (2001, February) *Mathematical Markup Language (MathML) 2.0.* World Wide Web Consortium.

A Century of Science Publishing
E.H. Fredriksson (Ed.)
IOS Press, 2001

Chapter 18

Developments in Technical Typesetting: TeX at the End of the 20th Century

Barbara Beeton
Editor, TUGboat, the Communications of the TeX Users Group

Introduction

The composition of mathematical and technical material has traditionally been considered "penalty copy", because of both the large number of special symbols required, and the complicated arrangement of these symbols on the page. While careful exposition has always been a valued skill for the mathematician or scientist, the tools were not available to allow authors to complete the presentation until relatively recently. The machinery has now come together: a desktop or portable computer; a text editor; an input language that is reasonably intuitive to a scientific author; a composition program that "understands" what mathematical notation is supposed to look like; a laser printer with a resolution high enough to print even very small symbols clearly. The composition engine is TeX, by Donald Knuth of Stanford University. This tool, originally developed specifically to produce the second edition of Knuth's *The Art of Computer Programming, Volume 2*, has been adopted by mathematicians, physicists, and other scientists for their own use. A number of scientific and technical publishers accept electronic manuscripts prepared with TeX and insert them directly into their production flow, while other publishers use TeX as a back end, continuing to accept and process copy in the traditional manner. TeX manuscripts are circulated in electronic form by their authors in e-mail and posted into preprint archives on the World Wide Web; they are portable and durable — a new edition of a work need not be typed from scratch, but can be modified from the file of the previous edition. In short, the impact on scientific authors is not just in the way their books and papers are published, but in the way they work.

From hot metal to cold type

By the end of the 1950's, the cost of composing technical material in the traditional manner was becoming insupportable for all but the most important or high-volume publications. "Cold type" was replacing Monotype for some journals and books of transient importance, with a corresponding degradation of the perceived professional quality of their appearance. The editorial model remained the same, however: manuscripts prepared by (usually) the author's secretary were rigorously copy-edited, then turned over to the compositor (who might be a skilled typist working on a Varityper or IBM Selectric Composer) for conversion to camera-ready copy. The machines used were similar to typewriters, but instead of keys, they had interchangeable "fonts" and the spacing was defined in very small increments. In the case of a Varityper, two half-cylinders, each containing three rows of characters in one typeface, were mounted on a head that could be pivoted to change the style; the Selectric Composer used a separate "golf ball" for each typeface. The resulting copy was proofread and errors lightly marked in non-reproducing blue pencil (these were the days before photocopiers); it was then returned to the compositor for corrections. Typed copy was corrected by keying patches and "cutting them in" — superimposing the correction over the erroneous original on a light box, using a very sharp knife or razor blade to cut through the two layers, and taping the good parts together with opaque tape; touchup with white paint was often necessary so that the camera would not pick up shadows from the cuts.

Obviously, this was not something that an author would willingly undertake.

The rise of the computer

The American Mathematical Society (AMS) undertook some experiments in the early 1960's with highly stylized input prepared on paper tape according to a mnemonic system in which mathematical notation and text were separated into two "columns": commands and mathematical notation at the beginning of the line, and ordinary text following a tab character. The results, processed by a service bureau, were adequate, but the process was cumbersome, and didn't yield the hoped-for level of cost savings.

Over the next decade, other organizations developed computer-based systems, several of which became commercial products. A compactly-coded input scheme by Penta required dedicated hardware and highly trained keyboarders. A system from Bedford used early CRTs and pointing devices to manually position symbols; it too required dedicated hardware and skilled personnel, and according to anecdotal reports, the same mathematical expression in two chapters of the same book, prepared by two input technicians, might come out looking quite different in the two places.

Other general-purpose typesetting programs such as RCA's Page-1 and Page-2 were becoming fairly widely used, but while they were quite good for ordinary prose and directories of various kinds, multi-level mathematics was quite beyond their capability.

In the academic world, the program TROFF, developed at Bell Laboratories as an adjunct to the UNIX operating system and the C programming language, was gaining a devoted following. The licensing of this system was extremely generous to academic users, requiring not much more than a token fee; however, the price to non-academic organizations (which included the AMS) was quite steep. Therefore, although TROFF and its companion equation processor, EQN, were very attractive, the financial implications were not.

The AMS had an opportunity to obtain the rights to a program by Science Typographers (STI) that would run on a general-purpose computer (an IBM 360 or clone). This system, like the Penta system, had rigidly coded input, but the ability to use the computer for other business processes made the investment more acceptable. An alternate input language was devised at AMS, based on the two-column (mnemonic) system developed earlier; it was thought that potentially this form of input might become usable by authors or their secretaries, and not require the highly-trained keyboarders that were hitherto indispensible. Input was initially on punched cards, with simulated distinctions between upper- and lowercase. Paper tape and mini-barcode Selectric type balls were also used to some extent. Bulk output was sent on magnetic tape to a service bureau for imaging on a VideoComp; an alternate output path involved conversion to Photon 713 machine code, with punched paper tape as the transfer medium. (Several acolytes of this system became quite adept at repairing torn or mispunched paper tapes in emergencies.) The STI program was used by AMS to prepare nearly all journals and many books from the mid-1970's through about 1984.

The birth of TeX

In 1978, the situation changed drastically. Donald Knuth, a computer scientist teaching at Stanford University, was invited to deliver the Gibbs Lecture at the annual meeting of the AMS. The lecturers for this series have been eminent scientists who are often known for their use of mathematics in disciplines other than mathematics; among the lecturers since the series began in 1924 were Albert Einstein, John von Neumann, Norbert Wiener and Paul Samuelson. The Gibbs Lecturer's topic is his or her own choice. Donald Knuth chose as his topic "Mathematical Typography" — this was the public unveiling of TeX.

Knuth's major published work is *The Art of Computer Programming* (TAOCP), a deep and broad survey of programming techniques and algorithms, originally intended to comprise seven volumes. However, by 1977 (when three volumes were in print), the programming discipline had advanced with such great speed that Knuth had to revise volume two. When he first looked at the galley proof for this revision, he was appalled. Unlike the first edition of the first three volumes, which had been typeset by Monotype, the revised volume two had been phototypeset. Not only did it not look like the first edition, its quality was, to Knuth, unacceptable.

After recovering from the shock, Knuth thought about the problem, and determined that he, as a computer scientist, should be able to use his computer to do something about this. He realized that he would have to develop fonts as well as the computer program, but figured that if he planned well, the project might take him six months to a year.

Knuth had taken great interest in the typesetting of his books, and also in how mathematical notation appears on the printed page. When he began to think about assuming the responsibility for composing the new edition of TAOCP, he began to look more closely at published literature, not only technical, but the products of fine presses, to learn to recognize quality so that he could produce it.

Knuth began to think about his new program early in 1977; his journal for May 5 shows two entries: "Read about Bell Labs typesetting system", and "Major design of TEX started" [6, p. 482]. By the middle of May, he had devised the principal mechanism for placing type on pages, as well as the main features of the input language he would like to use; he recorded his decisions in a long memo saved as a computer file named "TEXDR.AFT" (because the computer he was using wouldn't allow it to be called "TEX.DRAFT"). As soon as he finished this memo, he went away with his wife on a library associates' tour of fine presses around Sacramento. Throughout the development of TeX he continued his education in typography, eventually working with several eminent type designers and typographers, and in the process creating a computer typography group at Stanford that nurtured several members of the next generation of type designers.

The first iteration of TeX was written in the SAIL language, developed at the Stanford Artificial Intelligence Laboratory. This language was specific to the mainframe "edusystems" of Digital Equipment Corporation (DEC). These machines were among the first timeshared systems, well suited to the needs of computer science research and experimentation. Access to computer time was almost no problem, but to get the best response, Knuth shifted to "night phase" for a lot of his work.

In his design of TeX, Knuth visualized an arrangement of boxes, containing single characters or composed groups, and flexible glue, which joins boxes within the framework of a page. At a low level, TeX manipulates these components according to rules appropriate for text or for mathematical expressions, with reference to directives in the input file. The input vocabulary is mnemonic, with terminology usually selected to be familiar to a mathematician. Further, TeX is designed as a macro compiler, so it is possible to overlay the base commands with a different vocabulary, providing more complex operations through a single instruction. The most ambitious uses of this facility provide a user interface that consists entirely of logical markup and "hides" the underlying composition commands.

In mid-May 1977, Knuth left off work on TeX to develop the fonts that would be needed to put TeX's output onto paper.

Fonts for TeX

Stanford had an early laser printer, the Xerox XGP, with a resolution of about 180 pixels per inch; Knuth realized that with this kind of digital device, he could form fonts by treating each character as a matrix, filling in certain cells — pixels — while leaving others empty. A page of a book would then become a gigantic bit matrix.

The resolution of the XGP was not adequate, of course, to produce crisp images, but when Knuth looked through a magnifying glass at a sample produced on a high resolution machine (probably based on a cathode ray tube), he realized that the application of ink during printing will smooth out the edges when the raster is small enough. He observed that the critical density for ink smoothing was probably somewhere between 500 and 1000 pixels per inch [6, p. 35]; this value is very close to the density at which the human eye can no longer distinguish small irregularities.

It was important to Knuth to solve the problem of defining lettershapes in a purely mathematical way, so that as the precision of raster devices increased, the task of creating new fonts at higher resolutions did not have to begin again; the definition of the lettershapes would stay the same in a machine-independent form. The analogy he initially chose was to define the shape of a pen and describe in terms of cubic splines the path that it should follow. These shapes are defined in terms of parameters (such as pen dimensions and degree of slope) chosen by the designer; alteration of the parameters results in changes to the lettershapes. The first implementation of this program, Metafont, was usable early in 1979.

After considerable experimentation, and consulting with professional font designers, it became clear that the pen-path model was not how fonts were actually designed. Although type is based on writing, it is not the same, and a more satisfactory model consists in defining the outlines of the glyphs and then filling them in. The second version of Metafont adopts this model; released in 1985, it has remained unchanged since then except for a few bug fixes.

Using Metafont, Knuth developed a comprehensive family of fonts, known as Computer Modern, for use with TeX. In addition to alphabets in roman and italic shapes, in all the common weights, with and without serifs, there are a number of fonts devoted to symbols, so the collection of fonts is fully capable of handling nearly all mathematical typesetting needs. And if on occasion a symbol is required that doesn't yet exist, an author or publisher can use Metafont to create it.

One of the main problems in a raster environment is to determine which pixels are to be turned on; with Metafont, the rasterization is fixed at the time the program is run, and different renditions of a font are thus required for different output devices. The space required for storage of these files can be substantial. This is quite a different approach from the Type 1 (PostScript) and TrueType models, in which an outline is presented to a rasterizer at the time the composed image is rendered into output. These outlines are much more compact than Metafont raster fonts, and TeX users expressed a desire to both save space and get access to the wider variety of fonts available in outline formats. Since TeX itself requires only the font metrics, to make outline fonts usable by TeX, it suffices to create metric files in the required format and write suitable TeX-output-to-device programs to handle the imaging.

The Computer Modern fonts have been re-implemented in Type 1 form, and, at least in a publishing environment, TeX is now used almost exclusively with Type 1 fonts.

The spread of TeX

We left TeX in mid-1977, still under construction. Knuth's Gibbs Lecture in 1978 has already been mentioned. Reaction to this lecture, which introduced TeX and Metafont to a mathematical audience, was more enthusiastic than Knuth had expected. In particular, Richard Palais, then chairman of the AMS Board of Trustees, recognized the potential of these tools to typeset AMS publications. He interpreted their status as being ready for use, not still a research project. Arrangements were made for a small group of mathematicians and AMS employees to spend the month of July 1979 at Stanford to learn TeX, "bring it back and make it work". (These were my marching orders as I was presented with plane tickets and a copy of the first TeX manual.) Two members of this group were charged with developing TeX macro code for processing various AMS publications including Mathematical Reviews. The others were to create a package of macros suitable for use by authors, along with a user manual; this became AMS-TeX.

As it turned out, there were still some serious gaps in TeX, which, up to that time, had been designed for use by essentially one person, Knuth, to produce one particular, well-delineated series of books. As more people heard about TeX and experimented with the original version, the gaps became known more clearly, and many requests were communicated to Knuth for extensions and "improvements". Where such changes were justified by reference to well-documented examples, the required functionality was usually provided. In a few instances, such as more flexible handling of diacritics, Knuth rejected the requests, giving his reasons for doing so; in the case of diacritics, he said that it would be more appropriate and robust to provide fonts with already accented letters than to apply piece accents.

The first version of TeX ran on only one type of hardware — the DEC "edusystems" for which it was written. It was, nonetheless, capable of typesetting the long-delayed volume two of TAOCP, so this was done, and the second edition appeared in January 1981.

In order to make TeX available to a wider audience, it had to be modified for other hardware and operating systems. A prototype was coded in Pascal, a programming language popular at that time for instructing computer science students; Knuth's graduate students developed this version under his direction. At this point, Knuth decided that he wanted TeX to be more than just a typesetting program; as a committed teacher, he felt that it should also be a model of a large program that would illustrate good programming techniques. To this end, Knuth devised yet another concept, "literate programming".

In using this technique, program code is interspersed with documentation, in a sequence that is logical from the point of view of explaining what is going on. The source file of a literate program can be processed in two ways: the documentation can be stripped out and the code reorganized into the sequence required by a compiler, or the entire file can be converted to a form that can be typeset by TeX. With this tool, Knuth started again from the beginning, and recoded both TeX and Metafont, taking care to use a "least common denominator" version of Pascal, to ensure that the programs could be compiled and installed on any platform that provided enough memory for the programs to run. This excluded a few smaller, older machines, but most popular machines were soon able to boast a standard implementation of TeX — not, however, before the compilation of TeX had flushed out a few bugs in nearly every Pascal compiler. This version is known as TeX 2 or TeX84.

After refining the documentation, Knuth typeset the two programs; these were published as two volumes of the series "Computers & Typesetting" (C&T) — *TeX: The Program* and *Metafont: The Program*. Of the former, one reviewer said that it was the first program he had ever been able to curl up with by the fire and enjoy reading it. These two volumes are fundamental illustrations of the "open source" concept in programming.

Three other volumes complete the C&T series: two reference cum user manuals, *The TeXbook* and *The Metafontbook*, and *Computer Modern Typefaces*, a heavily illustrated book describing the fonts that Knuth created and providing a practical example of how Metafont might be used in practice. The five volumes were formally released in 1986 at a party held at the Computer Museum in Boston.

TeX became quite popular among mathematicians and scientists in the "hard" sciences, who require considerable mathematical content in their papers and books. It also acquired a substantial following among academics in Eastern Europe and other areas of the world where economic conditions do not permit purchases of expensive software. Two features are particularly attractive in this regard: first, TeX can be obtained with almost no monetary outlay; second, if suitable fonts don't exist, a user can create them (this has been accomplished for Greek, cyrillic, Amharic, and other scripts).

The heavy use of TeX in Europe made one limitation particularly onerous: TeX wasn't really designed to hyphenate words with accents and diacritics. In 1989, a delegation of TeX users from Europe approached Knuth at the annual TeX Users Group meeting and explained to him that some changes were needed to permit them to typeset their languages effectively. Although reluctant to make any more changes to TeX, Knuth was persuaded by their arguments, and he provided some major enhancements to support 8-bit input and effective hyphenation of languages other then English. This version is known as TeX3; after its release Knuth announced that, for his part, "TeX is frozen", and only the most egregious bugs would be corrected thereafter.

Knuth's custom has been to offer a reward ($2.56) to readers of his books for the first report of any error. In the case of TeX and Metafont, he also rewards the finders of programming bugs; this reward was doubled annually through the release of TeX3, and then stabilized at $327.68. Knuth now looks at bug reports only every two to three years; only one or two major bugs have been reported during each of the last few cycles.

TeX from an author's point of view

Arguably the best thing about TeX for an author is that it gives documents a professional typeset appearance.

Although becoming a skilled TeX user requires some effort, the ubiquity of computers and the decrease in availability of secretarial support in many academic departments provides incentive, especially for graduate students and younger faculty. For physics, perhaps even more than mathematics, the growth of preprint databases, such as the arXiv at Los Alamos (http://xxx.lanl.gov), is a further incentive to master TeX (arXiv strongly prefers TeX submissions). For this use, TeX has several advantages: the source is plain ASCII, so it will not become unusable with the next release of the processing program; it is compact; it is freely available for all popular platforms; it generates high-quality output; and it retains contextual information, such as the relationship between equation numbers and cross references.

There are some other advantages for authors. TeX's vocabulary and syntax for mathematical notation is straightforward; it is nearly equivalent to the descriptive language that two mathematicians might use when communicating by telephone. This notation is also known to several important symbolic algebra programs, which are able to generate output in TeX form for direct use by an author. An author who is fluent in the TeX mathematics notation can combine all these tools to record an idea as it develops; it has been reported that this capability has radically changed the way that some mathematicians work.

Some authors prefer a "point and click" or WYSIWYG approach to input. Even if they agree that the results from using TeX are superior to those from word processors, they still struggle with the learning curve. For such people, tools have been developed to provide menus and on-screen formatting of mathematical expressions, with TeX code stored behind the scenes.

The situation is not so clear with respect to the document structure. "Plain" TeX is a low-level typesetting language, and with it, one can obtain almost any desired result. Although several highly functional front-end interfaces have been created, some authors still prefer to use raw typesetting commands. On the other hand, for a publisher, especially a publisher trying to compile journals out of submissions from multiple sources, article sources prepared using uniform structural markup is essential. Some authors can't be bothered with such "petty" concerns, but more and more publishers are using the reward of more rapid publication when a submission conforms to the rules, along with the threat of retyping a submission, slowing down its production and incurring the possibility of new typographical errors, for submissions that cannot be inserted smoothly into the normal production flow. It is still a challenge to get all authors to actually read instructions.

TeX from a publisher's point of view

For most publishers, the TeX flavor of choice is LaTeX. This macro collection provides a user interface that defines logical structural markup for the top matter and sectioning elements of a document, and supports automatic numbering, cross-referencing, and interaction with standard tools for compiling bibliographies and indexes.

While not as rigorous as SGML or XML, the LaTeX framework is reliable and permits authors to produce a well-structured document onto which a publisher can superimpose a house style. There are a few rough edges, however; the handling of author addresses in basic LaTeX, for example, does not conform to the style of some publishers, and in extending this area, different publishers have made some mutually incompatible decisions. Nonetheless, there is a common, dependable core, and public-spirited users have made extension packages for many desirable features, usually (if not always) doing their best to ensure inter-compatibility with other commonly used packages.

What (La)TeX doesn't provide is rigor. SGML and XML documents are required both to be well-formed and (at least for SGML) to conform to a DTD. There is no such requirement for (La)TeX documents, and authors are free to ignore the conventions of a document style if they so choose; TeX is quite forgiving in processing a mixture of logical markup and physical typesetting commands, as long as they properly reduce to TeX's somewhat arcane syntax rules. The disadvantage in this is that transformation other than by TeX for presentation in modes other than on paper (e.g., in HTML, or via audio) becomes quite difficult, and in some circumstances nearly impossible.

There are nonetheless some things that a publisher can do to increase the likelihood that a TeX manuscript submitted by an author can be processed with high reliability and minimal special handling. (1) Provide well-designed "author packages" and easy-to-follow instructions. (2) Make sure that the fonts the author is using are fully compatible with the ones used in-house. (3) Provide at least introductory TeX training to all production staff handling TeX submissions, and have at least one person with solid TeX expertise on staff to answer questions from authors and production staff; don't try to rely entirely on outside consultants. Of course, this changes the nature of the production environment, but that has changed already, and no traditional technical publisher would forgo thorough training in house style and copy-editing techniques; only the tools are different.

There is one more danger in using TeX. There are very few symbol fonts available, and few authors are likely to be willing to purchase new ones when a reasonable set is available for free. This limits the choice of text fonts unless the publisher is willing to do extra work to recheck line breaks and similar features which are particularly suscriptible to font changes. The document styles that come with LaTeX are very recognizable, as are the fonts. A publisher is advised to invest in some expert design effort to create styles with a distinctive look, yet are still compatible with what the author is using.

The future

Many technical journals and some books are now published in electronic form as well as, or even instead of, on paper. The style suitable for paper is often not best for reading on a screen. Even if pages are put online as PDF files, the capabilities of an online environment — an active contents list, links to internal cross-references, etc. — should be incorporated into a document. For certain kinds of documents, particularly instructional ones, a different design is desirable, one that presents material in small chunks, not all at once.

Math has always been a niche market, and future developments are likely to come, as TeX has, from a self-interested source. TeX users — both authors and publishers — want to participate in the electronic revolution, and that will take a while to become routine. The major problem is the absence of suitable fonts. A two-pronged effort undertaken by STIPub, a consortium of scientific societies and publishers, is now addressing this gap. One part of this project is directed at Unicode, to increase the population of symbols with standard Unicodes; the other is to create a font containing these symbols and make it freely available to any and all users of the Web.

As noted earlier, the variability of a (La)TeX file means it is not ideal for repurposing. For this, XML and SGML are superior. MathML, an XML application that defines a structure for expressing math formulas in a Web-compatible manner, is now an accepted recommendation of the World Wide Web Consortium. However, TeX is much less verbose and more easily handled by a human than any of these *MLs. For an author to switch from TeX, some very capable input tools will have to become available; authors, having caught the TeX habit, are not going to give up without a struggle. In the long run, an internal *ML format for archiving will probably become the norm, with translation by various tools to formats suitable for presentation in different media. The development of such tools is proceeding slowly. Like TeX, which took ten years rather than the originally envisioned six months, they will arrive, but not as soon as one hopes.

TeX is no longer novel, but it is still one of the most reliable and flexible typesetting programs available, and one of very few that is capable of producing publication-quality math. Stability is a virtue in this context. However, some missing features would make it even more valuable, especially to users working in languages other than English. Several projects are underway that will extend TeX to provide such features. PdfTeX has added a few features that are directed at hypertext and online presentation, and outputs PDF files directly. E-TeX has incorporated into the present TeX program some new elements such as right-to-left typesetting. NTS (a "new typesetting system") is re-implementing TeX in a "more modern" programming language (Java, at last report) and then making additions. Omega uses Unicode for its input character set, and provides a number of filters to handle the special requirements of non-Western scripts. It remains to be seen which of these projects might result in a system that develops a critical mass of users to supersede TeX itself.

None of these TeX extensions directly addresses the special needs of flexible Web presentation. That will more likely be handled by some new internal format, like MathML.

In more mainstream developments, some of TeX's key ideas have been adopted for incorporation into new products. For example, TeX's line- and paragraph-breaking algorithm is now in Adobe's InDesign, by way of the hz program by Peter Karow and Hermann Zapf; however, this does not, and probably will never, handle math. Typesetting of math is too small an area, and much too demanding, for any of the major software houses to want to join in. There simply isn't any possibility of large profits, especially since a free alternative is available.

Where will math publishing be in twenty years? That is hard to predict. The only thing certain is that mathematicians and scientists will continue to have something to say to one another, and will demand that it be presented clearly and accurately.

References

[1]   Knuth, D.E. (1984) *The TeXbook*. Volume A of Computers & Typesetting. Addison-Wesley, Reading, MA.

[2]   Knuth, D.E. (1986) *TeX: The Program*. Volume B of Computers & Typesetting. Addison-Wesley, Reading, MA.

[3]   Knuth, D.E. (1986) *The Metafontbook*. Volume C of Computers & Typesetting. Addison-Wesley, Reading, MA.

[4]   Knuth, D.E. (1986) *Metafont: The Program*. Volume D of Computers & Typesetting. Addison-Wesley, Reading, MA.

[5]   Knuth, D.E. (1986) Computer Modern Typefaces. Volume E of Computers & Typesetting. Addison-Wesley, Reading, MA.

[6]   Knuth, D.E. (1999) *Digital Typography*. CSLI Lecture Notes Number 78, CSLI Publications, Stanford, CA.

A Century of Science Publishing
E.H. Fredriksson (Ed.)
IOS Press, 2001

Chapter 19

Biological and Medical Publishing
via the Internet

Matthew Cockerill
BioMed Central Ltd., London, UK

The early days

Biomedical researchers have been enthusiastic users of web technology since its early days. Even before the release of the first usable web browsers in 1995, scientists were downloading software from biological ftp (file transfer protocol) archives, accessing gopher servers (precursors to web servers) to search databases, and using email both to communicate with colleagues and to run sequence comparisons against biological databases such as *EMBL* in Europe, the *DDBJ* in Japan, and *GenBank* in the USA (http://www.ncbi.nlm.nih.gov/Genbank/GenbankOverview.html) [1,2].

The exponential growth which these nucleotide and protein sequence data-banks have experienced over the last 20 years (Figure 1) probably in large part explains biologists early enthusiasm for the Internet. It quickly became impractical to physically distribute such databases, both because of the amount of data involved and the frequency with which new data was being added. Making use of the data remotely via a network was a far more efficient solution.

When the web began to take off in 1994–1995, biologists (especially bioinfor-maticists) took full advantage, and biological websites of various kinds sprang up, almost all of them non-commercial, and maintained by scientists in their spare time. At this time the web was still predominantly non-commercial nature, and one of the most trafficked scientific pages on the Internet was Pedro's Biomolecular Research Tools (http://www.public.iastate.edu/~pedro/research_tools.html), main-tained by a graduate student, which kept track of many of the most useful biolog-ical web pages and online sequence analysis tools.

Bibliographic databases

Since the late 19th Century the US National Library of Medicine (NLM) has been compiling bibliographic details of medical research articles published each year into a printed publication, *Index Medicus*. In the 1940's, an alternative to *Index*

Medicus arrived in the form of *Excerpta Medica*, now owned by Elsevier.

Index Medicus has been distributed electronically since the late 1960's as the MEDLINE database, which now contains more than 10 million records. Similarly, *EMBASE* is the electronic version of *Excerpta Medica*. Neither *EMBASE* nor *MEDLINE* is fully comprehensive, and many scientists use both. See Ch. 16 for more on the history of *Index Medicus* and *Excerpta Medica*.

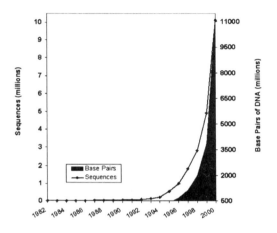

Figure 1: Growth of *GenBank*.

In the 1960's, Eugene Garfield, at the Institute for Scientific Information (ISI), created the *Science Citation Index*, which added an important twist to the idea of a bibliographic database, by including details of all the citations from the reference list of each indexed article. ISI and the *Science Citation Index* are described in more detail in Ch. 15.

By the 1980's, companies such as Ovid, SilverPlatter and DIALOG were offering paid-for access to *MEDLINE* and *EMBASE*, via their own proprietary software, typically on CD-ROM, or via a text-based online interface.

In 1988, as it became clear that molecular biology was producing an explosion of data that would require processing with advanced computational tools, the National Council for Biotechnology Information (NCBI) was founded as part of the NLM. One of the most important roles played by the NCBI is managing a collection of globally accessible databases of biological sequences and structures — of which the *GenBank* nucleic acid sequence databank is perhaps the most significant. In doing so the NCBI works closely with similar organisations in Europe and Japan who maintain their own databanks. The NCBI recently also became responsible for the data collected by the US human genome project.

One of the most significant developments at the NCBI in recent years has been the Entrez system for retrieving sequences and related information [3,4]. Entrez allows sequences, structures and related bibliographic records from *MEDLINE* to be retrieved, either by keyword searching, on the basis of a similarity based clustering scheme, or by explicit links between the various databases (e.g., from a protein sequence to a corresponding structure).

Entrez was initially released as a quarterly CD-ROM in 1993, but the following year a networked version was released, which meant that updates could be far more frequent. As web browsers took off in 1995, the web became the dominant mode of access to Entrez. Initially, only a small molecular biology related subset of *MEDLINE* was included in the Entrez database, but the popularity of even this limited free web-based *MEDLINE* searching was such that in 1997, the US government decided to make the whole of *MEDLINE* searchable on the web without charge. This aspect of Entrez, known as *PubMed*, was an immediate success. By the end of 1999 *PubMed* was handling 700,000 searches per day. It was clear that the power of the web to provide open electronic access to research information would profoundly change the way scientists communicated.

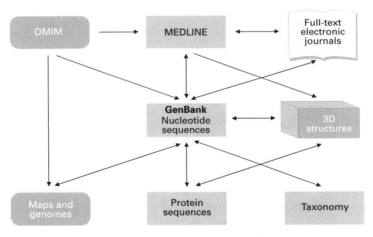

Figure 2: Links between Entrez databases.

The response of science publishers to the web

Traditional scientific publishers had been pondering the coming importance of electronic access to scientific research for some time. However, the speed of the web revolution took everyone by surprise. Publishers began to place their scientific journals on the web in large numbers, and disparate as these efforts were, there usefulness quickly outstripped what was being achieved by expensive proprietary digital library experiments such as Red Sage (http://www.ckm.ucsf.edu/projects/RedSage) [5].

By the mid 1990's, enlightened publishers had already begun to digitize the content that they published in a structured form such as SGML, and were able to take full advantage of the evolving capabilities of the web. The establishment of Adobe's Portable Document Format (PDF) as a standard also played an important role in encouraging online journal access, since PDF's are easy for the publisher to produce, quick to download, and when printed via a laser printer, produce results far superior to a traditional photocopy or fax.

The larger scientific publishers devoted significant resources towards building their own comprehensive electronic journal solutions. Examples of these services include Academic Press's "IDEAL" (http://www.idealibrary.com), Springer's "Link" (http://www.link.springer.de) and Elsevier's "Science Direct" (http://www.science direct.com). These services were typically targeted at existing print institutional subscribers, who by paying a small supplement on top of their existing subscriptions could get online access to their holdings. In some cases, as a hedge against online access causing immediate drop-off of print subscriptions, publishers encouraged libraries to enter into online access agreements which committed the library to retain all its existing print subscriptions for a 3–5 year period, in return for broad online access. Thus, online access became an important tool which these publishers could use to address their ongoing problem of attrition (losing old subscribers faster than new ones can be acquired).

Some smaller publishers (e.g. *Nature*, http://www.nature.com) also built their own sites, either in-house or via outsourcing. But many publishers did not have the resources to build a full-featured website from scratch. HighWire Press (http://www.highwire.org), a non-profit offshoot of Stanford University Libraries, filled this gap by developing systems to host online journals in a standard way. The first journal offered online through HighWire, in early 1995, was the *Journal of Biological Chemistry* (*JBC*). HighWire set a high standard with its online journals, and many society journals and others followed *JBC*'s lead. HighWire currently hosts 225 different journal sites. Most HighWire sites restrict access to subscribers only, but with HighWire's encouragement, an increasing number of these journal sites make their content freely available to non-subscribers after an 'embargo period', typically ranging from six months to two years, has elapsed. HighWire Press now (December 2000) boasts that its sites offer a total of nearly 200,000 full-text articles for download without charge. (For Highwire's list of open-access research archives, see: http://www.highwire.org/lists/largest.dtl)

Bibliographic linking

From a scientist's point of view, one of the major problems with the explosion of different journal websites has been the lack of reliable citation linking. In the early days, publishers would link to articles on their own websites, but would not link to other publishers articles, either for technical or political reasons. Some publishers even went so far as to block other sites from linking to their articles. Eventually however, the message got through to publishers that readers wanted to be able to follow any citation they came across and find the full-text article concerned, and the CrossRef initiative was born (http://www.crossref.org).

CrossRef, which exploits the Digital Object Identifier (DOI) standard, is designed to be a generic system for resolving citation links. Most major scientific publishers are participating in the CrossRef initiative, but has yet to be widely implemented. In the meantime, the increasing numbers of full-text links from databases such as the *Science Citation Index* and *PubMed* go some way to filling the gap.

Online communities

Not all scientific publishers used the web simply to make their existing published content available online. In the early 1990's, Current Science Group, then publisher of the Current Opinion series of review journals, developed *BioMedNet* (http://www.bmn.com), an internet-based community service for biologists and medical researchers. Initially, access to *BioMedNet* required the use of dedicated 'client' software, but as browsers such as Netscape became available, the service was quickly switched over to the web. *BioMedNet* not only offers the full text of the Current Opinion journals, but also brings together facilities such as a job exchange, discussion forums, news, a bookshop, databases and a scientific webzine, *HMS Beagle* (http://www.hmsbeagle.com), to which many scientists contribute. One of *BioMedNet's* most popular innovations is its enhanced MEDLINE service, which uses evaluations from Current Opinion reviewers to highlight the most interesting articles in MEDLINE. Access to most of these services is free, but requires registration, although access to review articles requires a subscription. By mid-1999 *BioMedNet* had more than half a million registrants.

The success of *BioMedNet* was repeated by *ChemWeb*, a joint venture between Current Science Group and MDL Information Systems Inc. (http://www. chemweb.com). *ChemWeb* offered registrants access to chemical journals and databases, along with community facilities similar to *BioMedNet's*. *ChemWeb's* unique feature, when it launched, was the use of MDL technology to offer structure-based searching of many of its databases. This allowed chemists to draw a specific chemical structure (using a browser plug-in), and then search for references to structurally similar molecules in any of *ChemWeb's* databases.

In subsequent years, many more scientific community sites (sometimes known as vertical portals or vortals) have followed in the footsteps of *BioMedNet* and *ChemWeb*. In biomedicine these include *Medscape* (http://www.medscape.com) and the *Community of Science* (http://www.cos.com), while in chemistry, the American Chemical Society launched *ChemCenter* (http://www.chemcenter.org) and the Royal Society of Chemistry, *ChemSoc* (http://www.chemsoc.org).

Many community sites have been started by existing scientific publishers, but in other cases they have been started by new companies. For example, VerticalNet (http://www.verticalnet.com), founded in 1995, operates a variety of industry-specific sites, including *Bioresearch Online*. VerticalNet's sites provide various kinds of community information and services, but their prime function is to act as a front-end for e-commerce marketplaces. Internet-based scientific e-commerce has proven to be a difficult area however, as witnessed by the closure in late 2000 of the Chemdex online life science marketplace, which less than 12 months previously had had a market capitalisation of more than $10 billion.

Databases

Publishers of commercial scientific literature databases were also quick to adopt the web. For example, the Institute for Scientific Information developed a web based front end for its citation databases, *Web of Science* (http://www.isinet.com/isi/products/citation/wos), and set up linking agreements with several journal websites.

Other bibliographic database providers followed suit, but free access to *PubMed* has changed the competitive landscape significantly.

Aside from bibliographic databases, the web has also allowed scientists to easily and conveniently self-publish databases which collate biological information of various kinds in specific niche areas. *Nucleic Acids Research* (http://www.nar.oupjournals.org) publishes an annual database issue [6], which catalogs some of these databases. A problem that frequently occurs, however, is that the curation of the databases becomes an unmanageable long-term burden on the lab or individual that set them up.

SWISS-PROT (http://www.expasy.ch/sprot/sprot-top.html) offers one model of a solution to this problem [7]. *SWISS-PROT* is a curated, non-redundant protein sequence database containing annotations that describe evidence of protein function (both experimentally and theoretically determined).

Begun in 1986, initially maintained by the laboratory of Amos Bairoch at the University of Geneva, and later in collaboration with the European Bioinformatics

Institute, *SWISS-PROT* grew to be a widely used resource, but by 1996, it was in funding crisis. The solution reached was to form a separate non-profit body, the Swiss Institute of Bioinformatics (SIB) to be responsible for maintaining *SWISS-PROT*. The SIB (http://www.isb-sib.ch) receives some funds from the Swiss Government, but supplements these with income obtained by licensing *SWISS-PROT* to the commercial sector. SWISS-PROT remains freely accessible to academics. It is likely that this model will be emulated by other high value but high maintenance databases in the future [8]. Alternatively, many existing databases may disappear or cease to be maintained. Many commercial alternatives are already appearing, from the growing number of companies such as Incyte, Celera, DoubleTwist.com and Rosetta Inpharmatics which specialize in such bioinformatics databases and tools.

Markup languages and file formats

The explosion in the use of internet and software tools to analyse biological information has led to an urgent need for standard file formats for the exchange of this data.

Many different ad hoc file formats, mostly text-based, have become widely used in molecular biology. Often these file formats are named after the software or database which make use of them (e.g. FASTA format, PDB format, SWISS-PROT format).

As discussed in Ch. 17, at the same time as these biological data formats were coming into use, important work was also going on in the development of standard markup languages, to allow data to be structured in a flexible way, while facilitating its exchange and its conversion to other formats.

In an attempt to bring some standardization to database formats, NCBI initially experimented with the use of an ISO markup standard known as Abstract Syntax Notation 1 (ASN.1). Recently, though, ASN.1 has been overshadowed by the emergence of XML as the predominant standard markup language. Many biological databases including *GenBank* now allow data to be downloaded in an XML format of some kind. XML is not really a file format, however. It is a meta-file format — a standard way of describing file formats. The full benefits of XML cannot be realised until domain-specific XML formats (known as Document Type Definitions, or more recently, Schemas) are agreed and used throughout the scientific community. Two of the most well-developed scientifically relevant XML formats include Chemical Markup Language (CML) (http://www.xml-cml.org), [9] and Mathematics Markup Language (MathML) (http://www.w3.org/TR/REC-MathML). After several years of experimentation, CML and MathML are finally on the verge of mainstream use. XML markup standards for biological data are at a much earlier phase in their development. Initiatives such as the Gene Expression Markup Language (GEML) (http://www.geml.org) [10], for describing microarray data, are an important starting point, but it may be some time before any such standard gains widespread acceptance.

Pre-prints and distributed archives

Biologists got their first taste of broad open access to research information through the web with the launch of *PubMed* in 1997. But *PubMed* includes only abstracts, not full text articles. Many physicists, on the other hand, had been accessing a large collection of full text research articles through the web at no charge for several years. The Los Alamos Physics Preprint Archive (now known as arXiv.org; http://www.arxiv.org) began in 1991 first as an email service, and subsequently as a widely-mirrored web archive, which allows researchers to exchange 'preprints' — articles that have not yet been accepted into a peer-reviewed journal. Initially the archive covered only high-energy physics, but its scope has expanded until it now covers all areas of physics, and also some areas of mathematics and computer science.

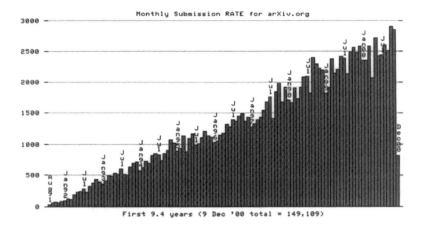

Figure 3: Growth of arxiv.org pre-print repository.

Within the physics community, there was already a long tradition of preprint circulation, in paper form, and as a natural electronic extension of this system, arXiv.org has been widely accepted by both physicists and physics publishers. Many of the articles made available through the arXiv.org servers do go on to be published in peer-reviewed journals, but in particular sub-fields of physics, arXiv.org is now the primary mode of access to the research literature.

In the chemical and biomedical sciences, no such established tradition of broadly circulated preprints existed, and although non-physicists have looked enviously at the arXiv.org example, it is not clear to what extent the same model can succeed in other sciences.

Many worry that in medicine especially, relying on an archive of research which has not been subject to peer-review could have dangerous consequences. Also, many scientists are nervous about submitting their research to pre-print servers, worrying that their work will subsequently not be accepted for publication in traditional journals, many of whose rules prevent authors from submitting work that has previously been made available elsewhere.

Nonetheless, several initiatives have started which aim to allow researchers in areas other than physics. These include the *British Medical Journal's* Netprints (http://www.clinmed.netprints.org/home.dtl) and *ChemWeb's* Chemistry Preprint Server (http://www.preprint.chemweb.com), and CogPrints (http://www.cogprints.soton.ac.uk), a preprint archive for Cognitive Science operated at the University of Southampton.

One recent development arising from the interest in pre-print servers is the Open Archives Initiative, an emerging set of XML standards for the interchange of metadata (such as titles, abstracts, and subjects/keywords) between research archives in different physical locations (http://www.openarchives.org). Originally envisioned as a way of connecting pre-print archives in the biomedical sciences, the initiative has expanded into a generic framework for exchange between distributed archives of scholarly literature of any kind. For example, one participant in Open Archives is the Networked Digital Library of Theses and Dissertations (http://www.theses.org/), which aims to bring together archives of digital theses and dissertations from universities around the world.

Another area in which the collection of metadata from many sources is becoming important is clinical trials. Publication of the results of clinical trials in conventional journals is problematic, since clinical trials producing inconclusive or negative results are less likely to be published. This can significantly skew the balance of results that appear in the published literature.

ClinicalTrials.gov is the US National Institutes of Health's response to this problem — a comprehensive archive of all in-progress NIH-sponsored clinical trials. Taking the same idea further, the recently released metaRegister of Controlled Trials (http://www.controlled-trials.com), published by Current Science Group in collaboration with the UK Cochrane Center, Glaxo-Wellcome and others, brings together information from many registers into a single web-searchable database.

When combined with the online publication of results from all clinical trials, however inconclusive, this approach promises to eliminate the problem of 'publication bias'.

Open access to research — PubMed Central and BioMed Central

The huge success of NIH's decision to make *MEDLINE* freely available, via *PubMed*, led to the recognition that open access to biomedical research was highly desirable from a scientific point of view.

Since it started, *PubMed* has continued to increase the number of links from *PubMed* records to fulltext articles (as of January 2001, *PubMed* includes links to full text articles from more than 1600 journals). But for many scientists these full text links lead to frustration, as the articles concerned are not accessible without a personal or institutional subscription. Journal subscription prices have greatly outpaced inflation for many years, and so even relatively well-off institutions cannot afford to subscribe to all the publications they would like. Currently, a major funding organisation such as the National Institutes of Health spends tens of billions of dollars each year on biomedical research, but then has to pay once again to get access to the resulting research articles for its scientists.

Against this background, in August 1999, after a period of consultation with the research community, Harold Varmus, then head of the NIH, announced the PubMed Central initiative (http://www.pubmedcentral.nih.gov). PubMed Central's mission [11] was defined as the creation of a permanent archive of peer-reviewed biomedical research which would be available to all, without subscription charges or other barriers to access. PubMed Central is not itself a publisher, and does not control the peer-review process, although it does set minimum standards for what constitutes peer review and therefore what can and cannot be included in PubMed Central.

Publishers were encouraged to allow existing journals to be archived in PubMed Central, but recognizing that many would be reluctant to do so because of the impact it might have on their subscription revenue, Varmus encouraged the scientific community to set up new open-access journals specifically intended to be archived in PubMed Central. Several aspects of the PubMed Central proposal were designed to speed the acceptance of new online-only journals. Firstly, all research archived in PubMed Central is listed in *PubMed*, and is highly visible to scientists since *PubMed* is the single most widely used biomedical bibliographic database in the world. Secondly, by providing an independent NIH-backed electronic archive, PubMed Central provides a credible guarantee of permanent accessibility for those electronically published articles, which a new small publisher could not provide alone. Finally, by openly supporting the development of new online only journals, the NIH provided a reasonable indication that electronic only publication, in new journals, would be treated fairly when making funding and career decisions on the basis of a publication track record — i.e., it reassured scientists that publishing in an established journal was not the only option if they wanted to obtain kudos and career advancement.

Several existing journals already participate in PubMed Central, including *Proceedings of the National Academy of Sciences* and *Molecular Biology of the Cell*, but these journals operate an embargo period, and so articles appear on PubMed Central only after a several month delay, during which time they are available to subscribers only. The *British Medical Journal* (*BMJ*), funded largely from membership dues paid to the British Medical Association and therefore not wholly reliant on subscription revenue, makes its content available through PubMed Central without delay.

Another publisher which has embraced PubMed Central wholeheartedly is Current Science Group. With the announcement of PubMed Central, Current Science Group saw the opportunity to create an alternative to traditional research journals and in late 1999 set up BioMed Central, a website which allows scientists and clinicians to publish research articles in any area of biology or medicine (http://www.biomedcentral.com). In total, BioMed Central offers a choice of 60 subject-specific online journals, each of which has a panel of expert subject advisers.

BioMed Central also works with groups of scientists to create electronic 'niche journals'. The editorial process for these journals will be controlled by the group of scientists concerned, who will make use of the online manuscript submission and peer-review tools that have been developed for the main BioMed Central journals.

BioMed Central is a commercial initiative — it plans to reduce the cost of publishing original research to a minimum through the use of the web and technologies such as XML which facilitate the automation of the publication process. It then plans to recoup the remaining cost through advertising, e-commerce linkups, and by offering value-added services which scientists are prepared to pay for, such as high quality databases and commissioned review articles. In doing so, BioMed Central aims to develop a new model for commercial scientific publishing, which incorporates open access to original research as a basic tenet.

The slowness of commercial publishers to allow open-access to newly published research has become a significant frustration for many scientists, who believe that the potential of the web to facilitate scientific communication is being squandered. Several thousand scientists have gone as far as to sign an open letter, pledging to boycott any journal that fails to provide open electronic access to the research it publishes within 6 months of publication. [12,13].

Building a permanent digital archive

As scientists increasingly rely on electronic means to view journal articles, librarians are in many cases considering cancelling their print subscriptions, and are being encouraged to do so by publishers, for whom printing and distribution is now an unnecessary expense.

However, this has prompted concerns amongst some librarians as to the longevity of the digital record. Past experience suggests that paper journals, stored carefully, will remain accessible on a timescale of centuries or even millennia. But keeping a similarly permanent digital record is not straightforward. Typical digital media such as magnetic and optical disks have a physical lifespan of just years, or at most decades. Furthermore, the pace of technological advance means that even if the digital medium remains intact, the equipment for reading it may have long ago become obsolete and unavailable (5 1/4" floppy disk-drives are already something of a rarity).

Concerns such as these have prompted a variety of proposals, ranging from Stanford Universities LOCKSS (Lots of Copies Keep Stuff Safe) project (http://www.lockss.stanford.edu) which allows libraries to maintain their own copies of important web content, all the way through to more outlandish suggestions such as periodically micro-engraving important data in analog form onto nickel disks, as proposed by the Long Now Foundation (http://www.longnow.org).

As reliance on online journals increases inexorably, this issue will certainly have to be addressed in years to come.

References

[1] Benson, D.A., Karsch-Mizrachi, I., Lipman, D.J. & Ostell, J. (2000) Genbank. *Nucleic Acids Research*, **28**, 15–18.

[2] Stoesser, G., Baker, W., van den Broek, A.E., Camon, E., Hingamp, P., Sterk, P. & Tuli, M.A. (2000) The EMBL Nucleotide Sequence Database. *Nucleic Acids Research*, **28**, 19–23.

[3] Woodsmall, R.M. & Benson, D.A. (1993) Entrez: Sequences and Entrez: References; NCBI's Genbank on CD-ROM. *Biotech Knowledge Sources*, **6**, 3–4.

[4] Baxevanis, A.D. & Landsman, D. (1995) The Internet biologist: Network Entrez. *FASEB J*, **9**, 994.

[5] An experimental digital journal library for the health sciences. *D-Lib Magazine* (1995, August) http://www.dlib.org/dlib/august95/lucier/08lucier.html.

[6] Baxevanis, A.D. (2000) The Molecular Biology Database Collection: an online compilation of relevant database resources. *Nucleic Acids Research*, **28**, 1–7.

[7] Bairoch, A. & Apweiler, R. (2000) The SWISS-PROT protein sequence database and its supplement TrEMBL in 2000. *Nucleic Acids Research*, **28**, 45–48.

[8] Bairoch, A. Should the model proposed by SWISS-PROT be considered by other databases? http://www.expasy.ch/announce/abpp98_1.html.

[9] Murray-Rust, H.S. & Rzepa, P. (1999) Chemical Markup, XML, and the Worldwide Web. 1. Basic Principles. *J Chem Inf Comput Sci*, **39**, 928–942.

[10] A useful list of resources relating to biological applications of XML. http://www.maggie.cbr.nrc.ca/~gordonp/xml/.

[11] Varmus, H. PubMed Central: An NIH-operated site for electronic distribution of life sciences research reports. http://www.nih.gov/about/director/pubmedcentral/pubmedcentral.htm.

[12] Brown, P. (2000) What must scientists do to exploit the new environment. *Freedom of Information Conference -The impact of open access on biomedical research July 6th-7th, 2000, New York, Academy of Medicine.* http://www.biomedcentral.com/info/brown-tr.asp.

[13] Public Library of Science. http://www.publiclibraryofscience.org.

A Century of Science Publishing
E.H. Fredriksson (Ed.)
IOS Press, 2001

Chapter 20

Changes in Librarianship

Björn Tell
University Librarian Emeritus, Lund University, Lund, Sweden

The professional job of a librarian has always been to collect, order and store documents in a variety of forms and to present them to his patrons. Libraries have been associated with cultural societies from the Sumerians, Mayas and Chineses to our modern times. The concept "document" has been changed by the impact of hypertext and the Web, as has the title of the librarian. We speak now of information professionals, business intelligence managers, super searchers, information analysts etc. Many persist in saying that "it is all on the Net, it is easy to find, and it is all free", and this has damaged the standing of the professional librarian. However, as the Internet expands, and the number of information sources grows, there is even more need for expertise to navigate and find gateways to the rich collections of value-added online services which are not free, and to serve as intelligent filters. The great professional knowledge of librarians and their personal networks will always be needed to evaluate information resources. The librarian himself creates his own job market.

Libraries have always been associated with culture in the broadest sense. For most literate societies, for Islamic, Chinese, Jewish and Christian societies such as ours, for the ancient Mayan and Greek people, reading has been the entrance to an orderly society. The societal memory has been the libraries, storing scripts in various forms and carriers from clay tablets to hypertext in a virtual cyberspace.

Paulys "Real-Encyclopädie des classischen Altertumswissenschaften" asserts that libraries, i.e. collections of books, were encountered in ancient times both among Oriental peoples, and by Greeks and Romans. The word for library — βιβλιοδήλη — is first mentioned by Kratinos the Younger, ca 400 B.C. The word seems to have got its present meaning from the great library of Alexandria.

Merchants of the Light
As we are preoccupied in the following about practitioners in libraries and their future, more than about the book collections, we would like to cite Francis

Bacon who understood the word "information" in the same way as we do, as he stated that information was "the light of the state". In his book The New Atlantis he describes how twelve "Fellows of Salomon's House" are sent out to "bring us the Books, and Abstracts, and Patterns of Experiments of all other Parts. These we call Merchants of the Light". In the following we will deal with some of these information marketing fellows, mostly called librarians.

By tradition the profession of librarian has been deemed to have a preserving effect, presumably caused by the sedentary and meticulously intellectual work that librarians carry out. It is not known how old Callimachus became by cataloging in the library of Alexandria, around 75 it is believed. But Magliabecchi reached, for his time, the respectable age of 81, by tenacious reading in the library of the Prince of Tuscany. That Leibniz was a librarian is not so well known, and he certainly stressed himself to death at the age of 70. That Casanova ended up as librarian at the Dux castle in Bohemia at the age of 73 must be attributed to earlier adventures around Europe. Of younger generations many are found to have become octogenarians. They have bestowed the profession a status, which few librarians of today can acclaim. In the following some more details are given to emphasise this.

Librarian as information provider...
Antoine Magliabecchi (1633–1714) began his career as a rather uneducated goldsmith, but his passion for knowledge drove him to buy books and acquire skills by his own efforts without formal instruction. He learnt Latin, Greek and Hebrew and had a prodigious memory, which permitted him never to forget what he had once read. Thus he had acquired a profound erudition when he came in contact with Michel Ermani, the librarian of cardinal Léopold de Médicis. Soon afterwards his merits were appreciated by grand-duc Cosme III, who nominated him custodian of his library. He was also permitted to transcribe the manuscripts of the Laurentienne library, and his legacy to us has been some reknown catalogs.

... and landlord for spiders
Known as the Varran toscan, he became a living library. Even if he never left Florence and hardly ever the library, he knew more than anyone did by reading the catalogs of the richness of great literary deposits in Europe. One day, it is said, the grand-duc asked him about a rather rare book: "Sire, Magliabechi answered, there is only one copy, which is in Constantinople, in the library of the Grand Seigneur: it's the seventh volume in the second book case to the right of the entrance". He never cared for mundane convenience, but the grand-duc permitted him to attend

the court. He was careless about his clothes, and satisfied his appetite with some fruits or salt fish. His furniture was just two chairs and a poor bed loaded with books, on which he only slept in wintertime, confining himself to a chair during summer. His house had two or three floors, and not only all the rooms, but also the corridors and stairs were packed with books, and the exact catalogue to all this was in his strange brain. Scholars from all over the world came to see and consult him. He was not very hospitable except to the savants and the spiders. He had legions of spiders in his place, and if a visitor moved around too unwarily and disturbed his friends he said with vehemence: "Don't disquiet my spiders", which he liked as much as he detested the Jesuits.

Even if he didn't leave any written work of importance except the catalogs, Magliabecchi built up an immense network by correspondence with numerous scholars of his time, so it can be said that he achieved great services to the humanities and other sciences because of the information he could provide. The appreciation of this self-taught librarian came to light by four medals, which were stamped to commemorate him, all of them showing his crooked nose. For one medal offered to him by Cosmo III, he was asked what inscription he wanted, and in his modesty and knowing his classics (in this case alluding to Persio) he proposed: "Scire nostrum reminisci" — My knowledge is just what I can remember — and with his formidable memory this was a true understatement [1].

Leibniz's astounding memory

Gottfried Wilhelm von Leibniz (1646–1716) is known as the great German philosopher who challenged Newton. In biographies he is mentioned as jurist, diplomat, and historian, as well as mathematician and philosopher. He lost his father at the age of six, and was left with a huge library of well-chosen books. His mother took care of his education. As soon as he managed Latin and Greek, he started to read the classical poets, historians, philosophers, theologians, and mathematicians. At the age of fifteen he entered the University of Leipzig. Like Magliabecchi he had an astounding memory. In old age he could recite the entire Eneide, which he hadn't opened since childhood. He liked to travel and already before the age of 30 most eminent scholars had met him and become his friends. He became a fellow of the Royal Academy. In 1676 he was nominated librarian at the Duc and Elector of Hannover, Braunschweig. It has been said that no philosopher or librarian before him has thought through, understood and elucidated the library spirit as exhaustively as he.

His reputation became European, and the numerous relationships he established through his network gave him a real influence over most of the scholars of his time. The workload he took on voluntarily and subsequent immense fatigues caused his death at the age of 70.

Casanova — not only a lover

Jean-Jacques Casanova de Seingalt (1725–1803) was 57 years of age when he became librarian at the court of prince Waldstein in Bohemia and started to write his memoirs. Besides his amorous escapades, he had become acquaintanced with Rousseau, Voltaire, Frederic II of Prussia, and Catherine II of Russia. He had talks with Louis XV, and was tenderly saluted by Mme Pompadour. Especially after his reknown escape from the leaden chambers of the prison in the palace of the Doge of Venice, which astonished the whole of Europe, he became "un homme à la mode". He had been imprisoned because of treason against the state. Even if he was a charlatan like Cagliostro, it has never been proven that during these years he did not provide a lot of secret services to his country, as he claims in his memoirs. It is obvious that the illiterate Waldstein highly appreciated having in his neighbourhood such a source of information and a man with such an enormous network, until Casanova's death in 1803.

Librarians as spies

The network of librarians has often been an invaluable source of information for governments in all times. During the Napoleonic wars in 1812 the Danish King Frederik VI wanted to know about the intentions of the Swedish army under General Bernadotte who was stationed in Germany. What would happened when the war against Napoleon was over? Would the Swedes start to attack Denmark? The king went to his Royal Library and selected three librarians to travel around Sweden. Under the pretext that they were searching for the oldest historical sources of Scandinavia they also had the task of informing him about the intent of the Swedes and to what extent they were a threat to Denmark. The Swedish counterespionage followed them closely and took note of their network activities. It ended when the king could feel assured of no threat. At least one of the librarians was so appreciated by his Swedish acquaintances that he became an academician.

A similar procedure was tried during the Vietnam war when the State Department sent a librarian to find out what happened with the young men who had fled to Sweden to avoid being drafted. Through the network of librarians she got the contacts she needed to report back to the US.

I have tried to show by these examples how librarians represent a valuable information resource. Their personal networks have been used in cases where it would have been very difficult to access quality information rapidly and accurately, since the sources rely on the selection a knowledgeable librarian has built up as an intelligent filter mechanism.

The oldest Nordic statutes for a librarian date back to the year 1120. They are found in its Necrologium Lundense in the Consuetudines canonice for the canons of the St. Laurentii chapter at the Lund cathedral. The library of the medieval canon society should be in the "custodia" of the cantor: "In ipsius cantoris custodia sit armarium, ... ne quis per neglegentiam perdatur" [2]. In many English libraries the name "custodian" or "keeper" is still valid for more status-pronounced positions of the profession.

Librarians, bibliophiles and bibliomaniacs

Before leaving the medieval time behind, another phenomenon has to be stressed. True librarians are also lovers of books especially for the qualities of format, style and binding, not to mention those who have developed an extreme preoccupation with collecting books, i.e., bibliophiles vs. bibliomaniacs.

From their point of view, the recent development of hypertext is something that has been experienced earlier as many medieval manuscripts and incunabula cannot be attributed strictly to just one author. We are in a sense back to the ancient codices where different hands could add commentaries and annotations in the margins, so-called "scholia", by which the different hands interacted with the original author. If this paper had been in hypertext, much of the exposition would have been in the background, accessible through a number of links. Even the references could have been hidden. The full reference could then be exposed just by pointing to the reference note in the text. The simple reason for not having done this is that hypermedia cannot be printed on paper and still retain their unique characteristics and advantages.

The invention of the printing press

Another point is the perfection of the medieval manuscripts, laboriously written by hand and largely inaccessible to most of the population at that time. They contained colorful, ornamented headings and artistic masterpieces of illustrations. The right play of light between white and black on the lines was achieved by varying the width of some letters. To give the same harmonious impression Gutenberg experimented with various widths of his movable letters such as a and n to adjust his work to the manuscript he was copying. Thus, the production of the Gutenberg Bible ranks as a landmark in the history of civilization. Only now such high quality of script together with colorful illustrations can be achieved by computers and distributed over the Net or by Print-on-Demand or by conventional printing. The tools to achieve computerized scripts of unprecedented beauty in a hypertext environment are a challenge to every literate person. The question remains as to what role the earlier custodians and keepers of the memory of society will play in the new environment.

Librarians in the Third World

In the Third World a librarian is usually thought of as a person who puts books up on shelves and takes them out, i.e., a semi-professional occupation which requires the ability to read and which can be allotted to females. When I was invited to Indonesia by Unesco to introduce new practices, Mr Habibi, later president, told me that as a librarian I should not think I knew, enough about the country to propose considerations for change. Instead, I should help by starting up a deposit of books and documents related to what was called appropriate technology. Indonesia did not have the book reading habits, that for instance, the British introduced in many Southeast Asian countries. The acquisition of know-how from sources such as books and documents was still in its infancy. Appropriate technology was a concept where little thought was given to the documentary support a librarian could give. That lack of appreciation in such a case might be related to the semantics of the name of the profession. Even today the conservative monks on the holy mountain of Athos in Greece use the name "bibliofylax", i.e. "the guardian of books", in order to stress the function to protect and prevent stealing as significant for the profession.

I mentioned above the reaction in Indonesia towards change in the information field, showing the inertia on the highest level. In contrast it can be revealed that a developed country like Australia simultaneously in 1973 took the opposite view. When I once showed what the European Space Organization was doing in the information and telecommunications field to its Prime Minister, Mr Gough Whitlam, he immediately asked his advisors: "Why don't we have it here?" That ambition on the highest level was triggered by me as a librarian [3].

Reports to governments

Thus, we have witnessed a process of development over the centuries in Western Europe that brought the information scattered in medieval monastries and universities first into libraries and then to the modern world of open press and publications available by telecommunications means. A new chapter for society had started to be written with information/computers and telecommunications. The contributions in this field to science and technology had finally been recognized on the governmental level during the 1960's. The so-called Weinberg report had a great impact: *Science, Government and Information*, which in 1963 was handed over to president Kennedy. That report was primarily the work of the librarian at Oak Ridge National Laboratory, François Kertez. In the US the Office for Science Information Studies in the National Science Foundation was given a leading role, and it urged the State Department to ask OECD to set up a special forum for discussions about a national information policy.

The OECD complied with the American request by setting up the Scientific and Technical Information Policy Group, where some governments chose to send a few librarians. Immediately government action in the information field came under fire from a renowned author, J.-J. Servan-Schreiber, who stirred up the ministers in OECD [4]. So, after the Third Ministerial Meeting on Science, the Secretary General in 1969 called an Ad Hoc Group on Scientific and Technical Information in order to explore the need for scientific and technical information and data in science, economy and society. Its report, *Information for a changing society. Some policy considerations*, and its recommendations, became a guide for the OECD member countries [5]. The importance of government policy at a high level was stressed, and focused on strategies which were likely to result in policies for implementation that were highly centralised and largely placed within government institutions.

One conclusion of the OECD study was that the "educational systems of the past have depended on exposure of youth to the information contained in static, archival form as provided by librarians before the advent of modern information technology. The dynamics of growth and obsolescence of human knowledge require more continuous process of education utilising information systems better adapted to changing values, knowledge structures, and human needs. Technology makes this possible. Education of youth will then be concerned with preparation for a lifetime of organised relevant learning. The information systems must be educable too, preparing the world's knowledge for ready assimilation".

With regard to information system needs, it was stated: "The demands of modern information systems for human talent are creating new professions and skills for which organized training is not yet adequate... Qualified and motivated manpower is the single largest restraint on the evolution of successful information services in science and technology". It went on to say that there are obstacles to effective recruitment: "salaries, working conditions and an outdated image of the librarian and documentalist. Concerted action by governments is needed to overcome these obstacles".

In view of the need for manpower the Group commissioned a study from Prof. George Anderla which resulted in the report *Future Needs for Information Specialists — A Forecasting Study* (1972), in which he foresaw a doubled exponential growth of scientific articles. Collection and evaluation of information should be an important function since that can hardly be automated. The need for analysis and synthesis would demand personnel, but the managerial, technical and operational functions of the new systems would also call for personnel.

The Unesco launching of the UNISIST program in 1971 had far more impact on governments because it was directed to a much larger circle of countries than just the industrialized ones [6]. A description of a world science information system was outlined, and the conclusion was that the establishment of such a system is not only necessary, but also feasible. Today, it can be said that with the access to the quantities of databases on the Internet, this could be part of the establishment of such a world science information system. However, the system's need for content analysis, i.e., design and use of indexing languages vs. operations in natural language, is far from meeting the expectations of a user who interacts with the system. The earliest electronic files consisted only of titles, bibliographic descriptions, and codes of index terms, sometime abstracts were also included. But there were restrictions because of shortage of storage space. "Indexing had to be of high quality if the information was to be retrieved at all, hence the obvious need for thesauri" [7].

The dawn of automated indexing

When automated indexing, the KWIC (KeyWord-In-Context)-index was invented in 1961 by Peter Luhn, some thought that it was just the beginning of more sophisticated automated indexing methods, so much of the librarian's subject analysis work of systematizing and classifying the increasing document flow could be alleviated. It is true that new search engines are steadily appearing for searching the Net both on keywords and free text, but we are far from being able to abandon human intervention to achieve good retrieval results.

Looking back, it is obvious that the big software firms have never really been interested in going into the intellectual part of information collecting, ordering, storage and presentation. Many systems have instead been developed in library environments, e.g. the MARC format by Library of Congress, the CDS/ISIS system by Unesco, DIALOG by Lockheed, MEDLARS by National Library of Medicine. However, when such systems worked, commercial firms were eager to follow suit. This is why we are now witnessing an explosive growth of Web search engines with rather primitive algorithms. "Some of these engines appear to have been developed by people who saw a need, but who had not the vaguest idea that there was already a history of development of tools to fulfil similar needs" [7].

So this is not a new question. Since the 1970's it has been circulating among librarians who were feeling more or less frustrated in a world where computers and information superhighways seemed to take over. The importance of information in the pursuit of knowledge had become obvious in a society marked by increasing complexity. Education is no longer reserved to locally situated learning institutions — instead it is becoming universally distributed by broadband communications. At the same time knowledge about information technology is becoming a freshware, because of the rapid developments.

Frustration and challenge

It is certainly a challenge for librarians to be questioned about their profession in this new age because they are not used to working in an environment where everybody with a PC thinks he can easily access the information he wants using database management systems on the Internet. So, people are exploring the Internet and getting an enormous number of things out of it. Information is delivered from multiple sources, covering a whole range of subjects.

All existing tools are not being used to deal with the incoming stream of unstructured or semistructured data, because people are unaware of how to use them. They see that something is wrong, but they do not know how to fix it. One reason is that the systems people have not taken advantage of all the capabilities of the PC clients, and why they usually use them as dumb terminals to the server that is supposed to do all the job of conveying information to their screen.

On the other hand, librarians need to make explicit all that they have learned through structured access, through thesauri, through hundreds of years of the development of the profession before it was automated. The voice of the expert librarian is not loud enough. Among all the available tools we do not yet have the retrieval tool that will do the job. Even if we strive for the perfect tool, there is an immense untapped utilization of the tools that already exist, and these could be put to better use today.

Filtering agent

The sheer amount of information available makes filtering a vital component of a librarian's work. Some of the system designers have proposed various algorithms and interface agents for information filtering [8]. Semantic analysis might be one mechanism for higher precision on the filtering system. The filtering service (operated automatically or by a librarian) is often used to confirm that the searcher knows what he knows, and that there are no surprises. If you receive something quite new, that is a threat.

Earlier we have touched upon problems in the Third World by emphasizing an example from Indonesia at the early stage of development. Since then the revolution in information technology has reached deep into the developing world. One way to create an understanding of the present opportunities has been to donate PCs as development aid to university libraries in the Third World. In 1997 the University of Barcelona offered 20 PCs and a connecting network to the library of the León university in Nicaragua which now is linked to the Internet. The Swedish Agency for International Development did the same for eight university libraries in African countries under the assumption that the library is the central and essential focal point for higher education.

At a seminar at the library of Lund University the librarians from the above countries demonstrated the development of IT in their countries in a number of case studies. The importance of continuing education by collaboration in library consortias was especially stressed. The facility the participating librarians showed for their presentations by expert use of the program PowerPoint was noteworthy. It is no doubt that such initiative in the university library field can close the North-South gap in the area of higher education, and that this leapfrog strategy to furnish brand new technology to libraries will pay off as long as the developing countries try to keep up with the IT development and handle it intelligently.

Social intelligence for a leapfrog strategy

Social science researchers such as Stevan Dedijer, Yehezkel Dror, William Colby and others started in the 1980's to talk about the need for social intelligence for broad policy decisions. Groups of highly qualified professionals in charge of strategic development should produce high-quality intelligence for decision makers [9].

The present information transparency makes it possible to take advantage of what has earlier been called social intelligence: that organisational capacity of a nation, a government, a corporation or any other social institution to acquire and use information to probe its environment, identify new threats and challenges, and adapt in a creative way to new circumstances, a concept that applies to decision makers at the highest level. To establish a support center for social intelligence is now a challenge for the research librarian in a developing country. This mere wording appeals more easily than librarianship to those who are responsible for a national information policy. The social competence of librarians will be needed for this task, especially in a participative democracy.

Business intelligence for decision-makers

The intelligence process developed within the government machinery became too important to be left just to governments. A development started of private centres to serve the increasing demands in modern life for economic, political and social analysis [10]. What was called management or business intelligence is spreading in private and state owned organizations and enterprises. Environmental scanning of business opportunities, competitors and so-called benchmarking is a must for survival. The decision-maker's scanning involves knowledge management and a librarian could be an invaluable element. Decision-makers have no problems in detecting and interpreting weak signals coming from the environment, but they tend to over-react to the situation. Only by having access to other perspectives from others, can this tendency to over-react be modified [11].

In any organization with a library, that element is part of the organizational context, but it usually keeps a low profile and tries not to interfere with the environments of the decision-makers. Probably this is a wise position to take, as the decision-makers should perform their own environmental scanning. But in this new world of opportunities there is a possibility for the librarians to act as a helping hand in the decision-makers' scanning. The basis for doing so is to know the decision-makers' situation and present them with variations of perspectives to help them in their particular situation.

So the more the librarian can be present in the decision-makers' everyday life, the more he/she can be of assistance in opening up vital information for them. However, there is an implication here for organizing the library service. The strategy of being present in the decision-makers' workday implies not being present in the library. Thus, many of the functions of the library have to be moved into the offices of the users.

A third opinion

The librarian's role is to offer a "third" opinion. At business meetings the librarian represents a different enacted environment than the others, and can contribute to supplementary perspectives to the decision-making process. This is an important role but it may be experienced as disturbing the decision-making a bit. Therefore, it is important that the librarian, in this context, is permitted and even expected to present perspectives that seems odd in the ongoing discussion. The value of being different must be recognized and appreciated, otherwise the role will be difficult to sustain.

Another of the librarian's advantages is his position to get to know several perspectives present in the organization and outside, so he/she can identify common denominators in these perspectives and let the rest of the organization share this knowledge. This will contribute to an increasing transparency in the organization. So, it is possible to look upon the librarian as a transparency-facilitating agent in the organization.

Library as business intelligence center

Some activities of knowledge transfer are more central to the library than others. As everyone in the organization is tied to the internally prescribed environment, there are few, if any, who care about what is happening in the blind-spots in between their own environment and the environment outside the entire organization. There is a huge remote environment not very well attended to. As the library is not biased by any particular organizational function it can use a much broader scope in environmental scanning and act as a business intelligence center of the organization.

But this role of the library in the organized environmental scanning to bring in the really odd, and in many cases threatening, discomforting knowledge, also requires a deep knowledge about the enacted environment of the decision-makers. Without being able to anticipate how they will react to the knowledge about a changing remote environment the information transferred by the library may do more harm than good in the organization. Therefore, it is important that the librarian communicates closely with the general management on these issues.

Hamrefors [11] is confident that the future will offer exciting new challenges for the library of an organization, and concludes that there are two important paths of development for the library to follow:

- Increase the presence in the decision-maker's enacted environment, learn these environments carefully and increase the asking of questions and to a lesser extent wait for questions to be asked.
- Increase the integration of the library process into other processes of the organization.

Conclusions

Thus, the future of libraries and librarians is challenging. The more the Internet expands, and the number of information sources grows and are offered free of charge to users, the more there is a need for expertise to navigate and find gateways also to the rich collections of the value-added online services which are not free, and to serve the users as intelligent filters. As the concept "document" has changed since the introduction of hypertext, so has the title of the librarian. We speak now of information professionals, business intelligence managers. super searchers, information analysts, competitive intelligence specialists, etc. These new professions have grown to serve companies that are increasingly aware that they can and must utilize intelligence disciplines to keep them aware of what their competitors, their markets and their suppliers are doing and how these activities could affect them in the future [12].

The great professional knowledge of librarians and access to their personal networks will always be needed. As can be learnt from history by the outstanding examples of famous librarians and their extensive personal networks demonstrated earlier, it could be maintained that the librarian himself creates his own job market.

References

[1]   *Museum Mazzuchellianum.* Venetis 1763. T.2, p. 233.

[2]   *Necrologium Lundense.* L. Weibull (Ed.), (1923) Lund, p. 33.

[3]   National information policy and the impact of social and technological change on national information planning. An advanced working seminar (The Tell Seminar), John Vaughan (Ed.) (1973) Canberra, National Library of Australia, pp. 157.

[4]   Servan-Schreiber, J.-J. (1969) *Le défi américain.* Paris.

[5]   Information for a changing society. Some policy considerations. Rapporteur B.V. Tell, (1971) Paris, OECD pp. 48.

[6]   UNISIST. Study Report on the feasibility of a World Science Information System. Unesco (1971) Paris, pp. 161.

[7]   Milstead, J.L. (1998) Thesauri in a Full-Text World. In: *Visualizing Subject Access for 21st Century Information Resources.* P. Atherton Cochrane & E.H. Johnson (Eds.) Urbana, Graduate School of Library and Information Science, p. 30.

[8]   Fidel, R. & Crandall, *The Role of Subject Access in Information Filtering.* Op.cit. p. 16.

[9]   *Intelligence for Economic Development.* Dedijer, S. & Jéquier, N. (Eds.) (1987) Oxford, Berg, p. 264.

[10]   Colby, W.E. Comprehensive Intelligence for Advancement. In: *Intelligence for Economic Development.* Op.cit. p. 44.

[11]   Hamrefors, S. (1999) *Spontaneous environmental scanning. Putting "putting into perspective" into perspective.* Thesis. Stockholm, Stockholm School of Economics, EFI.

[12]   Colby, W.E., Privatizing intelligence. In: *Intelligence for Economic Development.* Op.cit. p. 17-22.

A Century of Science Publishing
E.H. Fredriksson (Ed.)
IOS Press, 2001

Chapter 21

Peer Review: The Holy Cow of Science

Jaap de Vries
Publishing Consultant, The Netherlands

Introduction

Success in science depends as much on the scientist's ingenuity as on recognition of his or her achievements by colleagues. Positive evaluation of established results by one's superiors is the basis of any career. Published reports of recent findings, clearly having survived critical examination by outsiders, are its stepping stones. The sum total of admitted publications is the canonization of science. Peer review is the name of the infrastucture which supports the system.

Tens of thousands of scientific journals, in one form or another, delegate decisions on what to publish and what not to peer reviewers. Widely acknowledged as this practice may be. it is under attack. There is much dissatisfaction with the results, bitterly characterized by one of its critics as suppressing novel ideas and enforcing the rules set by a scientific oligarchy. Biotech and pharmaceutical companies may side-step the scrutiny of peers by keeping important scientific developments secret or making them public in the 'popular' press to boost their stock value. The system is undermined by the potential of the Internet to make instant and unsupervised publishing facilities available to all. Yet, not many editorial boards of scientific journals have shown awareness of the weaknesses of peer review by moderating its autocratic character. Industrial innovations will anyhow have to pass judgment by independent experts before being admitted to the market. And even the most fervent advocates of Internet freedom despair of the anarchy which would result from unlimited dissemination of scientific contributions.

1. Peer prerogatives

The development of scientific communication in the western world initially rested on Latin as the Lingua Franca. Throughout the Renaissance, travel, studying facsimiles in cloyster libraries, and attending lectures by famous scientists had been the only way to further one's understanding of nature and people. The educated few kept in touch with each other through correspondence and and travelling students, forming international schools of learning. The invention of the printing process opened the doors and let the less privileged in. Gradually, knowledge spread. For many of the new intellectuals, experimentalists and inventors using a language different from their own to publicize their exploits would be a waste of energy. The drive of these newcomers, patriotic sentiments and a general humanistic mood made Latin lose its right of way. However, in the heartlands of Europe growing interests in biology, mathematics, astronomy, physics and mechanical matters were shared by many. Linguistic borders could not remain closed. Polyglots like Marin Mersenne in Paris and Henry Oldenburg in London found ways to satisfy the urge for knowledge by inviting, translating and distributing personal communiciations from scientists everywhere.

Mersenne (1588–1648), a monk belonging to the Franciscan order of the Minims, made his cell in the monastry near the Place des Vosges in Paris the center of intellectual development, in France as well as in Western Europe. No inventor himself, his inquisitiveness was inspired by his religion. He felt that the discoveries of scientists would confirm the truths of his belief. He was a man of great personal charm and in his cell he entertained many of the great names of his days. His correspondence served to keep him appraised of as many novelties as his legion of admirers could muster and he himself distributed the news to whom it might concern.

One of his correspondents was the son of a German professor of medicine, who had found a niche in the scientific community in London. This man of many languages and immense curiosity was Henry Oldenburg (1617?–1677) a born diplomat and teacher. He became acting secretary to the Royal Society when this was established in 1662, and his communicative skills soon extended the Society as a meeting of persons into an 'invisible college': letters from all parts of Western Europe provided the subjects for discussion in the weekly meetings of the London group. Letters then became a medium in itself, their flow and contents moderated by Oldenburg. In 1665 he published, on his own accord, transcripts, if necessary translated into English, in a monthly journal, which he named *Phililosophical Transactions*: giving some accompt of the present Undertakings, Studies and Labours of the Ingenious in many Considerable Parts of the World.

Among Oldenburg's considerations there was one which appealed strongly to the scientists of his day. By making their findings public they could ascertain ownership. With so many industrious thinkers and experimentalists in so many countries, working in so restricted an area as science then was, similar paths inevitably led to similar results. Establishing priority was fundamental. Private correspondence or oral communications could not serve this purpose. Oldenburg first devised a scheme by which preliminary notes could be put in a sealed box in the

Royal Society's safe. But in his journal the date of the claim could publicly be tied down to the time of receipt. This feature of the printed paper has not lost significance. Today's peer reviewed scientific journals still stamp original articles with the date of receipt. Since so many other methods of distributing news are en vogue (conferences, pre- and e-prints) it can be argued that archiving is becoming their main function. According to the *Journal of Electronic Publishing* (1998; 4/2) already forty percent of all journal readings concern articles older than the current year and twenty percent of the consultations go back four to fifteen years.

Mersenne and Oldenburg, moderating the news on seventeenth-century's innovations, in terms of today acted primarily as editors or journalists. Their personal vision on what was important or not has, however, had major implications on the directions in which science expanded. This responsibility now rests on the editors of scientific journals. A few society journals excepted, most of them have delegated this to their advisers, their peer reviewers. Typically, for journals with international readership these are scientists of repute, affiliated to scientific organisations of considerable renown, (usually) department heads, male and of Scandinavian, German, Dutch, British or North American origin. Nobel Prize winners are the 'crème de la crème'. In the self-propelling world of science, as represented by today's typical scientific publication, the peers of today are yesterday's most cited authors in their fields. Today's most cited authors wil be tomorrow's peers. It all revolves around professional proficiency, sharing specific research traditions, the availability of money, publications in leading journals, honours received. There is more to peerdom than reviewing papers. Peers also award funds and/or promotions. In the literature some see science as a hierarchy run by one or more power elites, who control both the rewards and the means of publication.

Recognition by one's equals is the key to peerdom, knowing which ropes to pull and not treading on important toes are further requisites. Peers are network builders and when someone is asked to review a paper he carefully checks how his judgments may affect his position. The names of the authors may have been removed and he may exercise his judications in anonimity — for the insider the subject of the research and the bibliography cannot be mistaken as signs of its origin. Perhaps, in the future, this publishing party may be asked to review the paper that this reviewer or his group has in store. Are there any old scores to be settled? Conflicts of interest to be taken into account?

There are many different types of journals in many different scientific disciplines. If we assume that a journal publishing one thousand articles per year has a list of three hundred and fifty reviewers to draw from and that every article is seen by two of them, every reviewer will judge on average six papers per year. If all five hundred thousand articles published in the peer reviewed journals were to receive the same treatment, this would amount to sixty thousand peer/paper contacts and involve ten thousand peers. Since there are approximately five hundred thousand scientists active as authors (each producing four papers as a member of a team of four) to be on a reviewers' panel means that one is in the top five percent of scientists. Gross as these approximations may be (is it perhaps the top ten percent?) this is why peers do not demand payment and, on the contrary, invest an average of three hours of their (organisation's) time in the article under review. Affirmation of their status and foreknowledge of the accomplishments of their colleagues/competitors are their rewards. Hard pressed for time as he may be, a scientist asked to review a paper very rarely refuses to do so. The smaller the discipline, the higher the scientist's standing, the more he is besieged. Nobel Prize winners can afford to refuse or name a replacement, important department heads may farm (part of) the job out to their subordinates and the depth of the review is of course a referee's responsibility, but it would seem that a call to review is hard to ignore. In the end a reviewer is found for every single article of the hundreds of thousands published each year in the thousands of peer-reviewed journals.

2. Reviewing papers

Science as published in journals with international distribution is a representation of the beliefs of a specific group of scientists that their interests can be expanded if a given set of rules is followed. These rules are of Western European provenance, deterministic in essence, emphasizing linearity of approach. Every secret can be unraveled. There is no effect without a cause. What our senses do not perceive cannot be known. Findings are valid only if verified through replication. A scientist spurning these rules will be ridiculed or ignored. And it is part of the game that anyone's claim will meet with scepticism until substantiated by someone else. This is most true for 'hard' science such as (bio)chemistry and physics, and mostly true for the life sciences, such as (clinical) medicine and pharmacology. But where 'power elites' are in disagreement over the basic rules, as often happens in the behavioral sciences, the fight for a place on the forum between rivals may end in a feud.

The peer reviewer is in the center of it all. The harder the science, the clearer the rules, the easier this gatekeeper's job. He will focus on matters of interpretation rather than on procedures as his colleague for a psychology journal may feel compelled to do. He will reject fewer papers because his authors respect the framework he himself helped to construct. His mind will only be challenged occasionally when a paper leads to conclusions for which on first sight the arguments challenge the familiar logic. Is the author a step ahead of the rest of the field? Is he a crank? A genius? It is every reviewer's nightmare to reject a paper that later will appear to have revolutionised the world. However, as a rule, the reviewer is said to be wary of novelties; progress in the discipline should be orderly and not cause eyebrows to be raised.

On its way to print a manuscript will be scrutinized by a reviewer only if it has passed the journal editor's first appraisal. It may be rejected outright if it is obviously flawed or deals with a topic clearly outside the journal's scope. If admissible it is dispatched to the reviewers. Most journals select two reviewers for each paper. The selection is usually a match between the editor's impression of the article's subject, the ramifications of the bibliography and his knowledge of the competence of his reviewers. A former editor of the journal *Science*, Floyd Bloom, used as selection criteria the following questions. Who is a peer of this author in content area, in technique and when possible in experience? Which reviewers should be avoided for competitive conflicts and past disputes? How much of the submittal's data can one expect the reviewer to examine in detail? For example, should the statistical conclusions be re-calculated?

The *Journal of the American Medical Association* (*JAMA*) published instructions for peer reviewers. They should judge if the manuscript's contents are original, if the data are valid, if the conclusions are reasonable and justified, if the information is important, if the article is of general medical interest and if the writing is clear or can be made clear. Some journals may also request their reviewers to adequately support their judgments, and to be alert to the failure of authors to cite relevant work by other scientists, to respect the confidentiality of the manuscript under review and to return the manuscript immediately to the editor if a conflict of interest is apparent.

Imponderables are characteristic for the reviewer's work. There is no universal standard procedure. No studies are available to clarify the exact decision making process. The least that can be said is that, as in any human diagnostic activity, there must be false-positive and false-negative outcomes, leading to erroneous recommendations. Disagreement between reviewers is common and perhaps partly due to this.

If reviewers disagree the editor may want to consult a third reviewer or decide himself. Otherwise papers are accepted, with or without modification, or rejected. The reviewers' comments are passed on to the authors. It is not uncommon that a paper revised by its author, on reappraisal by the reviewers needs another revision followed by yet another re-appraisal. No wonder that between the date of receipt of the first version and the date of publication in these instances delays of as much as a year occur. In less problematic circumstances time lags of three to six months are the rule rather than the exception, the main cause being reviewers' overload or inertia. Authors hate these delays. Journal editors try to minimize them as much as possible in order to attract the best papers.

It is often said, but not verifiably, that a paper rejected by one journal eventually finds a place in another. Authors like to begin their publishing spirals by submitting their work to the most influential journal in their field. No wonder that these usually have high rejection rates, some boast seventy five percent. The higher the rejection rate, the more prestigious the journal.

3. Flaws and fallacies

Where, as in most cases, peer reviewers' names are witheld from authors, secrecy is regarded as the best way to ensure objective appraisal of the manuscripts. It is exactly this aspect of the process which elicits severe criticism. Some see it as diametrically opposed to the openness, freedom of speech and mutual trust which the academic community has proclaimed as universal ideals. They say its rationale is to obscure conflicts of interest of a personal, collegial, or financial nature and editorial responsibility. They quote a series of illustrious cases were faulty papers were admitted and later had to be disavowed but no one in particular could be blamed. Nobody knows who has been responsible for rejecting papers which later proved to be classics, such as listed in Campanario's article with the rhetoric title 'Have referees rejected some of the most cited articles of all times?' (*Journal of the American Society for Information Science*, 1996; 47/4, 303–310)

Some journals have adopted a 'double blind' reviewing process. Names of authors and their affiliations are concealed. Ideally, eliminating these elements would free the reviewers from possible prejudices. Investigations of the procedure have produced different outcomes. Some indicate that referees are more citical if they don't know the author's identity, which would result in lower acceptance rates for authors not belonging to the top-ranked universities. Often, however, reviewers are able to identify the author on the basis of clues in the bibliography, or personal knowledge of the author's work. Generally, the advantages of the double blind method have not been so convincing as to convert the majority of editorial boards to adapt their approach.

Acting as reviewers, eminent scientists sometimes reveal their human sides. Anecdotes dealing with errors made and prejudices shown could fill a book.

There was the well documented trick Douglas P. Peters and Stephen J. Ceci pulled on a range of reputable psychology journals. They resubmitted twelve research papers from prestiguous departments which these journals had published some time earlier. Names of institutes and authors had been changed into fictitious ones. Only three of the thirty six editors and reviewers of these journals detected the fraud. Of the nine articles left, eight were rejected, in many cases 'because of serious methodological flaws'.

Reviewers, obviously receiving papers in fields in which they are active themselves, may in their own work benefit from the information in these papers. There was the twelve year battle between Immunex and Cistron, ending in Immunex paying twenty one million dollars to Cistron in damages and handing over the patent rights to the interleukin-1 protein. Settled out of court the dispute centered on the fact that the journal Nature had sent for review an article submitted by a Cistron-sponsored team to an employee of Immunex and that subsequently Immunex had filed patent applications concerning this protein, in which some of the errors made in the article were replicated.

There was the complaint of the Brazilian biochemist Franklin D. Rumjanek who upon his return to Rio de Janeiro after having worked in England for six years and having published (in his own words) a 'reasonable' amount of papers, found that he had serious problems in getting his manuscripts accepted: neither the policies of the journals to which they were submitted, nor the quality of his work had changed.

In 1977 Rosalyn S. Yalow won the Nobel Prize for her work on the radioimmunoassay of a group of hormones, the first report of which some twenty years earlier had been turned down five times by different journals.

In an article analyzing the reviewing process for her own journal, Susan van Rooyen of the editorial board of the highly esteemed *British Medical Journal* (*BMJ*) to which yearly some five thousand papers are submitted concludes: "The process is by its very nature subjective, prone to error, or more kindly, to the kind of variation expected of any diagnostic test". The journal had after normal peer review, accepted a paper on risk factors for death in the elderly. The same paper was then sent to four hundred and twenty potential reviewers from the *BMJ* database; in it eight errors were introduced. Of the two hundred and twenty one who responded, none identified all mistakes and only a few spotted more than two or three of them.

Bias was so prevalent in their disciplines that they felt that the peer review system merited reform. This was the opinion of some forty percent of the responders to a survey conducted in 1989 among five thousand scientists by the Office of Scholarly Communication of the American Council of Learned Societies (ACLS). Of these almost two thirds responded.

Peer review is also felt to obstruct the publishing process. The Assocation of Learned and Professional Society Publishers (ALPSP) in 1998/1999 undertook a study on the motivations and concerns of contributors to learned journals. The members of this association sent almost eleven thousand questionnaires to contributing authors. Over three thousand were returned. Of these almost eighteen percent mentioned peer review as a major obstacle in their publishing endeavors. A major reason of concern was the delay caused by the reviewers followed by superficiality of reviews, hostile reviews and of unqualified reviewers. The responders also had the opportunity of making additional comments about the peer review system. To quote from the ALPSP's report: "...the issue of reviewer anonimity was raised quite frequently and there were comments both for and against it...the superficiality of reviews was cited as a concern and also a disappointment...there were quite a few comments which centered upon the dismissive attitude of reviewers to work from authors who were based outside the major centers of excellence".

4. Added value

On the steep road to success a scientist's first publication is an important step. Publishing results of one's work is the accepted escape from mediocracy. The paper is perhaps not immediately noted by every colleague everywhere in the world. But it is essential in getting a foothold in the faculty or department. Without publications to show young scientists may be asked to leave after a couple of years. And for promotion or a move the longer the list the better the opportunities. There is of course a difference in the ranking of the journals a manuscript can be submitted to, but everyone knows how difficult it is to pass the threshold of the top ones — the list must be built in any case.

A second basic and historically more prominent reason to publish is the scientist's aim to be associated with the developments in his field. Some will end with their name attached to a theory or discovery but every scientist regards the results of his findings as his own and seeks universal acclaim for them. Since many people (teams) may be on the same path towards the claimed results, it is important to be recognised as the first person (team) who made these public. Although for (potentially) lucrative inventions patents now serve as the safest way to secure property rights, in this respect not much has changed since Oldenburg's day.

Scientific journals accommodate the need to be visible and to put one's stamp on science. They provide a permanent record of the scientist's achievements. Important as they may be for career advancement, formal, peer reviewed publications are by no means the sole source of scientific information.

Science is, perhaps before all, a personal thing: a universe peopled with inquisitive, ambitious, competitive, often egotistic human beings. They need to look each other in the face, hear each other speak, be member of the group, draw attention of their peers, become peers themselves. Each person's efforts rest on a fundament of earlier endeavors. These are usually in the public domain. Other people may be building on them too. It is risky not knowing what people with similar interests are doing. It is also dangerous to deviate from mainstream research. Communication is the name of the game. There is more to it than publishing, for instance the meetings and symposia industry. International meetings in major interest areas easily attract twenty to thirty thousand attendees. Every self respecting subdiscipline of two hundred devotees meets every two to four years. A mid-sized congress brings two to three thousand persons together. One wonders what would happen to the airline and hotel businesses if scientists stayed home. But without the thousands and thousands of presentations, panel discussions and poster sessions featured by these meetings — not to mention personal contacts during breaks, at receptions and in bars — the grounded scientists would also suffer badly. Informal information, intelligence, is the butter on their bread.

But keeping informed begins at the working place. Colleagues have eyes and ears too. Coffee corners, departmental lunches, informal get togethers, briefings, budget discussions, collective research are situations in which information abounds. Preprints of articles intended to be published and received by (e)mail from colleagues for comment can also be an excellent source. Peer reviewed journals complete the spectrum. It is however not necessary, not even possible, to read all that is published in one's field. In most working places keeping up with the literature is delegated to a number of colleagues. In this respect the librarian (information officer) often plays a key role by alerting his patronage according to the interest profiles they have made known. Scanning citations and abstracts has become an art by itself. It is also no uncommon practice to glimpse at the contents lists of those few journals one trusts to publish leading papers, or issued by the society one is a member of. One may restrict one's reading to articles originated in specific institutes or even to those with familiar authors' names. And it is often quite possible to stay aware of developments by not seeing primary journals at all but reading review articles, meta research and digests in special journals or serial book publications, materials which may have been authored by peers but have escaped peer review as such.

Peer reviewed articles are the outer shell of the learned world. They apotheosize the power elites and are instrumental in the distribution of funds. To advance the insider's knowledge they are less essential. Science as the expression of human curiosity and industrial impetus will not be doomed if peer review dissipates. This might even be a blessing in disguise, at least for the medical community. The British Medical Journal's editors have boldly stated that peer review is erroneously credited as "being a good method of keeping poor quality work from publication, whereas the evidence suggests that with persistence even the most flawed work will eventually find a home. Considerably less than five percent of papers in current journals contain a message that is both scientifically sound and relevant to doctors".

5. Horror vacui

Opportunities to publish in journals have always been regulated by the inherent constraints of the medium. There was an end to the amount of paper which could economically be distributed. Contrary to a popular misbelief commercial science publishers did not expand their positions rigorously, cheating the academic library out of their last cent. Anyone involved in this business has an archive of non viable proposals, pushed upon them by members of the scientific community's subdivisions in dire need of establishing their own specialty journal. Commercial publishers certainly pulled a few tricks which earned them a reputation of greediness. But there must have been benefits for the other party as well. And as quasi monopolists they do not in principle differ from journal-publishing learned societies. If 'there is no such thing as a free lunch' there is also no such thing as a publication designed to make a loss.

It is no wonder that if the Internet is felt to threaten the existence of printed journals, publishers whatever their lineage find themselves in the same boat. What they are facing has been outlined by a working group composed of members of the American Association for the Advancement of Science and the (British) International Council for Science which in 1999 presented a proposal on standards and practices for electronic publishing in science to the International Association of Scientific, Technical and Medical Publishers (STM) [see Ch. 25]. Internet offers many advantages to the individual who wants to make his ideas public. The added value of the electronic medium was summed up. The speed with which it can disseminate information The size of the audience it can reach efficiently. The enhanced indexing and search capabilities. The hypertext linkages to a wide range of material. The ability to be updated and corrected as needed. The interactivity, which enables real-time exchanges between authors and readers. The multimedia functions incorporating video and sound into text.

Publishers of traditional media may read this as follows. Every scientist, crank or genius, neophyte or professional, may freely publicize his accomplishments with features they cannot (unless at great cost) provide. Their quasi monopolies will flop. Is it strange that they find many influential scientists (openly or discreetly) on their side? Peers have much to loose too. It is they who are editors of the journals (often at substantial remuneration). They are sitting on editorial boards. They are reviewing the articles submitted to the journals they serve. But these journals also serve them, making them visible as the top of their league and giving them the power to decide on what will be published and how. They can make or break careers.

The publisher-peer complex has one last line of defence. Scientific publications cannot be taken seriously if not peer reviewed. The line has its weaknesses. Publications can be scientifically valid if not vetted by peers. Ironically, this was the outcome of the brainstorming of the same STM working group. They specified that for any document to be considered as a valid scientific publication it must be durably recorded on some medium. It must be publicly available (not necessarily free of charge). It should remain in the same form and at the same location, so that it is reliably accessible and retrievable over time. A bibliographic record must be attached to the document and if new versions appear, to each of these. Versions should be certified as authentic and protected from change (even when occasioned by the author).

The proposal of the working group mentions quality control (in whatever form) as a necessary feature only for documents which, after having progressed from a preliminary to a definitive stage are meant to "contribute to the production of useful knowledge" and thus must be certified. "To maximize its usefulness for science, a publication needs to have been vetted to ensure qualitiy and to establish a high level of trust among readers. This process is equally essential for electronic documents — indeed perhaps more so in view of the vast quantity of available information." Certification is, however, not regarded as a prerogative of the traditional peer reviewer. The proposal entrusts publishers, authors, professional organisations, research and archival institutions, funders of research with future quality control and with organizing the relevant infrastructure.

But here is the twist. The (STM) publishers' admonitions are not supported by the broader scientific community. In the ALPSP study referred to above significant concern was expressed that peer review should continue, "as its loss would be very detrimental to the quality of published work". Almost seventy percent of the responders were satisfied with the system in general terms against thirty percent who were more or less dissatisfied. Recommendations for improvement were rare. "Only a few people said that the idea of electronic peer review is appealing." And: "Overall, the only scenario that all authors would like to see happen more than it is at present is open peer review post publication". What they perhaps had in mind is something like the succesful (but time-consuming) editorial process adapted by the journal *Behavioral and Brain Sciences*, where printed articles are co-published with up to 30 peer commentaries, plus the author's response. As the editor, Stevan Harnad notes: "Peer commentary is no substitute for peer review; the journal is very rigorously peer reviewed. The Internet offers the possibility of implementing peer review more efficiently and equitably and of supplementing it with what is the net's real revolutionary dimension: interactive publication in the form of open peer commentary on published work."

6. Peers will be peers

The number of (refereed) electronic journals in science, engineering and medicine has increased rapidly in recent years An electronic repository of preprints (the Los Alamos Physics Eprint Archive) pioneered by physicist Paul Ginsparg receives some 2500 submissions and services 30.000 hosts a week. It forced the American Physical Society to open an Internet link between one of its journals and the archive, also making manuscripts available before peer review. The interactivity, which is a basic element of the archive, in some aspects fulfills (peer) review functions. Authors are reported to be meticulous in updating their articles with changes suggested by colleagues. The project obviously benefits from the traditional self-discipline of physicists, which earned them low rejection rates in peer reviewed journals. It may be difficult to copy in areas where seventy five percent of submissions to journals is returned to the authors on first sight.

This is, however, exactly what is going on at the moment. As a director of the National Institutes of Health, Harold Varmus in 1998 created turmoil by planning to establish a stand-alone pre-print server for non-reviewed articles. He was subsequently forced to incorporate the concept into the existing PubMed bibliographic service of the National Library of Medicine, but the beginning was there. It may gain momentum by an initiative, which in 2000 intended to attract groups of researchers wanting to create their own niche journals on-line and allowing pre-prints to be stored in and retrieved from an e-print server closely co-operating with PubMed. Initiator Vitek Tracz, has already made his marks in the publishing industry. With BioMedCentral he promises to "make the publishing process much more efficient and flexible in both format and economic terms". Research reports should be published electronically with all the features the medium allows and be "available to all — globally, free and without barriers tot access". Will it work? It had not exactly a flying start. Equally hesitant to burn their ships behind them seemed scientists when, late in 2000, challenged by Varmus (by then ex-NIH) to refuse cooperation with publishers who would not make their publications freely available on PubMed six months after the date of publication. Varmus may have misjudged politically inspired misgivings regarding the monopoly the US-based repository would have. He may have underestimated the toughness of publisher/editor/author allegiances, embedded in years and years of intellecual, professional and financial interdependency. But publishers were scared. There will be quite a few authors who simply do not appreciate the complexity of the marketplace. There will also be 'maverick' reviewers: those without established positions in the publisher-peer complex, dissatisfied with the way things work and believing that they should be paid for their efforts. And what about librarians who will cancel subscriptions on journals if the contents of these will be freely available? How crucial is a six month delay anyway for most printed publications if there are so many other ways of spreading vital news? If the number of responders to Varmus' call will gain critical mass commercial and institutional publishing traditons will fade away. And how will this affect the peers?

The editors of the *British Medical Journal,* when denouncing the value of peer review did so on the occasion of introducing an e-print server for clinical medicine and health research. They chose as a title for their article: Moving beyond journals: the future arrives with a crash. Prediction or prophecy? Perhaps just a premonition phrased to shock indolent readers. In their article a dichotomy between researchers and practicians is revealed. The latter "are likely to continue to want to receive predigested, well presented accounts of research that matters for their practice… a role that journals are likely to continue to have in the future". This does not sound like slamming doors in peer reviewers' faces. The distinction between researchers and practicians is also somewhat casual. It is self evident that in well-delineated scientific (sub)disciplines validation and presentation of preliminary research reports is subordinate to their 'news-value' and that e-print facilities will be appreciated. But the existence of peer-reviewed journals in heavily researched areas demonstrates that the availability of 'predigested, well presented accounts' is not without some consequence.

The balance between authors, peers and publishers is precious. It may shift. But will peers lose their pivotal role? Scientists use alternative validation systems in their day-to-day routines. For these to replace peer-reviewing, albeit in categorial environments such as specific disciplines or professional organisations, they need to be accepted as trustworthy. Adequate infrastructures must be established. The Internet may facilitate all this. But more is needed than isolated initiatives to cannibalize functioning validation structures such as the reviewing of scientific papers. Peerdom may don a different cloak but organized science needs its hierarchies.

Related readings

[1]   Bloom, F. (1998) *Human reviewers: The Achilles Heel of Scientific Journals in a Digital Area.* Presented at INABIS'98 – 5th Internet World Congress on Biomedical Sciences at McMaster University, Canada, Dec 7–16th. Keynote Address.

[2]   Boorstyn, D.J. (1991) *The Discoverers.* Harry N. Abrams Inc., New York.

[3]   Editorial, (1999) Moving beyond journals: the future arrives with a crash. *BMJ*, **318**, 1637–1639.

[4]   Daniel, H.D. (1993) *Guardians of Science.* VCH, Weinheim.

[5]   Harnad, S. (1998) Learned inquiry and the Net: the role of peer review, peer commentary and copyright. *Learned Publishing*, **11**, 283–292.

[6]   Lundberg, D. and Williams, E. (1991) The Quality of a Medical Article. *JAMA*, **265/9**, 1161–1162.

[7]   Meadows, A.J. (1974) Competition and the urge to publish. In: *Communication in Science.* ch. 2, pp. 35–65.

[8]   Moran, G. (1998) *Silencing Scientists and Scholars in other fields, etc;* Ablex Publishing Corporation, Greenwich Connecticut, London, England.

[9]   Peek, R.P. and Newby G.B. (1996) *Scholarly publishing: the electronic frontier.* American Society for Information Science, The MIT Press, Cambridge Massachusetts, London, England.

[10]   Peters, J. (1995) The hundred years war started today: an exploration of electronic peer review, *Internet Research, Electronic Networking Applications and Policy,* **5/4**, 3–9.

[11]   The Association of Learned and Professional Society Publishers, (1999) *What authors want.*

A Century of Science Publishing
E.H. Fredriksson (Ed.)
IOS Press, 2001

Chapter 22
Watersheds in Scientific Journal Publishing

Jamie Cameron
Publishing Consultant, UK

The history and development of scientific journals is slow and gradual as often happens in other walks of life, but there are two periods of concentrated change where many things changed quite quickly. The first of these was around the middle of the last century after World War II, and the second in the late 1990's. The first centres on the explosion of Scientific, Technological and Medical Research and tertiary education in these areas, which occurred in the late 1940's and 1950's. The second is the advent of the Internet. Behind these two periods of accelerated change are economic, behavioural and technological considerations. For the first, the widespread economic growth after the war made possible the growth of scientific research, amounting to an explosion, and a similar growth in tertiary education — the last, of course, not limited to the sciences. In the behavioural area the issue of validation and authentication was increasing in importance and there was growing pressure for research workers to publish their work in refereed journals. The main issues of publishing technology were in the production of journals, where the move away from hot metal was beginning. Another factor for the significant growth in the middle of the 20th century was the impetus the war provided, largely for the applied sciences.

We can look relatively calmly and dispassionately at what happened in the middle of the last century. However, we are still in the middle of the Internet revolution and no one can forecast the outcome — not that it stops a number of people trying, with varying degrees of vociferation and widely differing if not contradictory conclusions!

For the second watershed, the main issue is, of course, technological with the advent of the Internet. Economics also play a part because the infrastructure of the Internet was available to research workers, funded by governments, and therefore did not require a significant investment from the Institutions, whether academic or industrial, where research was taking place. As far as behavioural aspects are concerned the electronic availability of journal material enables research workers in different subject areas to use this material differently. Before the availability of the facility of the Internet different disciplines used journal literature in broadly similar ways, whereas now significant differences are emerging. For example, Physicists use non-refereed pre-prints much more than other disciplines; Biomedical researchers require as short as possible a gap between completing research and "publishing" the results as the subject progresses with increasing speed.

The first watershed: post-war explosive growth

We should now look in more detail at the tremendous changes that took place in growth and development of journals and journal publishing in the decades immediately following the war. There was essentially an explosion of progress in science, technology and medicine in the 1950's, 1960's and 1970's. It was realised that the raising of educational standards was essential to cope with the increasing technical demands of modern society. This pressure was not, of course, limited only to science, technology and medicine.

The war itself played a significant part in this as it placed a tremendous emphasis on research and technology to a much greater extent than any previous conflict. For example the invention and development of the jet engine led to a revolution in air transport. The devising and breaking of codes, in which Bletchley Park in the UK was prominent, accelerated the development of computer science and technology. The harnessing of atomic energy led to the widespread use of nuclear power and energy in various areas. The invention of penicillin revolutionised the treatment of infection and led to the development of the growing family of antibiotics, which are now in widespread use.

This situation also led to an unprecedented increase in the numbers of institutions of tertiary education, where the sciences and technology were arguably predominant. Another example was the US government's commitment to college education for those leaving the Armed Forces — The Veterans Bill — which led to the growth of existing universities as well as the establishment of many new ones. However, the phenomenon was universal throughout the developed world.

Following on from this came, of course, a comparable growth in research, largely government-financed, but with occasional grants from industry. Also, a growth in the number of government research establishments, where there was a large amount of unclassified work, which could be freely published. The same also applied to research establishments set up or developed by science based industry in, for example, electronics and pharmaceuticals. This led, of course, to a tremendous increase in the output of research papers and an increased sub-division of traditional subject areas.

Up until the war the vast majority of STM research had been published by the learned societies but they were slow to adapt to these radical changes in the ever increasing needs of people to publish refereed papers as well as to consult them. There were a number of reasons for this. They tended to be unable, or unwilling, to make the investment required in launching a new journal or indeed significantly expanding an existing one. They argued, in many cases quite justifiably, that the funds generated by a successful journal should not be reinvested in the journal, or indeed new journals, but should be spent on benefits to members. Also, the decision-making process tended to be bureaucratic with the necessity for consultation with publication committees, council etc., while it became increasingly obvious that, to be successful, decisions on launching journals had to be taken quickly, to satisfy in a fairly objective way the demands of research workers in a rapidly growing area, as well as to pre-empt activity by other publishers. Publishing is essentially an extremely entrepreneurial activity, and a risk taking one, and this does not always sit happily in the structure of a learned society. In time many societies separated their publishing activities from the main work of the society and established them as separate commercial organisations. An example of this is The Institute of Physics Publishing in the UK, which is run almost entirely separately from the Institute of Physics. Nevertheless, by all these arrangements the profits from the publishing activity went directly to the society. Finally, societies at this stage were very national in their outlook and again it became increasingly clear that journal publishing had to be international in aspect to be successful. This is not to say, of course, that societies do not still hold a significant position. Their number has increased to reflect the emergence of different subject areas. Indeed, one can argue that in the current debate about methods of publication, they have increased in prominence and importance by asserting the moral high ground which is attractive to research workers, particularly in academic life.

The role of university presses at this time should be considered. Apart from Oxford University Press and Cambridge University Press in the UK, operating to all intents and purposes like commercial publishers and well established in producing books and journals in Science, Technology and Medicine as well as the humanities, the most significant growth place took in the USA. This is not say, of course, that they do not exist elsewhere in the world making valuable contributions to knowledge. The emphasis tended to be in the humanities with greater concentration on books rather than journals and particularly those books with more limited appeal which were therefore less attractive to commercial publishers.

It also became clear that the whole area of scientific, technical and medical research could no longer be simply national and had to be conducted with international co-operation. It also emerged that the language of science was English, largely due to the prominence of the USA, owing to its sheer size and the fact that it had suffered significantly less economically than Europe during the war.

At the time there was an incredible opportunity for the growth of journals featuring primary research (in the English language), when those people pushing back the frontiers of knowledge wanted to publish the results of their research. The gap was largely filled by commercial publishers whose lists blossomed in the 1950's and 1960's. Again, notable examples are Pergamon, Blackwell Scientific Publishers, North Holland (developed from the Royal Netherlands Academy of Sciences) and Elsevier. Initially, commercial journal publishing was essentially a European phenomenon, because in the USA this activity was dominated by the large learned societies, with a market and pool for authors of one language, whereas Europe operated with a multiplicity of national languages — varying, of course, in importance in research and publication. The majority of American journal publishers in this area were run by European ex-patriots, examples of whom are Walter Johnson and Bill Jovanovitch with Academic Press, Eric Proskauer and Mauritz Dekker with Interscience. Indeed many commercial publishers on both sides of the Atlantic were initially not comfortable with journals. Wiley very nearly sold the journals of Interscience when it acquired the company, and took many years, if not decades, to exploit this very profitable activity which was led by its European office where people were more sympathetic to journal publishing. An exception to this was W.B. Saunders, the medical commercial publisher, who began to launch journals at the same sort of time as the Europeans.

Another opportunity presented itself by the policy of some commercial publishers, of which Blackwell Scientific and Pergamon are obvious examples, to publish journals on behalf of societies as a way of entering this lucrative field. Depending on the terms negotiated with the society, a reasonable profit could be made in the first year, but launching an independent journal would take possibly three years to become profitable, extending to five in the 1980's. Additionally, as it became clear that journal publishing, as with other STM publishing, required particular skills which were invariably not present in a learned society, professional publication of their journals became attractive to them. For some years it had been traditional for learned societies to look to their journal publishing programme for financial support, and the professional skills of running a publishing operation became more appreciated. It is also seen as a way of optimising the financial contribution this activity made to the society. Book publishing made a much smaller contribution and was only practised by a minority of societies and that to a much lesser extent.

A vivid illustration of the learned societies' attitude to journal publishing is presented by the Interscience polymer science journals. The American Chemical Society did not recognise the potential of this area of chemistry. It left the way clear for the establishment and growth of the Interscience journals in polymer science, which rapidly became the established international forum for papers in this area.

There are two other factors, which significantly influenced the development of journal publishing at this time and indeed are still significant today. The first of these was the fact that society publishers tended to impose rather strict limits on the length of the papers that they would publish. In many cases this was unrealistic and it encouraged research workers to submit their papers to commercial publishers who on the whole were more flexible. Another important phenomenon was the existence of page charges, which authors submitting papers were required to pay to the journal publishers. This applies almost entirely to American publishers and is not widely practised on the eastern side of the Atlantic, at least among commercial publishers. The background is that many research grants included a significant amount of money enabling authors to pay these charges. The practice varies between subject areas and is more common in the pure than applied sciences.

The changes taking place in these decades were more gradual than those immediately following the war. The single most important factor was that during the second half of the 20th century the funds available for research vastly outstripped, by orders of magnitude, the funds available for disseminating the results of that research. Whereas earlier librarians had looked for reasons to subscribe to a journal, they were now looking, with varying degrees of desperation, to find reasons to cancel or not to renew subscriptions. The mechanism for reaching an acquisition decision varied widely, for while the library processed the order, influence varied between the librarian and members of the faculty of university departments. The same is essentially true of classified research, the results of which are not "published" but are simply distributed to a smaller and restricted number of people. The result of all this was that academic libraries became unable to subscribe to all the appropriate journals for the disciplines and research in their institutions. Libraries had become really the only market for journals as the habit of individuals purchasing journal subscriptions had really died out since the war. The only exception to this was the position of members of a learned society where its members could either buy the society journal at significant discounts or even receive it as part of their society subscriptions. Industrial libraries were initially affected by this situation to a lesser extent because of the crucial importance that the development of the research in a particular subject plays in the profitability of a science based industry. Also, in both academic and industrial libraries, the vastly increasing numbers of issues of journals resulting from the growth in research created significant problems for storage and access both for academic and industrial libraries.

It is an obvious point, but not always sufficiently emphasised, that research is valueless if it is not promulgated and communicated to others in the same area, by publication. Indeed, additionally, for serious consideration, this research must be refereed and reviewed for a reputable journal of high standing which has a panel of strict referees. This conflict of interests between the availability of funds to undertake research and those to disseminate it affected everyone in the chain of scholarly communication — authors, editors and referees, publishers, purchasing institutions and finally, readers who, of course, constituted the same population as the authors. Another issue became clear at this period, also not sufficiently recognised, which is that the prime role of the learned refereed journal is one of assessment and validation rather than communication. There are many true and apocryphal stories of the number of readers of the average journal article but it is certainly very small. The only way, in general, that research can be recognised and rewarded is by the publication of refereed papers. The more of these and the better the quality the greater the opportunity of advancement a research worker has in his/her profession. Manifestations of this are promotion to reader or professor in academic life, or tenure if this is an issue, or general increase in profile and reputation leading towards recognition which arguably culminates in rewards like the Nobel Prizes.

No discussion of journal publishing can ignore the rather controversial topic of Impact Factors. Nor indeed can it ignore the role of Gene Garfield and the development of the Institute of Scientific Information (ISI) and *Current Contents*, who first realised the value of abstracts and exploited the commercial opportunity of circulating these to the market place. From these developed the technique "of impact factors", which is essentially a formula for indicating the number of times papers in this journal are referred to or cited elsewhere. While a number of people, publishers, authors and librarians alike, have a rather sceptical view of the value of this, it is nevertheless regarded as a useful yardstick by funding agencies. It has been used by the Research Assessment Exercise in UK when trying to assess the value of the contribution of research workers in a given department and the quality of a journal in which they publish. It is also highly valued by journal editors as the only allegedly objective yardstick for assessing the reputation and standing of their journal, and it is an incentive for authors to publish in those journals with high impact factors. However, the system contains many flaws. In American culture journal papers tend to have many more references than their European counterparts and it is not, alas, unknown for professors to require their research students to refer to their own papers when writing theirs. A classic shortcoming of the system was the work at Southampton University on cold fusion, which, because it was controversial, had very high impact factors even though the research results were soon discredited.

So there was increased pressure on research workers, at least in academic life, to publish papers in refereed journals. The pressure from research workers, who continued to push back the frontiers of Science, Technology and Medicine, continued relentlessly and indeed these areas of activity became more and more important in every day life, commercial and national economic success and in government policy. In spite of criticisms sometimes levelled at journal publishers, the main pressure to start new journals or expand existing ones came from the research community. As the years went by publishers were forced to become rather more cautious about starting new journals. The maximum number of possible subscriptions was reached rather more quickly, in most cases around five years, with the return on investment being harder to achieve with annual profitability coming in three to four years and cumulative profitability perhaps four to six years. There are, of course, significant exceptions to this generalisation. Again, in general, the only way for publishers to increase the profitability of a journal was to increase the size and frequency of the journal (invariably responding to pressure from the research community) and therefore the price, which it was initially possible to do without losing too many subscriptions. As the years went by this dichotomy between the growth in funds for research and the money available for disseminating it and the pressure it created on the market for journals became more intense.

New journals tended to arise either from the growth and expansion of what started off as a fairly specialist subject or where two or more subject areas began to overlap and coalesce. An example of the first is the family of journals published by Wiley on finite elements and computational methods in engineering which spawned sub-divisions devoted to fluids and then geomechanics. An example of the second is the journal published by Wiley on statistics in medicine. People who had qualified in medicine and were doing medical research needed to use the statistics in, for example, epidemiology and the study of infectious diseases, had their papers rejected by the established medical journals because of the mathematical content. On the other hand statisticians who were doing work in the area of medicine were unable to publish their papers in the established statistical journals because they were tainted with obviously practical applications! Apart from being profitable to the publishers this journal has played a significant part in the advance of certain areas of medicine such as cervical smears and the incidence of disease. A significant number, if not the majority, of successful journals, arise from pressure from the research community to start a journal because the existing journals do not cater adequately for their needs; it plays a prime part in the establishment of what is known as the "invisible college", where people throughout the world working in a particular area can make themselves known to each other and then communicate as well as publish their refereed results reasonably quickly. In spite of these initiatives from the research community the reaction from those experts to whom publishers went for advice tended to be negative — "not another journal" — and I have found it quite a useful aphorism to say that a book publishing decision is based on the amount of positive or favourable comment on the idea, but a journal decision is based on the lack of negative reaction! It has certainly worked for me!

It became increasingly difficult for research workers to keep abreast of developments in their fields. Secondary services proliferated and grew in size and importance. Examples are *Chemical Abstracts* run by the American Chemical Society, *Engineering Index* (now *Engineering Village*), the *Commonwealth Agricultural Bureau* (now *CABI*), and *Excerpta Medica*. These disseminated to their subscribers information about journal papers in any given subject area and varied in specialisation. The entries would contain details of the authors of the paper, the summary or abstract, and the key words (now known as 'journal headers') and were operated by learned societies, government or commercial publishers. Some secondary services rewrote the abstracts and others did not. The entries were, of course, indexed in a number of ways to enable the reader to look for a paper or to see what was being published in his/her area of research or even papers by a particular author. These were, of course, originally all in print but were extremely suitable for electronic form and adapted very quickly to the new medium.

This continued growth in published literature and the increase in numbers and sophistication of secondary services has led to the development of the discipline of information science, which more accurately described the increasing demands placed on the librarian, who was required to keep abreast of the unprecedented growth of information and to search for specific items for the research workers.

To try and cope with the plethora of research results and published papers, review journals assumed increased importance, as they constituted a guide to the literature and activities in any particular area. Special issues of existing journals also played a comparable role for those particularly interested in the area covered by the special issues. It became increasingly impossible for the researchers to flick through the tables of contents of the journals in their area to see what papers there were there which might interest them. Whereas this activity of browsing and that of searching for particular papers or papers in a particular area had been closely connected in the past, it now became further separated as the techniques for undertaking them differed. The big disadvantage of this situation, which is generally accepted, is that serendipity, or the chance encounters with unexpected papers possibly in adjacent subject areas, became more and more difficult, if not impossible, for those who did undertake it as the selection of journals they chose to consult had to become more and more limited.

Another development was the increasing importance of letters journals or short communications to overcome the problems of the lapse of time between the completion of research and the writing of the paper and it appearing in published form. This traditionally was nine to twelve months and as much as eighteen to twenty-four months for some society journals, but was significantly improved when the frequency of the journal was monthly or even fortnightly. The pressure was particularly acute in the biological sciences where not only was the development to the subject area extremely fast but additionally, and related closely to it, of course, the importance of attribution of research results to research worker or being "first in the field" was particularly important. These papers often covered partly completed research work and were reviewed particularly quickly and not perhaps as exhaustively as a full-length paper. This form of publication fairly quickly spread from the life sciences to other branches of Science, Technology and Medicine.

The second watershed: the electronic publishing revolution

Before embarking on this complex and crucial topic something has to be said about the dynamics and rather curious economics of journal publishing. We should look at the various parties involved in what is now known as the 'scholarly communication chain' — authors, editors, reviewers, publishers, purchasers (essentially acquisitions librarians in academic life or industry) and finally readers.

First the authors or contributors. What they want from the system is recognition of their work in order to achieve professional advancement which comes from the refereeing process and publication in, ideally, prestigious journals. Additionally, they want the results of their research disseminated to as wide an audience as is reasonably possible, because research which is not promulgated (published) is of no value to a researcher or his institution, and they want to be informed of relevant research results from other parts of the world.

What are referees looking for? By and large the situation is that if they referee other peoples' work, other people will referee theirs ("you scratch my back, I'll scratch yours"). Also, they have a genuine interest in research undertaken by others in similar fields because that is essential to their own progress and advancement.

Editors undertake their task partly for the prestige of being the Editor of a significant journal in the field and this probably particularly applies to journals of important learned societies.

The publishers needs are quite simple — return on investment.

Librarians, apart from the increasing difficulties of managing their budgets and coping with demands for expenditure which exceed their funds available, want a regular, accurate and timely service from the publisher, or rather the subscription agent, which is the organisation they deal with for their journal purchases. This 'trouble free motoring' which is so crucial to them includes such things as accurate information on prices and frequencies well in advance, issues arriving on time as advertised and everything clearly documented. What they do not want, for example, is the insertion of extra issues or volumes of the journal in the middle of the year!

Readers are looking for information, as recent as possible, about research work in their field elsewhere in the world so that they can be kept up to date with developments.

The economics of journal publishing are probably unique. Publishers pay nothing for the raw material and relatively small amounts to editors and referees in view of the amount of work and skills involved, though this becomes less true as and when a journal becomes more profitable for the publisher and some form of profit share becomes possible. Publishers then sell the finished product, in the form of issues and volumes of the published journals.

The electronic revolution affects different subject areas somewhat differently. The main trends apply to all STM journals. I leave aside those serials where assessment is not an issue — e.g., law and finance — which contain high-value and time-sensitive information. The important qualification has to be made that there are significant changes occurring almost every six months and there are significant exceptions to any generalisations that can usefully be made by those who have achieved — or claim to have achieved! — significant progress in understanding and analysing these areas of technology, economics and behaviour.

There is no general agreement on how this revolution will affect the scholarly information chain and there are widely differing and constantly changing views on almost every aspect as technology behaviour and economics change and develop. The best that can be expected is (hopefully!) a reasonably balanced but nevertheless personal view. What is certainly uncontentious is that electronic communication in all its forms has facilitated the whole process of producing journals. Papers can be submitted electronically, either on disk or on the Internet, and can be sent to referees electronically and returned via the publisher to the contributor in the same way. The whole refereeing process can be organised in any number of ways, either using the Net or using software packages specifically designed for this purpose. However, there is a limit to the time that can be saved, as the bulk of it is spent by the referee fitting this task into his schedule and then spending the time on reading the paper carefully.

One of the professed advantages of electronic distribution is the details and the quality of market feedback in that the publisher would be able to tell exactly who is reading which papers of a journal. However, in most cases, the amount of information proved much too large to be digestible and in any event it was in many cases impossible to detect whether someone accessing a paper actually read it or discarded it without reading it. It is, of course, possible to detect trends in particular subject areas where papers are accessed noticeably more than others.

A problem which this revolution has created, or accentuated perhaps, is that of archiving. In the past this has been the province of libraries, national and local, but the responsibility at the moment is unclear. Apart from discussions as to whether it should be, for example, the publisher or the librarian, there is the question of changes in technology which might make certain material inaccessible in the future. A possible solution might be initiatives for compulsory deposit of electronic material in national libraries, much in the same way as they receive deposit copies of print publications. The technology problem however remains.

Associated with this is the question of the local archive whereby an Institution has subscribed to a periodical from a publisher in electronic form only but then does not renew this subscription. If the institution is downloading material directly from the publishers' server, should they not be able to continue to download material for those issues to which they have already subscribed? It would be unreasonable to disallow this but there would be a small cost to the publisher to maintain and supply what might be described as 'back issues', but no generally agreed business models for this have emerged as yet.

So what of the future? Extreme points of view argue that publishers can now be by-passed altogether and research workers can put all their results independently directly on to the Net. Some of the motivation or reasoning behind this point of view is the high cost of print journals bearing in mind the fact that publishers pay nothing for the raw material. This totally overlooks the significant time and expense that publishers spend on collecting material, having it refereed, editing it, packaging and distributing it whether electronically or physically. Also, this point of view does not satisfactorily address the enormous problems of navigation and searching for material on the Net, which this mass of material would create — or rather aggravate. Additionally, it ignores the value that, for example, research workers and funding agencies place on papers published in prestigious journals. Another argument suggests that libraries can be by-passed and research results will be communicated directly to the research worker on his/her PC. However, the technological sophistication of this electronic age is extreme and becoming more so, which indicates that there will still be a role for the librarian or information scientist, albeit a significantly changed role.

So, the disappearance of published journals as we know them would certainly have an extremely damaging affect on the quality of research round the world and would not be welcomed by the vast number of research workers who see significant value in journals in one form or another. In fact research into user behaviour of journals suggests that a significant body of opinion, even amongst younger research workers, value the printed journal highly.

The picture is further complicated by the fact that the technological demands of the electronic revolution makes, has brought into the chain a number of organisations whose background is not in scientific publishing and communication but in, for example, IT and telecommunications. It can be argued that this phenomenon has created a significant technological 'push' in that there are many more sophisticated technological possibilities which make available functions — or functionalities as we must call them these days — for which those of us in the scholarly communication business can not immediately see an economic use.

Any sort of summary of this complex, contentious and ever changing situation would not be appropriate and arguably foolhardy. However, at the moment there are two points which, I think, can usefully be made, whatever changes take place in the roles of the various players and the scholarly communication chain in the future. The first is that whatever happens, the function of assessment or refereeing, together with that of formal and recognisable attribution, must remain if scholarly communication is to have any value and to continue its current useful role. At the moment this function is fulfilled by publishers, who have no God-given right to fulfil this role, but it must be done somehow and be seen to be done satisfactorily and constructively to preserve the element of quality control which is essential in scholarly communication. The second is the whole question of navigation; the ability to search — and find — relevant and significant research results is crucial to the optimal progress of scholarly research. This function at the moment is fulfilled by a combination of primary and secondary publishers and is once again an essential part of the scholarly communication chain, whoever undertakes this function in the future.

In some ways, the wheel has come full circle, with research workers communicating globally and electronically with each other, much as they did face to face in establishments like the Royal Society in London, three hundred years ago.

A Century of Science Publishing
E.H. Fredriksson (Ed.)
IOS Press, 2001

Chapter 23

The View from the Middle: Subscription Agents, Intermediaries and the ASA

John Merriman[a] and Rollo Turner[b],*
[a]Formerly Director, Blackwells Periodicals Division, UK
[b]Consultant and Secretary General of the ASA, High Wycombe, UK
ASA: www.subscription-agents.org

Introduction

Subscription agents may not be amongst the oldest professions but they are hardly new either. The first recorded agent was Everetts in 1793, Dawson in 1809, Harrasowitz first opened its doors in 1875, Faxon in 1881 and Swets in 1901. The ASA itself only started in 1934 as a UK body, the Association of Export Subscription Newsagents. Its aim was to control the 'unlimited price competition in supplying institutes, messes, libraries, clubs etc.' How successful it was is not recorded and I suspect that such blatant cartel formation would now be considered illegal! Trading conditions have changed since then but it was not until 1982 that it became The Association of Subscription Agents. In 2000 the name was again changed, this time to The Association of Subscription Agents and Intermediaries to reflect the fact that in the electronic environment a much wider diversity of organisations are involved with the supply and distribution of the serial literature.

The growth of subscription agents

From their beginnings supplying newspapers and serials to the establishments of empire in 1934, members of the ASA have changed dramatically. The numbers of subscription agents accelerated in the 1950's and 1960's when the growth in the scientific literature expanded so dramatically. At the same time and the underlying

---

*Rollo Turner writes in a personal capacity and the views expressed here are his own, not those of the ASA or its member companies.

cause of all this growth, was the very rapid expansion in higher education establishments throughout the world and a great need therefore to fill all the new libraries with the latest research literature. To this agents responded willingly and provided the basis of the remarkably efficient distribution chain for scholarly and research serials that we know today.

Many subscription agents began developing 'consolidation services' where the publisher supplied to the agent and the agent shipped all the issues each month to the customer to avoid some of the problems with postal services at this time. The availability of such services was and still is very popular in many markets and was a significant factor in the growth and history of many of today's agents. Consolidation services remain popular to this day though it is likely that the rapidly increasing availability of electronic journals spells the gradual demise of such services.

One of the more interesting aspects of this period was the realisation by publishers that there was a growing market for subscriptions in libraries all round the world but that at the time they lacked the marketing knowledge and sales ability to market to these new libraries. What was needed were subscription intermediaries who would find the library customers, carry the publishers journals in their catalogues, obtain orders, deal with payments in local currency and arrange for delivery with an as yet undeveloped postal system in many parts of the world. The commercial publishers therefore enthusiastically helped subscription agents by rewarding them for the new business being generated and because it massively reduced their sales costs. Journal publishers never developed sales forces until the coming of electronic consortia and electronic journals in the late 1990's.

The society publishers as a whole tended to look on this new library market with alarm: after all a single library subscription might replace scores of individual members subscriptions! As a result the societies were much slower into these markets at the time and have traditionally had a rather different relationship with agents as a result. (The parallel with today's challenges with electronic journals are quite striking. Then at least it quickly became apparent that society members rarely gave up their individual journal copies in favour of the library's copy.)

Until the mid 1970's the subscription industry grew both in terms of the number of customers (libraries) and hence the numbers of subscriptions but also in terms of the number of titles on offer. (For a good assessment of numbers of titles and the role of libraries see Tenopir and King: *Towards Electronic Journals*, SLA Publishing, ISBN 0871115077, 2000.)

Certainly library budgets were in general increasing at a rate that was more or less sufficient for libraries to build collections of much if not all of the important literature in their particular fields of interest — a time that now seems long gone!

Throughout this period the ASA helped its members through a variety of services but perhaps the most useful was the exchanges of experience at the ASA's regular meetings. These enabled trading relations to flourish between agents to ensure that literature from every corner of the globe could be supplied readily and inexpensively through the intermediation of one or more subscription agents.

The market hits recession

And then came the oil crises in the early 1970's. Suddenly industry and governments found costs rising and the money for higher education and especially library budgets started to go into reverse! However the march of science continued unabated as universities strove to protect their new and prestigious departments at the expense of library budgets and doubtless many other areas as well. Foreign exchange restrictions became commonplace amongst many countries as governments sought to use what foreign exchange there was to buy oil, not journals. This may have been the start of a problem with libraries budgets to buy research material but no such problems were apparent in the funding of research which continued to grow and within it the exponential rise in the number of papers (and journals) published continued. Publishers continued to launch more, and more specialist titles. Suddenly the market had changed dramatically by the late seventies. Gone were the ever rising circulations of ever more journals — cancellations started to arrive in increasing numbers until by the mid to late eighties publishers no longer talked of growth rates and new journal launches. A new vocabulary took over and talk was about attrition rates and price rises to offset falling subscriber numbers.

For agents this changed their relationships with publishers. Prior to 1975 (a key year in agents history) subscription agents were helping publishers sell journals on an international basis into an expanding market. After 1975 it became much more the case that agents were trying to hold on to the subscriptions they had and no longer could libraries be relied upon to buy the ever increasing numbers of new journal titles. Although on a international basis the market may have still been expanding there was a noticeable slow down of activity as far as agents were concerned and the emphasis switched from new subscriptions and new libraries to renewals. The agents were now no longer operating in a rapidly expanding markets and publishers began to notice the impact on their established journals circulation figures which at around this time probably reached their peak. In 1974 a large journal publisher (Pergamon Press) decided to reduce its terms to subscription agents. In recognition of the role of the agent and also highlighting the changing market a portion of the discount could be reclaimed if agents engaged in more promotional activities. In other words Pergamon needed to find new subscriptions because they were no longer rolling in through the agents as in previous years. Although this unilateral decision by Pergamon was probably made as much because of the state of the company at the time — Robert Maxwell had just regained control of the company which had almost certainly suffered as a result of the DTI investigations and adverse publicity — it certainly sparked a lively debate in the industry. Regrettably from the agents point of view it set the trend for gradually declining terms over the next two decades. On the positive side it undoubtedly helped to fuel the drive towards efficiency and better communication in the industry which saw the start of a number of important new developments in the next few years.

The drive for efficiency

If the period up to about 1975 can be considered the expansion phase for agents the next decade or so saw a number of innovations which greatly helped agents, publishers and librarians handle subscriptions more efficiently and achieve a better understanding of each others role in the marketplace.

Agents and the start of the Serials groups

Paradoxically it was during this period that the ASA began to become much more proactive in the industry and agents started to take a leading role in promoting innovation. The first major achievement was in the recognition that the serials industry was very different from books and indeed just about every other industry too! Apart from the ASA, journals were not represented in any other trade or professional body amongst libraries or publishers and in an attempt to address this Blackwells (now Swets Blackwell) identified the need to hold a forum to address the many specialist issues surrounding the serials industry. This forum was held in Oxford in 1975 and the guest of honour was none other than Robert Maxwell! The meeting was highly successful and repeated in 1977 and out of this meeting the UK Serials Group (UKSG) formed to become the UK forum for the serials industry with the fundamental tenet that trade and library professionals should be equal. Perhaps as a direct result of this the great strength of the UKSG has been the help and support from the trade and especially the subscription agents. Now the UKSG has some 600 institutional members holds numerous meetings and a hugely successful annual conference and has exported the concept of the serials group around the world.

Price is an old, old problem

Given the amount of column inches devoted to journal prices on list serves etc in recent years you might be forgiven for thinking that this is a new problem.

It is not. Back in the 1960's librarians were worried about the prices of journals and in response to this subscription agents started publishing price indexes of journals for their customers so that they could keep track of the changing prices of journals in most subjects. One agent, Blackwells, published their price index in the LA Record on an annual basis and this became a very valuable tool for both librarians and publishers. Although this analysis started in 1966 it developed through the 1970's into a highly useful tool for budgeting by librarians and pricing by publishers. It was soon further developed into the sophisticated system for predicting prices employed by most agents since the eighties and which has at times been accused of becoming a self fulfilling prophecy!

New technical standards

At a time when most industries were still struggling with the introduction of computers subscription agents were looking to automate the ordering process. The subscription business is seasonal with massive peaks at renewal time so automation of the process was clearly going to be beneficial to both agents and especially to publishers. In the early days some of the big agents such as Ebsco and Faxon were providing their own standard automated renewal order but clearly an industry wide standard would be desirable. The ASA accordingly organised a meeting to examine the challenges in February 1986 entitled Joint Seminar: Electronic Communications between Publishers and Subscription Agents which was attended by 53 organisations of whom 40 were publishers. This in turn led to the setting up of the International Working Party on Magnetic Media Transfers who produced the International Standards for Exchange of Machine Readable Subscription Orders. This then led to the foundation of ICEDIS (International Committee on Electronic Data Interchange for Serials) the standards making body in this area which continues its work today, still with the active support of subscription agents and the ASA as well as publishers. The first EDI X12 transmission was conducted in 1990 between Faxon and the Royal Society of Chemistry.

This work was highly important to the industry because it introduced automation and helped keep costs down at a time of otherwise rapidly escalating costs and prices. It also greatly improved efficiency leading to fewer subscription breakdowns and necessitated closer co-operation between publishers and agents.

Consolidation

The situation on journal prices and library budgets seems to have intensified rather than eased in recent years which has led to increasing pressure on the distribution system and subscription agents especially. Being an effective subscription agent is a curious mix of expertise, customer service and the economies of scale. With the increasing pressure on margins experienced by agents in the 1980's, it is not a surprise that economies of scale became the dominant factor and the ASA membership underwent radical change as members merged or acquired each other, a process that continues today. Fuelled by increasing automation and the need to provide large customers and suppliers with the kind of service which comes with scale, the larger subscription agents gradually acquired many of the smaller agents, dramatically reducing the numbers of specialist subscription agents with a reasonable level of business in journals. At the same time many of the academic bookshops who dealt with a small number of subscriptions for one or two clients began to get out of the business as it became increasingly difficult to compete with the specialist and much larger subscription agents (though there are still a substantial number of booksellers handling a small and probably declining number of subscriptions). For all that though the smaller specialist agent continues to survive and in some cases prosper where their expertise, market knowledge or particular specialism is seen as particularly valuable by their customers.

By the mid 1990's the subscription industry was in trouble: cancellations were on a spiralling downward path as journal prices continued to escalate. Agents were being required to provide more and more flexible services to customers whilst experiencing continued pressure on discounts from publishers. The increasing size of the larger agents and publishers meant that any failure by one of the larger players could be catastrophic for the industry as very nearly happened when Faxon ran into difficulties in 1993 before being rescued by the Dawson acquisition in 1994. During the 1990's after a series of years seeing price rises substantially in excess of retail price inflation, which currency variations often made much worse, the industry appeared to be approaching some form of crisis and the future was beginning to look increasingly challenging. And then came the Internet, the World Wide Web and electronic journals.

Distribution moves centre stage

The Internet is doubtless many things to many people, but as far as agents and publishers were concerned in the mid 1990's it was treated as if it was simply another way of distributing content. Distribution is the business that agents have always seen as their specialist role so it is perhaps no surprise to see how quickly they responded to the arrival of Web driven electronic journals available on subscription.

Agents saw this new channel to the market as both representing unparalleled opportunity and as a threat. The threat came from the realisation that in order for electronic journals to work properly the publishers needed much more information on customers than they had ever required before. It meant publishers had to know their customers which in the past had been the role of the agent. Furthermore the access to the content by the customer was directly with the publisher and in view of these facts many agents initially feared that this might lead to the marginalisation of agents. This in fact is no more true for electronic content than for paper. Both require the publisher to have some knowledge of the customer in order to develop content and this is the area in which agents have traditionally thrived. The opportunities however were considerable as there was likely to be a requirement for an enormous diversity of new services by both librarians and publishers.

New services from agents

To begin with agents tended to mirror the paper world in much the same way as publishers had, and concentrate on supplying information to publishers, undertaking the purchasing administration (very considerable for electronic journals) and so on. But then came the start of the new services: in 1996 the first into the field were Blackwells with their Electronic Journal Navigator service which was soon followed by Swets (now Swets Blackwell), Dawson (now RoweCom) and Ebsco. This provided a gateway to subscribed electronic journal content, a common search interface across the content based on simple search routines involving electronic tables of contents. Generally these services linked to the publishers website but some of these agents gateway services also hosted the content on their own servers for a few publishers.

New intermediaries formed

A few years earlier many other computer oriented businesses had spotted the market for a means of electronically publishing paper journals. Probably some of the first in this field were OCLC and Bids both of whom had a university background and rather wider responsibilities to the higher education community they served. These were the early electronic intermediaries who offered publishers and librarians a wide range of new services based around the Web. They were rapidly joined by more commercial and also successful companies such as Catchword (now part of ingenta) who started to produce electronic journals for publishers and distribute worldwide with a commercial model that worked well for many small and medium sized publishers. Others like ingenta (then Bids who were already active in this area), Turpin and HighWire soon joined them. These new companies were a different type of distributor but they were still intermediaries between the library and publisher. Their commercial model tended to be rather different to that of the subscription agents offering in that they charged the publisher for their services and made no charge to the library (although the publisher did). The distribution chain was now being stretched with libraries ordering from agents who ordered from publishers, who provided the subscription information to their intermediary, who supplied the library sometimes through an agents gateway service. In other words these new companies were a true part of the distribution chain dealing directly with the library's agents and publishers to provide service.

By 2000 many of these intermediaries had joined the ASA which changed its name in that year to reflect these new members needs and slightly different outlook in a rapidly changing market. As the world of electronic journals became ever more integrated more and more intermediaries joined the ASA especially those who distributed databases such as Edina and MIMAS for example rather than primary journals, but who face many similar challenges.

Administration challenges

The relentless march of the technology of electronic journals had somehow out-paced the administrative systems designed to cope with paper journals. Electronic journals required considerably more knowledge of the customer than publishers currently possessed to be able to sell or supply them at all. Persuading a customer to take up an electronic subscription was no guarantee that it would be used, and the use was difficult to measure in practice although in theory at least it could, unlike paper, be measured. Electronic journals required licences, technology and expertise not found in the paper environment. All of which increased the complexity of ordering electronic journals which meant that agents and their customers had to learn new skills. This process is still going on but all sides have been quick to see that in the long term there is potentially more value to be had from a subscription to an electronic journal than the continuation of a paper subscription. As a result agents were suddenly in demand by publishers to ease this transition and to regulate the flow of the required information, authorisation, access routes, and licences.

Consortia

The last few years have also been characterised by the rise in library consortia. Initially these consortia negotaited with subscription agents for the supply of the printed journals and, in return for volume were succesful in driving down the price of journals supplied through their agents. Recently there has been a very large increase in both the number of consortia and their size as consortia have started to negotiate with publishers for better terms for the supply of electronic journals. In the UK this has been done through NESLI whose Managing Agent comprises a partnership of two ASA members, one a subscription agent (Swets Blackwell) and the other an intermediary (MIMAS) connected with the HE sector. In other countries library consortia have not always made use of agents services in negotiation, but very frequently the agents' systems and knowledge of the subscription market have helped many consortia members (and publishers) take advantage of, and even structure the deals.

Common licensing

To all of this the agents responded innovatively and as fast as the enormous amount of change required to some very large and complex subscription systems would allow. Very early on subscription agents saw the need for an international common set of licences that would enable publishers and libraries to agree terms with ready made standard clauses (though the specific price and terms would still always need to be agreed between the parties concerned). By standardising the language and ensuring all aspects of a good agreement were included in the standard licence the job of both publisher and librarian was made easier. This innovative approach was based on the preceding work of the PA/JISC agreement and takes the standard licence approach another step further. This work was performed by John Cox and sponsored by Blackwells, Dawson, Ebsco, Harrassowitz and Swets.

E-commerce

Another of the more interesting innovations has been the rise of RoweCom who as a small company in the mid 1990's challenged the orthodoxy inherent in agents' business models. Now a much larger company having taken over Dawson's subscription interests in 1999, they continue to offer e-commerce systems which may point the way to how libraries, agents and publishers will purchase in the future. There is probably still much work to be done in this area but the first step in developing commercial e-commerce based services has already been taken.

The Future of Subscription Agents and Intermediaries

Predicting the future is only safely done in retrospect so anything said here is likely to prove an embarrassment in a few years time! However here are a few areas where we see intermediaries as having a pivotal role in the future.

Amongst the most important changes that are already occurring are in the areas of rights management. There appears to be a crucial piece of the distribution chain missing. It is now in principle possible, and rapidly becoming practicable, to link all electronic journal articles to the references contained in those articles and indexing services to the articles via CrossRef, the highly innovative new development from PILA, and the use of DOI currently championed by the DOI Foundation. It is again possible, via SFX technology, to link journal articles to university holdings, research databases etc. It is possible via Z39.50 for example to search across databases rather than within each database separately and to directly call up the discovered articles or content. What is not so obvious is how the publisher and the customer knows whether the customer already holds a subscription or needs to pay. Technology here is only part of the solution since this needs a link to the many commercial systems between customer and publisher. Not all subscriptions are directly with the publisher, many may be through aggregation services, subscription agents gateways, secondary information providers and so on. Currently authorisation tends to be dependent on the channel to the publishers system. For example if it comes direct there should be few problems but if the route taken is via a secondary service, linked to an aggregation service the publisher may not know that this individual user has rights to the requested information through a library subscription. Here the agents with their vast databases of subscriptions may well hold one of the keys to future development since they will undoubtedly be able to speed this process. But it will take time and probably further co-operation between all parties to achieve it.

The one stop shop

As has been hinted at above, the Web seems to work best from the users and customers point of view when everything is connected to everything else. To make such massive interconnectivity work there is a need to provide some form of overall commonality to the search strategies and access mechanisms and commercial systems. This is an area in which agents and intermediaries can and should become active to provide the type of systems that encourage the acquisition of, and access to, content of all sorts from journal articles to databases and books. Not surprisingly this is likely to be a bitterly contested area with some publishers unsure whether becoming the channel to the market is a better long term goal than publishing the content itself. But ultimately whatever the rivalries and strategic positioning it will happen as it is so clearly in the interest of the customers who, eventually pay for the services. This whole area of handling authorisation, acquisitions, discovery and access is where we see agents moving to in the future, in other words they will continue to be the channel to the market leaving the actual products and information generation to others.

But as these intermediaries devise ever more sophisticated and interesting new services it will be less clear exactly who is doing what for whom in an ever more interconnected world. For example are one-stop-shop electronic access systems for e-journals and articles an access system for libraries, or could they be more usefully seen as a marketing channel for publishers? It is likely that these arguments will persist.

There are already interesting beginnings being made here. Swets Blackwell has joined CrossRef, Ebsco has taken up SFX technology, RoweCom continues to develop its e-commerce type solutions, ingenta is developing an interesting new mix of services from article delivery to electronic publishing and portal development, to name just a few.

Library developments

As consortia continue to grow their administration requirements become greater. If they obtain common content for their members perhaps common access arrangements may follow. Certainly the content acquired through consortia needs to be linked to that acquired in the more traditional way by their members. There is a role here for intermediaries specialising in linking, access administration and acquisition since in general these tasks have substantial economies of scale. In other words the cost per organisation served falls dramatically as the number of organisations increases.

In conclusion

In the future it will not be surprising to find some intermediaries devising their services for the content suppliers as their customers in mind and others with the needs of libraries and users as their clients. Some will of course continue to do both, but in the new world of massively interconnected services and systems the intermediary has and will continue to have a key role to play both in helping publishers distribute their content and services effectively and to librarians in helping them purchase and access content.

A Century of Science Publishing
E.H. Fredriksson (Ed.)
IOS Press, 2001

Chapter 24

Developments in Scientific Communication
The virtual marketplace as a prerequisite for growth

Hans E. Roosendaal, Peter A.Th.M. Geurts and Paul E. van der Vet
University of Twente, Enschede, The Netherlands

1. Introduction

Scientific communication is in flux. One of the most important consequences is the transformation of the familiar information chain, i.e. from author to publisher to library to reader. This transformation is of a structural nature: the information chain is being fundamentally transformed to support the present demands for knowledge growth and management [1].

Current policies and practices in science and communication are, in the words of Mahoney [2], not ideal for an optimal exchange and refinement of our knowledge. However, this is more than needed in our present, knowledge-intensive society. Communication can only be effective and efficient if its configuration appeals to the research and education community, also in its relation to society at large (Simonton [3]). Differences in configurations between disciplines must be accommodated, as these differences should not impede knowledge transfer in transdisciplinary or interdisciplinary research.

It is often stated that the present excessive rate of production of original scientific work cannot but in the end retard scientific progress [4]. We need new methods of scientific communication that allow speeding up the advancement of science. Research time to explore the abundance of information and data seems the main issue here, which is the focus for improving the effectiveness and efficiency of the scientific communication system.

Technology serves as an important driving force as it enables further developments in the research and education process. Technology empowers the key stakeholders in scientific communication to induce structural changes in their communication configurations. These changes will clearly involve issues of strategic repositioning and organisational change.

For our analysis of the transformation of the value chain we have adopted a methodology leading to a structural analysis rather than a tactical analysis. This is achieved by describing the scientific communication market by four forces of complementary pairs: the *actor*, the *accessibility*, the *content*, and the *applicability* pair.

These forces allow an overall description of the dynamics of the market. This description provides a framework for the various aspects of time, space and action that are relevant within this context. Within this set of forces we have defined a set of four functions for scientific communication. These functions are the *registration*, *archive*, *awareness* and *certification* function. The present focus of development is on the registration and the archive function, and the development of the archive function in particular raises organisational issues. Within the context of research and education developments, e.g. towards learning communities equally involving teachers and students, the certification function will also require fundamental rethinking (compare also Ch. 25.).

With so many stakeholders involved, and given their widely different roles within the system, the ownership issue becomes a complex one. A solution must be found for the strategic management of the scientific communication market. This means finding the right balance and interface between private and public interests, and this balance must be consistent with the main aim of serving research and education while preserving the integrity of its means of communication. A virtual organisation may provide the solutions.

2. Boundary conditions

Scientific communication serves the progress of research and education. The overall objective of scientific communication is growth of knowledge by improving the effectiveness and efficiency of research and education.

For some time, we are witnessing a development in research towards tighter planning of research at large and the development of 'strategic research'. This trend to strategic research can be witnessed in the research policies of the industry world-wide.

Also national governments world-wide and supranational bodies have started, continued and strengthened a fundamental reorganisation of their higher education programmes and are influencing the research programmes by their funding strategies.

These trends also have consequences for the educational tasks of the universities and other institutes of higher education. Curricula need to be tailored towards this new research philosophy.

Recent developments in information and communication technology give rise to a multitude of combinations of synchronous and asynchronous interaction. This opens possibilities of distance learning and lifelong or continuous learning, in particular 'web based learning' [8].

Demands from research and education for scientific information will widely overlap, not least for advanced students. They will partly draw on the same sources and make use of the same technical infrastructure. The introduction of distance learning and lifelong learning will lead to a change in the student population of many universities. The university will attract students during a sizeable portion of the period of employability: an economic ground for a major reorganisation.

Investments in information systems will have to adapt to educational purposes next to research. Such information systems will include course management systems and course material. At many universities this will lead to the development of integrated study and information environments requiring document servers, browsers and archives. These will have to meet the same technical requirements as for scientific communication. In short, the universities will develop a publishing and archiving facility equivalent to the one needed for information for educational purposes. This development will greatly influence the information chain, resulting in a new balance of roles between universities and other learned institutions and scientific publishers. The added value is not anymore in information proper but in its effective and efficient communication, or knowledge management.

The question arises whether such a development can be achieved within the present scheme of distinction between 'formal' and 'informal' communication. We envisage a trend towards more formalising of 'informal' communication. This trend adds to the protection of the intellectual property of the individual researcher within a research institution.

3. The market

Scientific communication, in the most general sense, takes place between researchers, as authors and readers. The objective is to exchange (units of) information. The market place of scientific communication consists of authors and readers as generic actors or stakeholders. They author a unit of information, e.g. such as a scientific article or a set of data. They also want their product to be made available to all readers. Furthermore, their product is their main expression of accountability within the research enterprise. In this way they claim priority of discovery. This is a long-standing practice. Already since the end of the seventeenth century this priority of discovery is the norm and prior journal publication its criterion.

It is understood that the driving force for this market is that authors want to publish **more** and have their product widely available, while readers want to read **less**, but want to be informed of all that is relevant for their research at hand [5,10].

Thus the scientific communication market consists of authors and readers (actor pair) as generic stakeholders. They require availability and retrievability (accessibility pair) of all sorts of units of information. Their objective is to generate questions and to provide answers (content pair) in order to apply them in their research (applicability pair).

The forces can be grouped in a tetrahedron with in each vertex a force. This tetrahedron represents the following equation:

F (*scientific communication market*) = F (*actor, content, accessibility, applicability*)

There are four triangular planes with one force in each of its vertices. By observing that only those planes are relevant that contain both the actor and content forces, this tetrahedron then collapses into the two-dimensional diagram of Figure 1.

The vertical axis describes primarily the market dynamics and modes of transaction whereas the horizontal axis describes different aspects of the content being negotiated in this market. The market is defined as the place of balance of these forces, as an 'agora' of scientific conduct and discourse.

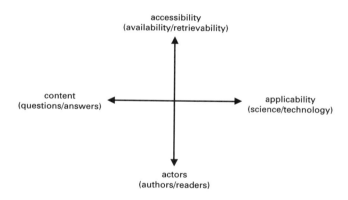

Figure 1. Forces of the scientific communication market.

The familiar main functions of scientific communication are *registration, awareness, certification* and *archive* functions [5,6,11]. In a similar way as with the market, we can visualise these functions in Figure 2. These also can be grouped in a tetrahedron. This tetrahedron represents the following equation:

f(*scientific communication functions*)= f(*registration, archive, awareness, certification*)

And again by observing that planes are void when they do not contain the registration and the archive function, this tetrahedron then collapses into Figure 2.

Here we also arrive at two axes: the vertical axis describes registration and awareness which can both be seen as different aspects of scientific observation, whereas the horizontal axis describes certification and archiving which can be seen as different aspects of scientific judgement.

Figure 2 shows that there are communication functions that are *internal* to the research and education process and that there are communication functions that *external* to the research and education process. The registration function is both a direct and external function, the awareness function is indirect and internal, the certification function is direct and internal, and finally the archive function is an indirect and external function. There is a half plane of two external functions, and a half plane of two internal functions. Similarly, there is a direct half plane and an indirect half plane. Following the familiar classification of the communication functions into author and reader functions we see that the author functions are the direct functions and the reader functions are the indirect functions. By their nature, registration and archiving as external functions to the research and education process can be easily outsourced within the market to the product space, viz. the publisher and the library.

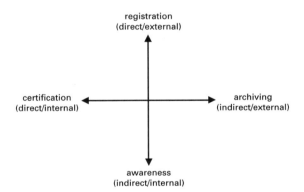

Figure 2. Functions in scientific communications.

The use of the four functions provides a consistent analysis of formal and informal scientific communication. It may be questioned if these four functions, together with the transactions between them, provide a comprehensive description of scientific communication. This question is even more relevant as we consider educational communication as being part of scientific communication. Comprehensiveness is a condition for the structural approach that we have taken, in particular if we want to apply the functions to arrive at conclusions, based on structural continuity, on strategic repositioning in the market.

External functions: registration and archiving

Within a digital communication environment the focus of development is still primarily on the two external functions. The function of registration is already fully matured with the exception of the intellectual property aspects of integrity of the communication and copyright issues. For the archive function we have observed that both publishers and universities are creating digital archives or warehouses of information material under their control allowing distribution of this information through a variety of different media. First attempts are being made to connect these archives into a more distributed system. This necessitates the introduction of conditions for transparency, raisings the issues of responsibility distributed and of organisation. Will such an archive allow the author and reader to integrate the information into a personal archive? This is no doubt desired and should be one of the main objectives of such an archive. From Figure 2 we see that the archive function serves as a transactional function or 'sluice' between author and reader. This raises the issue of integrating informal communication into the platform of such an archive, which in turn leads to an integration of formal and informal communication. This becomes particularly relevant if we take educational communication into consideration as well. This means formalising informal communication into one and the same platform and management system as is used for formal communication. A result of these developments will be that the now distinct roles of publishers and universities will be merged and will become nodes in the overall management of scientific communication.

Internal functions: certification and awareness

The certification function has been and still is under continuous discussion. A wide variety of schemes is being proposed. It is particularly the certification function that might be subject to strong development under a strategic research regime. It has to be investigated how 'economic' aspects related to the concept of 'centres of excellence' will influence certification of research results. Gross [9] already describes peer review as a negotiation on the level of claims permissible in a scientific article: "The higher the level, the higher the article's status; the higher the status, the more difficult the negotiations". And indeed, under conditions of strategic research the negotiations might well become even more difficult, and the role of the referee needs further attention [10,11,12] (see also Ch. 21). The transformation of the value chain needs to address the issue of certification, and the question arises if certification can and will remain primarily restricted to research internal methodological arguments (internal heuristics) or that more and more external elements of a more economic nature will be added (external heuristics). In this context, economic means that it may be more rational, and thus sufficient, not to aim for the best results in the methodological sense. Such a development could change the rules for the advancement of science, and has already changed these rules by creating 'centres of excellence'.

This will also be reflected in the way science will be communicated. To illustrate this point, over the last decades we have witnessed a clear change in emphasis from the collection of information proper, such as data, towards the application of data which requires new schemes of clustering.

The most difficult function, the awareness function — the real engine in the communication process — is also being tackled. Research on the modularity of scientific communication has been undertaken and looks a promising development. Research on science indicators is key to analysing this function. Science indicators also play an important role in the discussion on certification.

4. Technology

It is difficult to claim completeness for an overview of technological developments because computer science literature is difficult to access. In older disciplines such as physics and chemistry, access is facilitated by authoritative secondary literature. In computer science, most journals are indexed that way but, unlike what is the case in older disciplines, journals are not the primary means of communication. For many computer science journals, the time lag between first submission and actual publication can be two years or more. As a result, a journal article is outdated when it appears and serves only archival purposes. Instead, computer scientists communicate by means of conferences and of workshops with a specialised audience. A relatively large proportion of computer science publications thus becomes scattered over many 'grey' sources like proceedings that often are only distributed among the workshop participants. Such publications are not indexed at all. Computer science contributions to issues in scientific communication are produced in many subfields that hardly communicate with each other. As a result, computer science contributions are under-utilised. A perfect example of the importance of organising scientific communication processes.

However, one of the issues discussed is of special relevance here: the modularisation of scientific publications as a consequence of web-based publishing. Web-based publishing liberates us from the limitations of the linear, mainly textual presentation of scientific findings and turns a publication into a small web that may include not only text and figures but also data sets, computer programs, sounds and videos. Authoring tools for such multimedia presentations will have to be developed, as well as tools to convert media into each other to enable readers to choose presentation style and media types. Such tools will in most cases be unable to convert the full message from one medium into another. For instance, natural language is optimal for conveying the subtle modalities of a conclusion while a figure is optimal for conveying a configuration. Media conversion thus may well lead to a loss of information, but this need not be a problem when the loss is controlled and known to the reader. Media conversion is first and for all a formidable technical problem. In a realistic scenario, it involves two conversion steps: one in which the content is converted from the original medium into some media-neutral language, and a second step in which the content is expressed in the target medium. Both steps are currently fraught with difficulties, but the second step appears easier than the first. The first step would however, be largely unnecessary when authors would use a formal language optimised for machine manipulation. Developments in this direction are anticipated.

External functions

Authors who distribute their papers through their own websites often continue editing these. This makes citing awkward because it is not guaranteed that the citation remains correct or adequate over time. Since the citation system is one of the pillars of scientific communication, the practice of constantly changing personal publications must be complemented by an archive of registered, 'frozen' publications. Modular publications require separate registration of the modules. We will need systems for reliable authentication and time stamping, and probably also for encryption to ensure integrity of communication. Software needed for such tasks has matured to some degree. These methods rely on the computational complexity of certain calculations and thus become ineffective as soon as a major increase in processing speed is realised, allowing ever more complex calculations to be performed within a reasonable period of time. Moreover, quantum computing is expected to make every current cryptographic protection method ineffective. At present, there is no solution in sight.

Protection of intellectual ownership, strictly speaking, is a matter of organisation, but technology provides the means to both protect material and circumvent protective measures. We think that a purely technical solution to the problem of protecting material is an illusion.

Careful archiving cannot exist without the guarantee of durability and accessability. Paper (microfilm) is a durable medium and paper journals are distributed in hundreds or thousands of copies to institutions that themselves fulfill an archival function. If even half of these institutions would loose their archives, sufficient copies would still be available elsewhere. Digital material is less suitable for archiving. The number of servers holding the same material is orders of magnitude smaller than the number of paper archives, which, on itself, makes digital archiving less dependable. Also, digital material is deposited in a physical form that at best has a guaranteed lifespan of fifty years. Unlike its paper equivalent, digital content is very often stored in a proprietary format. Worse, the evolution of hardware and software makes information carriers and formats obsolete and practically unusable at an alarming rate. It has been suggested to employ a system of emulators that makes machines and software systems behave like machines and software systems of an earlier generation. The obvious criticism is that, this way, we end up with a stack of emulators on top of each other, with the risk of multiplying errors. The alternative is to convert archived documents to new formats each time the software needed for accessing the document is renewed. This would create a long chain of sequential conversion processes, so that here, too, one could be stacking errors on top of each other. Neither the technological nor the organisational problems in creating durable electronic archives are presently solved. This is an urgent and serious problem. In Europe, several national libraries have started research programmes to tackle this problem, among them the Koninklijke Bibliotheek (the national library of the Netherlands).

Internal functions

Quality assessment of scientific publications, in whatever form they are distributed, will remain a matter of human judgment. Technology can help by offering systems to route new findings to peers and to assemble their reviews at the site where a decision is taken. As publications move away from the traditional paper presentation, refereeing methods will have to keep pace. The possibility to publish data sets as parts of a publication will inevitably result in a pressure on authors to do so. This, in turn, will exert a positive influence on the quality of publications. Web technology makes it possible to improve the way peer review is organised. An example is the digital-only scientific journal *Electronic Transactions on Artificial Intelligence*, which employs a certification system that involves publication before review and (anonymous) publication of the referee reports [13] (Ch. 25). Readers can send in their own comments, both to the original submission and to the reviews, and all contributions are hyperlinked to constitute a small web. The web that thus grows from each submission is itself a valuable source of information. Furthermore, the fact that submission and reviews are all public is expected to have a positive influence on the quality.

On the horizon are systems that assist quality assessment by providing automated support to the comparison of experimental results reported by different sources. These systems help identify causes for divergent findings obtained in actual experiments, and they also help predict what the consequences of different experimental setups may be. Fully quantitative simulation of experiments already yields this information, but is very often not feasible because our knowledge of experimental conditions is not sufficiently precise. Comparative qualitative and semi-quantitative analysis of experimental outcomes is now being investigated [17].

As in the case of establishing the scientific journal, awareness was the prime motivation for CERN researchers to develop the Web. Awareness is one of the main forces behind web technology. One of the more compelling scenarios is that of a computer-supported discovery environment, a desktop computer with continuous access to the web, optimised for scientific work. In this scenario, each research group requires the presence of a librarian able to find resources of whatever form (publications, programs, videos, knowledge and databases) as member of the group [14].

Awareness requires communication and landmarks. Landmarks serve to alert scientists to material of potential interest. Examples of landmarks are scientific journals or websites read on a regular basis, tables of contents, and review articles. A next step is to collect what one is looking for from a collection or archive: a question of 'information retrieval'. The past decades have seen a proliferation of approaches. The issue of deciding between different information retrieval approaches is traditionally discussed in terms of precision and recall. These as a rule leave costs out of consideration. We think that the question is better approached as a microeconomic optimisation problem. For instance, improving recall only pays when the costs are lower than the costs likely to be incurred by missing relevant documents. Such problems are typically addressed by means of techniques from the field of statistical decision making, like the use of ROC (receiver operating characteristic) curves. Costs involved in indexing and searching can usually be determined with relative ease but costs incurred by missing documents are hard to calculate. Measurements aimed at decreasing the imprecision in our current knowledge of the cost factors are urgent. Full-text search methods have matured to the point that they can be cheap and effective when finding only a single document or a few documents of relevance. The main shortcoming of full-text retrieval is that it is designed for texts, whilst the proportion of text in scientific publications is expected to decrease. If we are interested in finding most or all relevant documents, there is no known, cheap technological solution. Web-related efforts employing metadata in fact return to the expensive practice of manual indexing using predefined search terms.

One of the problems in existing information retrieval approaches is that the search space becomes too large or too complex. The user needs navigational aids, for instance virtual worlds like the virtual books of Marti Hearst and the virtual music theatre developed at Twente [15]. This idea is particularly fruitful for scientific communication, where a virtual world that embodies a useful abstraction presents the scientist with a familiar environment in which he can 'travel', collecting information underway. What we mean by useful abstraction is exemplified by the illustrations published in a journal like *Scientific American*. Such illustrations are not faithful representations of reality. Rather, by means of lines, colours and other artistic manipulations, they emphasise particular aspects and ignore others. What the navigation aid will be like depends on the discipline and on the task at hand. Some obvious examples: for an organic chemist, a molecule; for a materials scientist, a phase diagram; for a crystallographer, a model of the crystal or the unit cell; for a molecular biologist, a virtual cell; for an environmental scientist, a model of the Dutch Shallows.

Obtaining information is one step, using it the next. Information-intensive disciplines like molecular biology increasingly rely on the availability of web-based resources like data bases and programs that can be run remotely. In the course of its work, a research group will typically want to 'wire together' a set of distributed resources, both in-house and remote, to perform a particular job like to predict the outcome of an experiment, to interpret a new finding, or to compare own findings with findings reported by other groups. The lifetimes of such configurations will vary between a few hours and several months. The obstacle currently in the way of relying on routine configurations is a multiplicity of formats. Standardisation is one way to solve this problem, but standardisation has a bad track record in many disciplines. An alternative to standardisation is middleware that can be configured dynamically by feeding it a description of the resource [18]. As in the far more difficult case of media conversion (discussed above), the middleware converts incoming information into a language optimised for machine manipulation. Outgoing information is converted from this internal language into the foreign format. The internal language is standardised locally, that is, within the system and within the group that uses the system. Its symbols are defined semantically, for example in the case of molecules as standing for a bond, an atom, and so on. The format of a foreign resource is precisely specified both syntactically and semantically. The syntactic specification identifies record and field delimiters and the strings that hold the information proper. The semantic specification tells how the information proper has to be converted into or from the internal format. The converters (incoming and outgoing) can be generated automatically from such a specification. Access to a format specification and connecting to a resource will suffice to automatically generate a converter and allow downloading or uploading data in a transparent way that does not bother the user.

5. The future

Does the market need a new division of functional tasks or a new functional division? In the context of this article we will restrict our remarks concerning future developments to this issue.

We have noted before that in the present market the principal stakeholders have outsourced a number of functions or tasks to other stakeholders such as publishers, libraries, and agents. (These functions are performed mainly at the operational level and add only restricted intellectual value in the selection and processing of information). There is also a substantial degree of 'insourcing' to institutions such as learned societies, universities or research and education institutions. This regards in particular the external functions of registration (publisher, learned society) and archive (publisher, library), and the logistics aspects of the internal certification function (publisher, learned society).

Changes will be rational rather than paradigmatic. This means a change at the structural level resulting from function development (leading to increased added value) rather than a tactical development. Structural continuity is assumed: the present system will evolve in a rational way along with the developments in the market.

This will affect the balance of functions in the market, in particular with regard to the certification function. Changes in the certification function will then translate into changes of the registration and archive functions. In the end, this will affect the possible schemes and degree of outsourcing. Our analysis based on structural continuity may provide insights to deal with possible strategic repositionings which could result.

The 'knowledge industry' is a complex network of different stakeholders of authors and readers, organised in different kinds of research and education institutions, of universities, libraries, learned societies, publishers, intermediaries such as subscription agents, and not least of the enabling industry and software houses. In this context we have seen developments to mergers between the institution's computer centres and other information facilities like libraries.

This existing network is characterised by a high degree of subsidiarity: the stakeholders enjoy a high degree of mutual strategic interdependence. The outsourcing concerns primarily the transfer and the management of content in the market. It is primarily focused on accessibility in the market. An issue is if this task of facilitation management should not be reintegrated into the market as we have seen that in a digital environment we cannot conceptually separate accessibility from applicability and content. The trend in the market does not allow a simple operational separation either.

The market will thus be organised in a different way and evolve into a virtual organisation, i.e. a special case of an organisational network which is an identifiable whole 'vis à vis' external stakeholders [16]. An important characteristic of a virtual organisation is its distributed ownership. This distributed ownership distinguishes it from a co-operative conglomerate or a joint venture. A virtual organisation is mainly representing a balance of forces in the market.

Can the present scientific communication market perhaps be seen as a virtual organisation? It shows aspects of distributed ownership. However, the market, if defined as the 'information industry' is a different entity. It is only a separate, outsourced and incomplete operational subset of the entire market. An analysis of the communication market on this basis will necessarily lead to invalid conclusions. Adherence to this organisational model of separating out the 'information industry' may well lead to inflexibility in the development of the entire market and is the source for the information crisis.

Looking back at the historical development of the scientific journal as the vehicle for scientific communication, we see that the Royal Society of London, and other learned societies for that matter, represented a virtual organisation. In particular, the research enterprises of that time were almost tautological with individual researchers, or small groups of researchers. Indeed, all forces in the market and all functions were integrated in the concept of the learned society with its members and institutions.

If we include in the market not only the transfer of information after the research process, but also the exchange of all kinds of information during the research process, e.g. in round-robin experiments or direct teacher-student interactions, we are tempted to conclude that the scientific communication market, including all its partners, qualifies as a virtual organisation. And it is consistent with the used definition of scientific communication to include all kinds of information.

The issue is that if we also include information exchange during the research process, we consider communication within the entire research and education process: research, education and communication are viewed as parts of one organisation. If we limit ourselves to information exchange after the research and education process only, and this would be inconsistent, we must see communication on the one hand, and research and education on the other hand, as two distinct organisations. In the latter case, communication is purely restricted to separate functions; in the former case we also consider the transactions between the functions.

One (virtual) organisation implies reintegration of those functions, and thus tasks, that are presently outsourced to 'external stakeholders'.

The question then arises whether a new division and subsequent separation of functions is feasible. The present discussion illustrates that scientific communication, as a whole, cannot be organised independently from the research and education market. What can, and thus probably will, be organised independently is the communication network, i.e. the technological network, including information of a variety of nature and forms. This will be a distributed network and its core will be the distributed archive. The main tasks that presently can be foreseen for such a network are content management, storage, management of communication and structure of communication. It has been proposed that a modular structure for scientific articles will replace the present linear structure [5]. Such a modular structure is supposed to strongly enhance the accessibility and thus applicability of elements of information and to allow a seamless and smooth integration with modules of other articles, or other information sets and collections.

These developments require a reorganisation of the knowledge industry and consequently a new division of tasks and responsibilities between the stakeholders. Following the conditions of a virtual organisation of such a unified, distributed system, strategic management needs to be clearly separated from operational management. This is an important issue for all stakeholders concerned. It will call for new alliances or consortia between the stakeholders, where they presently form separated subsets or groups within the market.

For a veritable virtual organisation this would further imply co-operation within the boundary conditions for a virtual organisation. These conditions carry important consequences for the present stakeholders in the knowledge industry and in particular for the stakeholders of the more restricted information industry, especially with regard to the distribution of ownership as content and applicability are major forces of the transformed value chain.

References

[1]   Meadows, A.J. (1998) *Communicating Research*. Academic Press, San Diego.

[2]   Mahoney (1989) In: Gholson, B., Shadish Jr., W.R., Niemeyer, R.A. & Houts, A.C. (Eds.) *Psychology of Science.* Cambridge University Press.

[3]   Simonton (1989) In: Gholson, B., Shadish Jr., W.R., Niemeyer, R.A. & Houts, A.C. (Eds.) *Psychology of Science.* Cambridge University Press.

[4]   Stigler, G.J. (1965) *Essays in the history of economics.* University of Chicago Press.

[5]   Kircz, J.G. & Roosendaal, H.E. (1996) Understanding and shaping scientific information transfer. In: *Electronic publishing in science.* Shaw, D. & Moore, H. (Eds.) Proceedings of the joint ICSU Press/UNESCO Expert Conference, February 1996, Paris. Unesco, pp. 106–116.

[6]   Kircz, J.G. (1998) Modularity: the next form of scientific information presentation? *Journal of Documentation,* 54(2) 210–235. Final draft: www.science.uva.nl/projects/commphys/papers.

[7]   Readings, B. (1996) *The university in ruins.* Harvard University Press.

[8]   Collis, B. (1996) *Tele-learning in a digital world: the future of distant learning.* London, ITP.

[9]   Gross, A.G. (1994) *The rhetoric of science.* Harvard University Press.

[10] Roosendaal, H.E. (1996) Scientific Communication and the Science Process. In: *Proceedings of the International Summer School on the Digital Library, Tilburg, The Netherlands, August 1996.* Van Luyt-Prinsen, J.G. & Meijer, E. (Eds.) Ticer B.V. pp. 1–12.

[11] Merton, R. (1973) *The Sociology of Science: Theoretical and Empirical Investigations.* University of Chicago Press.

[12] Radnitzky, G. (1989) In: *I. Lakatos and theories of scientific change. Boston Studies in the Philosophy of Science, Vol. III.* Kluwer Academic Publishers.

[13] http://www.ida.liu.se/ext/etai/

[14] de Jong, H. & Rip, A. (1997) The computer revolution in science: steps towards the realization of computer-supported discovery environments. *Artificial Intelligence,* 91, 225–256.

[15] Nijholt, A., Hulstijn, J. & van Hessen, (1999) A. Speech and language interactions in a web theatre environment. In: *Proceedings of the ESCA Workshop on Interaction Dialogue in Multi-Modal Systems.* Dalsgaard, P., Lee, C.-H., Heisterkamp, P. & Cole, R. (Eds.) Aalborg: ESCA/Center for PersonKommunikation, pp. 129–132. The Virtual Music Center can be visited on WWW via http://wwwseti.cs.utwente.nl/Parlevink/.

[16] van Aken, J.E., Hop, L. & Post, G.J.J. (1998) The virtual organisation, a special mode of strong inter-organizational cooperation. In: *Managing strategically in an interconnected world.* Hitt, M.A., Ricart, J.E. & Nixon, R.D. (Eds.) Wiley and Sons, Chichester.

[17] Vatcheva, I. & de Jong, H. Semi-quantative comparative analysis. In: *Proceedings IJCAI-99.* pp. 1034–1040.

[18]   van der Vet, P.E. (2000) Building web resources for natural scientists. In: *Interactive distributed multimedia systems and telecommunication services.* Scholten, H. & van Sinderen, M.J. (Eds.) Springer, Berlin, pp. 205–210.

Hans Roosendaal is professor of scientific information in the Faculty of Philosophy and Social Science, and the Department of Computer Science. Currently he is a member of the Executive Board of the University.

Peter Geurts is a methodologist and works at the Department of Public Administration and Public Policy.

Paul van der Vet works in the Department of Computer Science and the Centre for Telematics and Information Technology (CTIT).

This article is a condensed version of: "Developments in Scientific Communication: Considerations on the Value Chain", by Hans E. Roosendaal, Peter A.Th.M. Geurts and Paul E. van der Vet, to be published in: *Information Services and Use.*

A Century of Science Publishing
E.H. Fredriksson (Ed.)
IOS Press, 2001

Chapter 25

Open Reviewing, Closed Refereeing: Where's the Publication?

Erik Sandewall
Linköping University, Sweden

1. The ETAI approach to scientific publishing

The *Electronic Transactions on Artificial Intelligence* (ETAI) was started in 1997 as a novel kind of scientific journal. Besides using the Internet to distribute articles after they had been accepted to the journal, which is in itself only a practical matter, the ETAI proposed to use the Internet for a more substantial change in the process of communicating research results. The basic idea was to split the traditional peer review into two successive steps. The first step, called 'reviewing', is an open discussion on the Internet about the results in the proposed article. Both questions and critical comments are made openly, the identity of the all participants in the interactions is visible, and all questions and answers are available on a web page associated to each of the submitted articles.

Reviewing in this sense typically goes on for a period of three months, after which time the author has a possibility of revising the article based on the feedback that she or he has obtained.

The second step, called 'refereeing', is similar to traditional reviewing: two or three referees recommend acceptance or rejection of the article, and their identity is kept confidential. However, unlike traditional reviewing, refereeing is intended to be a pass/fail decision, which means that the referees are expected to perform that task rapidly and with relatively small effort. We recognized that traditional reviewing serves two purposes, namely both to provide feedback to the authors, and to establish a quality criterium for the journal. In the ETAI system these two functions are separated into the two phases of the acceptance process.

There were several reasons why we proposed to use this new reviewing system. First of all, we considered that it would be more fair to the author. Since both the critique and the author's responses are visible to the peer community, each author gets a stronger guarantee of a fair hearing. Even for controversial approaches, which may not be fully appreciated at the time they are first proposed, the new process guarantees that the author's result is on record and can gain full recognition during later years. In the traditional system, of course, once an article has been rejected it can not easily count for merit or for priority during later years.

Another reason for the new system was to give greater recognition to the reviewer's contribution. In the traditional system the reviewer is by necessity not rewarded, exactly because the work is done anonymously. This may be one reason for the frequent complaints about a decreasing quality of reviews, and even (sometimes) about a forthcoming collapse of the peer-review system. In our system the amount of confidential, unrewarded work is kept at a minimal level.

During the three and a half years that it has been in operation, the ETAI has enjoyed a steady increase in recognition and in the contribution of articles. A number of important issues have come up in this context: the dynamics of on-line discussions about research articles, the economics of operating this kind of communication medium, and the software technology that is needed in order to make it run smoothly. All of these issues are being addressed in other articles. Here I only wish to discuss one other topic that had to be addressed in the course of setting up ETAI, namely the question of what constitutes a publication.

2. Consequences for the definition of publication

The ETAI system of publication raised several questions of a formal, or even philosophical character. First of all, what is the status of an article during the period when it is being discussed? It has not yet been accepted to the ETAI journal, and therefore it is not a 'published' article in the sense often used in science. On the other hand, it 'is' in fact publicly available, so in the sense of the lawyer and in the common-sense meaning of the word, the article must be published in order to make it possible to discuss it.

This question is not only a terminological one. It is also of outmost importance for the authors that the results that are presented in the article are considered as being originated by the authors at the date when the article was first communicated to the peer community. If scientific priority would only count from the date of 'acceptance' to the journal, subsequent to the open discussion, it would of course become possible to pick up results and use them elsewhere.

This problem could only be solved by considering the article to be first published, then reviewed, then refereed, and only then accepted to the ETAI as a journal. Whereas other journals have a policy of not publishing previously published results, ours has a policy of "only" publishing previously published works — but after due reviewing, improvement, and refereeing.

3. The need for university electronic presses

Who is then the publisher of the article at the point preceding the discussion? Certainly not the journal, since the journal has not yet accepted it at that time. Also, if the original version of the article was to count for priority, how could one guarantee that the author would not cheat by improving the results in the article retroactively? For example, if the article was only available on the author's own webpage, then he could easily do that, and the legitimacy of this publication system would suffer seriously.

Our solution to this problem was to propose the creation of a separate kind of entity called a 'University Electronic Press'. In brief, the purpose of an E-press should be to receive articles from authors, publish them on the Internet (in the sense of making them publicly available), and to guarantee that the article will stay available for a sufficiently long period of time and that it would not and could not be changed during that period. In particular, it should not be possible for the author to change it, and even more strongly: it must be evident to the whole world that it was impossible for the author to tamper with the article after it had been published.

There is no reason why a particular journal, such as the ETAI, should rely on only one E-press for the first publication of the articles that are submitted to it. One journal may rely on several E-presses, and one E-press can support several journals when this system becomes more widespread. However, it is clear that a journal such as the ETAI can only exist if there exists 'at least' one E-press where submitted articles can be published.

For this reason we created Linköping University Electronic Press (http://www.ep.liu.se). We also set up a set of rules stipulating the criteria for E-presses that would be used by the ETAI, so that it was clear what should be the responsibilities of an organization in order to serve the ETAI as an authorized E-press. It took a while for additional E-presses to be set up, but now several others are being institutionalized.

4. The definition of 'electronic publication' and 'electronic publisher'

The publication system that has now been described requires a new way of using the word 'publication'. In the course of this process we therefore made a concrete proposal as to what ought to be the meaning of the term under the new conditions. This proposal was part of the background materials for the International Working Group that was formed in 1999 and whose report is also included in the present book (see Appendix). In particular, the emphasis on persistence as an important criterium for publications was part of both reports.

However, there was a difference on one important point. In our work, we also considered a philosophical difficulty that is a direct result of the emphasis on persistence: if a publication is something that is only present on the Internet, and which is therefore ephemeral by its very nature, then 'by what definition' can you say that it is persistent — how can you say that it is the same today as yesterday?

Our solution to this problem was first to define the concept of an electronic 'publisher'. The definition of an electronic 'publication' was then a derived one: something that is put out by an electronic publisher. In this way it was possible to establish a set of criteria that an organization must satisfy in order to be called an electronic publisher: it must administrate a set of document identifiers whereby each document obtains its unique identifier; it must maintain an archive whereby the original contents of each document can be inspected when needed; it must keep published articles on-line; it must maintain a validation system whereby the integrity of each document over time is guaranteed beyond any doubt, and so on.

Apart from this particular consideration, the definitions that are proposed by the International Working Group are similar to ours. This means, in particular, that there is already at least one actual case where the new approach proposed by the Working Group has already been used for several years, namely in the ETAI Journal.

5. From publication to research knowledge management

It is not an exaggeration that scientific publishing today is facing a revolution. The shift from print to electronic distribution of journals is only a very small step compared to the changes that are still ahead of us. The reform of the reviewing system in order to make proper use of the new technical possibilities is an important step. The conceptual changes that have been discussed here are also necessary steps in order not to hinder the new developments needlessly. But much more is on the horizon: changes in the granularity of research articles, further increase of interaction between authors and readers, integration of the result publication activity with the rest of the research process, integration of secondary information (measurements, software, etc.) with the primary publication, and so on.

The long range direction ought to be defined by the term "Research Knowledge Management". Research is about gradually building up a shared body of knowledge; publication in a broad sense is the mechanism whereby we jointly administrate this body of knowledge in the scientific community. Viewed from this perspective, we only see the beginning of a forthcoming revolution.

Appendix

Defining and Certifying Electronic Publication in Science

A Proposal to the International Association of STM Publishers
Originally Drafted October 1999; Revised March and June/July 2000
Prepared by an International Working Group

Mark S. Frankel, Co-Chair American Association for the Advancement of Science, USA
Roger Elliott, Co-Chair International Council for Science, UK
Martin Blume, American Physical Society, USA
Jean-Manuel Bourgois, Magnard/Vuibert Publishers, France
Bernt Hugenholtz, University of Amsterdam, The Netherlands
Mats G. Lindquist, Lund University Library, Sweden
Sally Morris, Association of Learned & Professional Society Publishers, UK
Erik Sandewall, Linköping University, Sweden

Synopsis

The peer-reviewed article will continue to play a crucial part in the certification, communication and recording of scientific research. However, in the electronic environment it represents one point on a potential continuum of communication. Other points on that continuum (such as preprints) are becoming increasingly common currency, and there is unlimited potential to add to or even change electronic content after it has been made available. All of these versions can be described as 'publications' in the sense that they have been made public. However, this does not necessarily assist the orderly development of scientific knowledge.

The working group was therefore asked to produce some definitions which might be helpful to scientists in this increasingly fluid information environment. We attempted to identify the most important fixed points in the continuum, and the criteria which would need to be satisfied in order to make them useful.

The crucial fixed point, in our view, remains the final published version of an article after peer review (or any future equivalent). We have called this the Definitive Publication and believe that it should be clearly identified as such. In the electronic environment, certain other characteristics are also required in addition to peer review:

- It must be publicly available.
- The relevant community must be made aware of its existence.
- A system for long-term access and retrieval must be in place (e.g. Handle). It must not be changed (technical protection and/or certification are desirable).
- It must not be removed (unless legally unavoidable).
- It must be unambiguously identified (e.g. by a SICI or DOI).
- It must have a bibliographic record (metadata) containing certain minimal information.
- Archiving and long-term preservation must be provided for.

This is the version to which citations, secondary services and so forth should ideally point. However, we recognise that earlier versions of an author's work may be made available, and that in some disciplines these are already being cited by other authors. Such early versions might be all that is available to an author for citation at the time of submission of the author's work. However, versions which are not durably recorded in some form, or which do not have a mechanism for continuing location and access, or which are altered over time (without due provision for version control, as outlined below), should not be regarded as 'publications' in the sense that publication has been defined here, even if cited by an author.

We recommend that a version which does satisfy the above criteria should be identified as such. We have called this the First Publication. We recommend that a version satisfying the criteria of First Publication (and no other) may be referred to in citations or secondary services, but only until such time as it is superseded by the Definitive Publication. Versions which are made public by one means or another, but whose authenticity, retrievability and permanence are not ensured as outlined above, should not in our view be cited, taken as the basis of claims of priority, or used for purposes of professional evaluation. That version of the First Publication, if any, which has been submitted for certification should be clearly identified as such in the bibliographic metadata.

We recognise that many journals (including some of our own) currently cite documents, such as preprints, which satisfy few if any of the above criteria. We would welcome debate on the desirability, and indeed feasibility, of introducing a greater degree of discipline.

We recognise that content can change after, as well as before, 'Definitive Publication'. Absence of systematic version control will make life very difficult for scientists. We therefore recommend that errata should be recorded in the accompanying bibliographic record (metadata) and that substantive changes should give rise to a new publication, to which the bibliographic record should refer.

We acknowledge that many unanswered questions remain; no one yet knows exactly how new, dynamic forms of electronic communication can be permanently preserved. However, we would welcome discussion of these proposed criteria, and we would like to see scientists and publishers working together to establish the necessary framework. In particular, we would like to see joint work on the information (metadata) which should be associated with a publication, and on technological solutions for content protection and authentication.

Full text
The present task
In October 1998, the American Association for the Advancement of Science (AAAS), the International Council for Science (ICSU) Press, and the United Nations Educational, Scientific, and Cultural Organization (UNESCO) co-sponsored a workshop on developing standards and practices for electronic publishing in science. (A report is posted at http://www.aaas.org/spp/dspp/sfrl/projects/epub/report.htm.) On the basis of that workshop, two of its co-organizers were approached in February 1999 by the International Association of Scientific, Technical, and Medical Publishers to ask them to develop a position paper on how to define a scientific publication in the electronic era. (They had previously commissioned a report from a consultant on the topic.) They agreed, and formed a small working group from among the participants in the earlier workshop and an additional member representing the publishing industry to prepare the position paper. Members of the working group are collectively the co-authors of this paper.

Why it matters
The scientific journal plays a critical role in the advancement of science through its certification and communication of knowledge from author to reader. The electronic medium unquestionably creates added value in publication through the speed with which it can disseminate information, the size of the audience it can reach efficiently, its enhanced indexing and search capabilities, its hypertext linkages to a wide range of material, its ability to be updated and corrected as needed, its interactivity, which enables real-time exchanges between authors and readers, and its multimedia format, which can incorporate video and sound into text. These features are very attractive to scientists, and the number of refereed electronic journals in science, engineering, and medicine has increased dramatically since 1991.

The need to define what constitutes a 'publication' in science in the electronic era is of considerable importance. The enhanced possibilities of electronic publishing are challenging traditional norms and practices that equate scientific publishing with print articles appearing in peer reviewed journals. Without a definition of publication that takes into account the many forms of scholarly writing found on the Internet, the quality, integrity, and authentication of scientific information communicated electronically will be difficult to determine.

Publication is the hard currency of science. It is the primary yardstick for establishing priority of discovery, making the status of a publication a critical factor in resolving priority disputes or intellectual property claims. Academic tenure and promotion decisions are based in large part on publication in peer-reviewed journals or scholarly books. To make these decisions fairly and with confidence, scientists and their institutions need assurances of what counts as a legitimate electronic publication.

The status of a published electronic document is critical in determining the trust that fellow scientists will have in it. This is increasingly important in the Internet environment, where the explosion of information produces a pressing need for efficient and reliable means to distinguish between information that adds usefully to the knowledge base and that which does not. Scientists need to know the status of the information they encounter, whether they need to refer to it, critique it, or build on it to advance their own work. The document also needs to persist, since in science identifying a clear context for later responses is essential to maintain the quality and integrity of subsequent scientific discourse.

Our recommendations

A workable definition of 'publication' in the electronic era is needed to respond to these challenges. Such a definition should be useful to those evaluating the professional work of scientists, and to authors, publishers, librarians, archivists, and readers. The definition of publication that we are proposing has three primary objectives:

- To promote the advancement of science and the social good it serves.
- To contribute to the development of a system for managing scientific information in the electronic environment that will maintain and sustain an accurate and reliable record of science.
- To help resolve some of the existing uncertainty about the status, role, and function of electronic publication in science.

Our recommendations, therefore, are premised on what we believe would be most useful for science. They are not, however, intended to be definitive.(1) The issues are far too complex, the working group too small, and the time too short for producing such wisdom. Nevertheless, we hope that our proposal advances discussion of these matters, enough to push the issues forward to a new level of deliberation. We distinguish between informal notification of one's work (which we do not consider 'publication'), First Publication and Definitive Publication (2).

To have any value to the scientific community as a whole, a document should, at a minimum, conform to the following characteristics:

- It must be durably recorded on some medium.
- It must have a persistent access mechanism so that it is reliably accessible and retrievable over time.
- It must be immutable (i.e., it should remain in the same form).
- It must be publicly available.

However, in themselves these characteristics are not sufficient to make the document one which can securely be referred to by other writers; the following additional essential features are required:

- Authenticity must be guaranteed (i.e., versions should be certified as authentic and protected from change after publication).
- Assignment and persistence of an identifier that identifies the work unambiguously.
- A bibliographic record (metadata) that describes the work and its various versions, and which must be public and freely accessible for any given address location.
- A commitment to continuing public access and retrievability.
- Notification of the community that the document is available.
- Commitment not to withdraw the document.
- That version of the document, if any, which has been submitted for a process of certification should be identified as such in its bibliographic metadata.

In addition, to qualify as a Definitive Publication

- It should be vetted (e.g. refereed) to ensure quality, in order to maximize its usefulness for science and to establish a high level of trust among readers.
- There should be a more stringent requirement that the certified version of the document is not subsequently altered. Significant changes should be embodied in a new version with its own identifier and metadata record (the original and new versions should cross-refer). Errata should be registered in the metadata record.
- There must be a commitment to long-term archival preservation.

We realize that in making these proposals there are a number of challenges that lie ahead.

The challenges

Versions. In the traditional print-on-paper paradigm essentially the only version of a publication that merited that name, by virtue of being generally accessible, was a final definitive version which also had all the added value of editorial control, printing, distribution and marketing. This was, inevitably, the version referred to by subsequent authors. But in the electronic environment this is no longer true, and there are a succession of versions that can be made publicly available without this full array of added value. Nevertheless, their wide availability seems to us to make them a 'publication' in the English language sense. It is therefore important to be able to distinguish among versions, and to identify which, if any, should be treated as definitive.

Quality. To establish its usefulness for science, a publication needs to have been vetted to ensure quality and to establish a high level of trust among readers. This process is equally essential for electronic documents — indeed, perhaps more so in view of the vast quantity of available information. Publication in a peer-reviewed print journal provides this assurance; a reliable equivalent of this 'quality stamping' is necessary in the electronic environment. Various more or less formal processes are being explored and we do not attempt to determine here which might or might not be valid.

Persistence. Methods for archiving and citing electronic publications are challenged by the electronic medium. An archival record of validated scientific work must be accessible for future use, since even the most innovative science is useless if scientists cannot identify, locate, or obtain the work. Yet the ephemeral nature of online publications and changing Uniform Resource Locators (URL) makes citing and accessing information a moving target, unless additional discipline is added. Given the potential for multiple versions of the same document to be available electronically, decisions will also need to be made about practices for linking to and citing versions of a scientific paper.

Version control

We view the publication process as a continuum ranging from an initial 'public offering' of one's work, to claims of priority, to certification of knowledge, to subsequent updatings of work. This process occurs without regard to the medium used. For our purposes, however, we focus on how we believe this process should work in electronic online journal publication (3).

The process may begin when an author offers his/her work publicly, perhaps by presenting it at a conference, posting it on a personal Web page, forwarding it to an electronic listserv, or simply announcing it during a radio or television interview. We do not consider that these actions alone constitute 'publication' for the purpose of establishing the record of science. If scientists want their work formally recognized as contributing to knowledge, there are further steps they must take. In our view, the author has the exclusive right (and responsibility) to take these steps, or to arrange for them to be taken. Once an author decides to make a particular work available in such a way that his or her community of peers can refer to it, critique it, or build on it, then in our view it must comply with the requirements that we are proposing. Once that is done, it becomes a 'publication' (4).

First Publication. The author must identify the version that will be the basis for claims to priority (5). We refer to this as the First Publication, and it must be marked by the following properties:

- Recording. The document must be durably recorded on some medium.
- Permanence. The document must be stored in such a way that it remains accessible and retrievable over time.
- Persistent identification. The document must be identified in such a way that can be located over time, even if its Web location should change.
- Immutability. The document (including, where technically feasible, any links) should not be altered. (Minor amendments may be permissible to avoid unnecessary proliferation of different versions, but these must be clearly documented.)
- Version control. The document must be clearly identified as the version submitted to be considered for certification.
- Metadata record. The document should be associated with a record containing certain minimum bibliographic information (see below).
- Notification. The community of one's peers must be informed of the version attached to claims of priority.
- Commitment not to withdraw. To ensure an accurate record of science and to discourage a deluge of trivial material into the publication process, authors must agree prior to commencing the selection process that they will not delete the document and all record of its existence from the electronic literature unless there are compelling reasons for doing so. Authors may elect to retract (disavow) or may have to retract a document for scientific, legal, or other reasons, however. In cases of either deletion or retraction, authors should note the reason for doing so in the bibliographic record of that version.
- The version of the document, if any, which is submitted for certification should be clearly identified as such in its bibliographic metadata record.

Once the First Publication is determined, the process of selection and certification may begin.

Definitive Publication. Selection and certification is the validation process by which the scientific community identifies work that contributes to the production of useful knowledge. It requires a fair, organized, and recognized vetting process that leads to the definitive (certified) version of a publication. It includes a number of features:

- Peer review, which evaluates the scientific content of the First Publication.
- Feedback to authors from peers and editors intended to improve the quality of the publication.

In addition, formal publication (e.g., in a journal) will also include the following:

- Editorial judgements that help to determine the ultimate path taken by the document.
- Copy-editing and design, to improve the accuracy, readability and navigability of the publication.

Collection, whereby related articles are selected and gathered together in a recognized (physical or virtual) journal or its equivalent for the convenience of readers. These processes will add significant value to the First Publication over and above selection and certification. Some First Publications will not survive this selection process. But once certified, this version should be considered the Definitive Publication for purposes of establishing the record of science. The Definitive Publication must conform with the following additional requirements:

- There must be commitment to long-term archival preservation of the document. We make no assumptions here about how this might best be achieved and by whom; we recognise that substantial technical and funding problems remain to be resolved.
- It should never be changed and should refer to all previous versions, whether or not retracted.
- Errata subsequently revealed should be appended to this version, with the dates that errata were recorded inserted into the publication's bibliographic record.

Further research that builds on and upgrades this version with new data and findings produces a new publication that must enter the system, secure its own bibliographic record, and earn its own place in the scientific literature. Authors and publishers should jointly develop criteria for determining when changes in content should mark a new publication. The authenticity of all versions of the publication must be assured. This is critical, since electronic publications are easier to copy and alter than their print counterparts. At present, the technological solutions to achieve this tend to be costly and reader-unfriendly. However, technical and administrative measures may provide guarantees against changes to the content in circumstances where unrecorded change is absolutely unacceptable. Appropriate technical and administrative measures should be implemented, once they are available, so that readers have confidence both that the version they read has not been tampered with, and that if it purports to be the Definitive Publication, it represents precisely the document certified by the selection (vetting) process.

Persistent access mechanism

Public availability and retrievability are essential; if scientists cannot identify, locate, and access the item, whatever version they are seeking, it is useless to the community. There must be a persistent means for locating and accessing the work (even if its Web location changes) and, if applicable, for each of its versions. It is the responsibility of the publishing organization to guarantee this. Each publishing organization should have in place a back-up plan in case it is not able to continue to perform this function.

Making the work public means that searchers must be able to find it, whatever version they are seeking. It also means that if the address for the work as a whole is cited in another document, then the reader of that other document at a later point in time must be made aware of, and must be able to obtain access to, later versions of the first work, and not only to those versions that existed at the time the citation was made.

Whoever is responsible for making available the Definitive Publication makes a commitment to provide the persistent means to locate the current Web address for the document. We recognise that URLs may change. In the future, it is hoped that systems will be developed that make this an intrinsic part of the process of identifying and locating a document. The long-term acceptance and viability of the addressing scheme must be credible, including the existence and proper functioning of a system that produces the bibliographic record when provided with the address.

Archiving and long-term preservation

To be optimally useful to science, publications must be retrievable, now and in the future. Archiving and preservation are necessary to help us identify prior ideas and prior disputes, and to offer a context in which to frame and conduct the debate. The author and other organizations involved must, therefore, make a commitment to archiving and long-term preservation.

An archive of electronic documents will not be static. Changes in technology may require format conversion of archived documents on a large scale. Other, as yet unforeseen, management and updating operations may also become necessary. The rules of archiving must, therefore, include provisions for the freedom to make digital archival copies. It must further be recognized that the continuous migration of technology to higher levels of efficiency and improved capabilities may mean that the format of archived publications will have to be altered in order to be preserved.

Bibliographic record

Unrecorded changes to a document to which scientists refer are not in the best interests of science. Hence, modifications to the content of a publication should always be recorded in either of the following ways: (1) the creation of a new version, or (2) the posting of an errata list that is attached to the bibliographic record for the work. In either case the new version or the errata should be dated.

We believe that the bibliographic record, which accompanies or is associated with each version of a given work through the publication process, must give not only generic information about the work, but also minimum information both about that version and about any other extant versions of the same work. The record should contain a sub-record for each published version of the work, indicating in particular the date of publication and location information for that version. Distinct versions should be identified in the following cases or in combinations thereof:

- On submission to a process of formal certification.
- After changes in the contents or presentation of the work.
- When the work is translated into another language.
- If a part of the work is selected as a separate publication.
- Optionally, if the same work is issued in both electronic and print form (these may or may not be considered as distinct versions).

Each sub-record for a version must contain links to the contents of that version in at least one, but possibly several, formats (e.g., PostScript, PDF or XML). The contents obtained from those links must not be changed over time, but the locations where the contents are stored may change. For example, one organization may commission another to store the contents of some of its published works, thereby transferring contents from one location to another, but it must update the links in the version sub-records accordingly.

The bibliographic record may be, for example, a record in a conventional database sense, or an HTML page that can be viewed using a browser. It could also be an HTML page containing metadata or other hidden data that allow it to be processed effectively by software agents, thus combining the two previous alternatives. Regardless of how it is realized, the record contains references whereby the full contents of all existing versions of the work can be retrieved.

At a minimum, and when pertinent to any particular version, the bibliographic record should consist of the following:

- Author(s).
- Title of the work.
- Subrecords for all versions (at least one).
- Stipulation which of the versions is the First Publication.
- Stipulation which of the versions, if any, has been submitted for certification.
- Stipulation which of the versions, if any, is the Definitive Publication, by whom/what certified, and when.
- Stipulation of the version for primary citation. This will change as the manuscript moves through the publication process. Normally, it is the First Publication until the Definitive Publication appears, and then the latter.

Since electronic publications can be continuously updated, improved, and expanded, some system of version control must be in place so that readers are able to quote or cite them with certainty that they are referring to the "right" versions. The following suggested requirements for sub-records are intended, in tandem with the full bibliographic record, to assist readers:

- Version identifier and date of publication of the version.
- Statement of why the new version has been created, according to the standard criteria for forming new versions mentioned above.
- Date of retraction by the author, if applicable.
- Statement of why the version has been retracted.
- Location(s) where the contents of the version can be obtained. These locations must be updated if the location of the content changes.
- Details and date of errata, if any. Reference to other version(s) from which the present one was derived, when applicable.
- Reference to other versions derived from the present one (e.g., translations, subsets, etc.) when applicable.

Who should do it?

For many of these features, it will be desirable to establish uniform standards to ensure as smooth a transition as possible to the proposed system. This task should be undertaken after broad agreement has been achieved on the basic characteristics of the system. It is important to stress that our recommendations create functions and responsibilities that will require an infrastructure to carry them out effectively and efficiently. Stable and reliable organizations will be needed to undertake the tasks we are proposing; we do not consider it practicable for these tasks to be undertaken by individual authors on their own behalf. We offer no opinion as a group on what the most appropriate and effective infrastructure should be, but publishers, professional associations, research and archival institutions, libraries and funders of scientific research will all have key roles to play in designing and maintaining this infrastructure.

It is implicit in our proposal, however, that a work should only be considered as "published" for scientific purposes if the requirements specified above have been performed by an organization such as those outlined in the previous paragraph.

Summary of recommendations
All Publications
- Recording. The document must be durably recorded on some medium.
- Publicly available (not necessarily free of charge).
- Immutability (i.e., should remain in the same form). Access mechanism so that the publication is reliably accessible and retrievable over time (i.e., through a persistent identifier).
- Version control (bibliographic record must be attached to each version; minimum details indicated above).

When available and affordable technology permits (the development of which should be encouraged) the following should be added:
- Authenticity (i.e., versions should be certified as authentic and protected from change).

First Publication
- Version control. The version of the item submitted for certification, if any, must be clearly identified.
- Notification (the community of one's peers must be informed of the version associated with claims of priority).
- Commitment not to withdraw (authors must agree prior to commencing the selection process that they will not delete the document from the electronic literature).

Definitive Publication
- Quality control/author feedback (it should be vetted to ensure quality).
- Version control (the bibliographic record should identify all previous and

subsequent versions, whether or not retracted).
- Errata should be noted in the metadata record.
- Commitment to archiving and long-term preservation.

Notes
1. An analysis of how the law will affect or our proposals is beyond the scope of our original charge. We acknowledge, however, that the system we recommend will have to operate within international and national intellectual property regimes.
2. This is not to say that documents which do not meet the full criteria of 'First Publication', and the ideas which they contain, should not be treated with just as much respect as those which do. It may also be valuable to establish an agreed convention for referring to documents which do not qualify as 'First Publications'.
3. Although we acknowledge the value of broadening this analysis to non-journal materials and to media other than on-line, because of constraints on time and resources we do not consider these here.
4. We recognize that some journals and publishers currently have policies that would preclude their considering for publication documents that have previously been made public by authors in one or more versions, for example by posting to preprint servers. We can only observe here that our definition of online publication is intended to facilitate the widespread dissemination of scientific work.
5. While authors may claim priority of discovery at this stage of the process, the validity of that claim remains to be determined by the vetting process that follows.

Republished with permission
Previously published at http://www.aaas.org/spp/dspp/sfrl/projects/epub/define.htm
and in the ALPSP journal *Learned Publishing*.

Appendix

Appendix: Main Publishers' Sites and Data

Holding	Websites	Turnover (x 1 million)	Books	Journals
American Association for the Advancement of Science	www.aaas.org www.sciencemag.org www.scienceonline.org			
American Chemical Society	www.acs.org www.cas.org (chemical abstracts service) www.chemsoc.org www.iupac.org	$205 (1999)	39	35
American Institute of Physics	www.aip.org asa.aip.org (Acoustical Society of America) www.aapt.org (American Association of Physics Teachers) www.aapm.org (American Association of Physicists in Medicine) www.aas.org (American Astronomical Society) www.agu.org (American Geophysical Union) www.aps.org (American Physical Society) www.osa.org (Optical Society of America) www.rheology.org (The Society of Rheology) www.vacuum.org (American Vacuum Society)	$50 (1999)		98
Bertelsmann Springer	www.springer.de www.springer.at (Springer-Verlag Vienna) www.spektrum.de www.steinkopff.springer.de www.technikwissen.de (Springer-VDI-Verlag)	684 Euro	2600	500

Publisher	Sites			
Cambridge University Press	www.urban-vogel.de www.vieweg.de www.cup.cam.ac.uk (UK) www.cup.edu.au (Australia) www.cup.org (USA) www.journals.cup.org	£26	400	157
Harcourt, Inc	www.harcourt.com www.harcourt-international.com www.harcourthealth.com (Harcourt Health Sciences, Mosby Inc, W.B. Saunders, Churchill Livingstone) www.academicpress.com www.apnet.com www.idealibrary.com www.jems.com (Jems Communications) www.mdconsult.com www.mkp.com (Morgan Kaufmann Publishers)	$745		450
John Wiley & Sons, Inc	www.wiley.com www.wiley-vch.de www.capstone-press.com www.interscience.wiley.com www.josseybass.com (Jossey-Bass) www.pfeiffer.com (Pfeiffer) www.technical-insights.com (under construction)	$594		400
Oxford University Press	www.oup.com www.oup.com.au (Australia/New Zealand) www.oup.com.pk (Pakistan) www.oup.com.sg (Singapore) www.oup.co.uk (UK) www.oup-usa.org (USA) www.oupcan.com (Canada) www.oupchina.com.hk (China) www.oupmex.com.mx (Mexico)	£350	5000	110

Holding	Websites	Turnover (x 1 million)	Books	Journals
Pearson, Plc	www.pearson.com www.scottforesman.com www.abacon.com (Allyn & Bacon) www.awl.com (Addison Wesley Longman) www.ccclearn.com (Computer Curriculum Corporation) www.ciscopress.com www.prenhall.com (Prentice Hall) www.informit.com www.bradygames.com	£2.087 (1999)		
Reed Elsevier, Plc	www.reed-elsevier.com www.elsevier.com www.elseviersciencedirect.com (Database Journals Elsevier) www.bmn.com (Biomednet) www.chemweb.com www.endeavorlibrary.org www.excerptamedica.com (Excerpta Medica) www.sciencedirect.com www.thelancet.com	£652/ 991 Euro	433	1403
Taylor & Francis, Plc	www.taylorandfrancis.com www.tandf.co.uk/journals (Carfax Publishing) www.tandf.co.uk/members.html (Hemisphere Publication Services) www.brunner-routledge.com www.dunitz.co.uk (Martin Dunitz Publishers) www.europapublications.co.uk www.garlandscience.com www.gbhap.com (Gordon & Breach Publishing) www.psypress.co.uk (Psychology Press) www.routledge.com www.routledgefalmer.com	£116	1700	542

Publisher	Sites	Data
Thomson Corporation	www.sponpress.com www.thomson.com www.derwent.co.uk www.isinet.com www.isiresearchsoft.com	$697
Verlagsgruppe Georg von Holtzbrinck	www.holtzbrinck.com www.bfwpub.com (College-Gruppe Bedford, Freeman & Worth) www.diesterweg.de (Verlag Moritz Diesterweg) www.macmillan.com www.metzlerverlag.de www.nature.com www.sciam.com (Scientific American) www.spektrum-verlag.de www.urbanfischer.de	579 Euro (1999)
Wolters-Kluwer N.V.	www.wolters-kluwer.com www.wkihs.com (Wolters Kluwer International Health & Science) www.adis.com www.fandc.com (Facts & Comparisons) www.kli.com (Kluwer Law International) www.lww.com (Lippincott Williams & Wilkins) www.ovid.com www.wkap.com (Kluwer Academic/Plenum Publishers) www.wkap.nl (Kluwer Academic Publishers)	752 Euro 1300 800

Index

Appendix